The
SOUND
OF HIS *Voice*

365 Devotionals of hearing
God speak into our ordinary lives

JUDITH ANN HENDRICKSON

PRESS

Acknowledgements

I am so grateful to the Lord who speaks in so many ways that we can hear even His whispers.

I want to also thank the people who have encouraged me to put these daily devotionals into a book:

To my dear pastor husband who supported me, believed in me and listened for the theological content of each devotional as I wrote them.

To my children and grandchildren who gave permission for me to write about them as I saw God speak through them.

To my editor and friend who gave inspiration and made room in her schedule to patiently edit each devotional throughout the writing.

To my friends who supported and encouraged me as they shared how these simple devotionals spoke into their lives.

To the prayer warriors who faithfully prayed for me while I was writing and kept me accountable.

To the team at Xulon Press who said they would hang in there with me until I held this book in my hands.

Foreword

It is a privilege as Judy's husband, to write a forward to her book of devotions. We have been married almost 50 years and I believe I am qualified to speak regarding her character as a follower of Jesus. I could say a lot, but will limit myself to three comments.

First, her faithful walk with God: My dear wife is the most consistent Christian I know. Day in and day out, she is the same. She is a positive, content, and self-less human being. What you see is what you get. She is the same in private as she is in public. In a word, Judy is as fine a Christian woman as you would want to know. That is the finest compliment I could give *my bride.*

Secondly, the spiritual gift that shines through these devotions is what I would call Judy's *stream of consciousness* spirituality: She sees and hears God in ordinary, everyday life. It is truly a gift from God that she has cultivated over the years. I have observed firsthand, how these devotions seem to *drop from heaven* as Judy listens to what the Lord is revealing to her. In these devotions she is sharing this gift.

Thirdly, it is what I would call Judy's *unassuming* personality: I sense no pride or desire for recognition in the publication of these devotions. Judy had to be persuaded that her devotions are a gift from God to be shared with others. I can assure you that this book is the result of her obedience to the Lord.

I pray that these devotions will be a blessing in your spiritual life. May the gift of being able to see and hear God in everyday life become more real in your walk with God. I thank God for what He has taught me through the life of my *best friend* and *spiritual director.*

This book is dedicated to Alan, my best friend and husband of nearly fifty years, our children Mark, Ann, and Kurt, and their families.

Introduction

As a pastor's wife, I have experienced the rush of the city and busyness of church life. I never dreamed I would live in the quiet of the north woods that is far away from our 3 children, their spouses and 7 grandchildren. But now it is home where I find God whispering to me. It is also a quiet place where pastors and spouses, missionaries and other pilgrims come for retreat, seeking spiritual direction for their lives. It is the fulfillment of a dream that God gave us many years ago.

Ever since I can remember, God has spoken to me in my stream of consciousness. I specifically recall being in the woods, picking wild raspberries with another gal, while sharing things the Lord was teaching me from the berry patch. I noted the importance of going back over the path I had taken as I had missed so many berries that could only be seen from a different perspective. The Lord was telling me to glean from my past as well as present. Some of the biggest berries were hidden in thickets and I had to bend low and be willing to get pricked too. I could see how important it is to be humble and be willing to even be wounded by others if there was to be good fruit in my life. I asked my friend what God was saying to her from our experience in the berry patch and suddenly realized that He doesn't speak in that same way to everyone. Each one hears Him in their own "language" which may be quite different from the next person. I began writing things down that God was teaching me and writing devotionals to send out to friends and relatives. Soon others wanted to be on the list and it became a daily ritual. I was humbled that God could use even these simple thoughts and impressions. As you read these devotionals, you may hear in a slightly different language from the Lord, but I hope you will see in new ways how God is continually speaking. Our part is to be open and receive from Him the way He chooses to reveal Himself to us. The "Daily Challenges" could be the door for you to open and begin to hear His personal whispers to you.

It is my prayer that you may know how much He loves you and desires to speak to you and commune with you.

Judy Hendrickson has put together an inspiring daily devotional that will serve as a catalyst to see God at work all around you in your daily circumstances. Your inner world will be expanded and filled with awe and beauty as you live the lives God has called you to, wherever you are, and whatever your work might be. This book will bring encouragement and peace to lives. I encourage you to make this book a part of your daily dialogue with Jesus.

Grace Copley Spiritual Director, Edmonds, WA

Judy, I love your daily devotionals. I just sit back in my chair and close my eyes with the image of wildlife and woods and godly men and women blessing the socks off people after they start their day with God and your devotionals! It is a comfort to know someone like you who knows how to make lemonade out of lemons and be positive and vulnerable at the same time. Judy, you are sunbeam from the Son!!! Thank you!!!

Marty Curley, Children's Pastor, Grace Center, Franklin, TN

Judy Hendrickson has the unique and uncanny ability to see God in the everyday experiences of life, and to draw deep spiritual truths from the common – and often mundane. If you are yearning to walk more and more in the light of the Lord's presence and experience more of the adventure described in Psalm 89:15-16, this collection of devotionals will be manna for your soul.

Bill – Business as Mission consultant/practitioner

Judy is a pastor's wife and mother of 3 children and 7 grandchildren. She lives in the North woods of Minnesota where she and her husband run a prayer house for pastors and wives, missionaries, and other pilgrims who come for prayer and renewal. She has taught Women's groups, led retreats, mentored etc. but prefers the hidden life. What she hears the Lord speak to her in her everyday life she writes and sends out a devotional daily. Her desire is for others to enjoy God's loving presence and hear His voice speak to their hearts.

Perhaps all of us at times have felt there was a ceiling on some of our prayers and that they didn't seem to go beyond it! I was reading in Isaiah 64:1 (NIV) where the prophet cries out, "Oh that you would rend the heavens, that you would come down, that the mountains might tremble before you!" When we talked to our daughter's family on Skype the other day they could see us plainly and hear us clearly but their voices were very garbled to us. We tried so hard to understand what they were saying but most of it sounded like someone talking with a mouthful of marbles! I wonder sometimes if it isn't like that with us and the Lord. He sees us very clearly and hears every cry of our heart but we don't always hear Him clearly. We need a better connection! After we talked with our daughter, a friend called on Skype and I could hear her perfectly. I felt like I was in her house sitting across from her and talking. Isn't that what we truly desire in our relationship with the Lord? We want to see Him and to know His voice that speaks clearly into our heart. May He break through all our barriers and defenses so that we can enjoy sweet communion with Him.

Challenge for today: Set apart a time today to sit in quiet, just listening for the Lord's voice.

Recently ten *Ladies of the Lake* gathered for brunch and fun, bringing along with them a white elephant gift for a game. It was a sharing game as each one had a hidden question in an Easter egg that they were to read and have everyone answer. The one with the best answer won a gift that was in a brown paper bag. Every gal brought something they didn't think had value to them and wanted to get rid of it. But it seemed that the one that got their gift was pleasantly surprised and liked the gift. Isn't that the way it is at times with us? We have gifts that we don't think are valuable and just kind of ignore them or consider them unimportant. And yet, it may be the very thing that would bless someone else, which may surprise us! One gal didn't think her pedometer and a hard cased credit card holder was valuable but the one who received them was thrilled. We are to use the gifts God gave us to bless others and we are not to minimize or neglect them. It says in Rom. 12:6 (NIV) "We all have different gifts according to the grace given us." Let us use those gifts. He knows whom He wants to bless through our gifts so let us use them for His glory and purposes.

Challenge for today: Let your God given gifts bless someone else.

Some days do not turn out as we expect and I ended up at the Ophthalmologist as I was having floaters and spider like shadows in my left eye. I thought of just ignoring it as I was self- diagnosing that it was the beginning of cataracts. But when I got flashes of light appearing like a lightening show I changed my mind. As the Dr. examined my eye he found a tear in my retina and a couple hours later I was having Laser treatment. What if I was content to just self-diagnose and not ask the authority? Lots of damage may have occurred. We can think we are good at diagnosing our own problems but why not go to the One who really knows and sees us deep within. He has not only the proper diagnosis but the exact treatment. For it says in I Cor. 4:5, (Amplified) "He will both bring to light the secret things that are now hidden in darkness and disclose and expose the (secret) aims (motives and purposes) of hearts."

Challenge for today: Ask God to help you see something in your life that desire Him to change

While I was shopping one day I questionably bought a pair of camouflage jeans for our granddaughter. Usually, I call to ask my daughter-in-law before buying but was running out of time. When my granddaughter unwrapped them, I could tell she did not like them so I assured her I would give them to someone else. The Lord brought to mind a girl her age at church and I gave them to her. She was so thrilled and wore them right away to school and even had a matching camouflage headband. I messed up in giving the wrong gift the first time but the Lord does not. We may sometimes think He has not given us the right gift when we are dissatisfied or looking at what He has given someone else. But He knows exactly what is good for us and what would bring the most glory to Him in our lives. We may not even understand today why He has chosen a certain gift but later on it becomes clear. I think it is especially true with trials that are not wrapped in pretty paper but later down the road we find it was the very thing that increased our faith. It says in James 1:17 (NIV) "Every good and perfect gift is from above, coming down from the Father of the heavenly lights, who does not change like shifting shadows." How wonderful when we can give Him thanks for every one of the gifts He has given us. May our hearts acknowledge that He is in charge and knows what is best.

Challenge for today: Thank God for a gift that you have found hard to accept and receive with grace.

One day we went to see my husband's surgeon for his year post-op check- up for his hip surgery. The surgeon showed us his x-ray and it was just perfect. Al has a cobalt chromium rod with a ceramic head and it was adhered to his femur bone with no space in between. That is exactly what they want to happen and they were perfectly fitted together and look as one now. Oh what a beautiful picture of us when we abide in the Lord. We become one with Him and depend entirely on Him and then become fruit bearers. We are not able to do anything of value on our own, just as the rod has to adhere to the bone to even move. Our will then becomes one with Him and our desires become the same. He has told us to just ask whatever it is we need and He will provide. As it says in John 15:7 (The Message) "If you live in me (abide vitally united to Me) and My words remain in you and continue to live in your hearts, ask whatever you will, and it shall be done for you." Let us stay close in His presence and draw our strength from Him.

Challenge for today: Spend time with Him today just being with Him in quiet.

As a group gathered recently, it seemed as if laughter spilled out everywhere! We ate more than we needed and shared humorous stories together. Now each person present came with heart concerns and things that weighted them down. But in the laughter the burdens were lightened and it was like a medicine for our soul. No, that doesn't make problems go away, but gives us an emotional release and a break so we can just keep carrying on. Proverbs 17:22 (Amplified) says, "A happy heart is good medicine and a cheerful mind works healing, but a broken spirit dries up the bones." Laughter is healing and actually boosts our immune system. Did you know that it is mentioned over 50 times in the Bible? Laughter and humor should not be absent from our lives but as we choose to be thankful we find humor. Just the other day I was in the doctor's office and a woman asked a man how he was feeling. He responded in a weak voice, "pretty good." The woman said, "Well, your vertical aren't you??!!" Both of them laughed and perhaps saw the silver lining.

Challenge for today: Find something to laugh about!

Last Sunday I noticed how pretty a widow in our church looked in a black and silver jacket. As I looked closer it was the very one that I had given her. This time it looked great on her, with the colors bringing out the silver in her hair. But on me it had looked awful, draining the color right out of my face. We are all unique individuals before the Lord and not like anyone else. What is good for one may not be good for another. That should teach us not to pray for things another person has, for it may not be fitting for us at all. We are not to compare ourselves with anyone else in the Body of Christ for it says in Galatians 6:4 (NIV), "Each one should test his own actions. Then he can take pride in himself, without comparing himself to somebody else, for each one should carry his own load." Our part is to trust that He knows best and to be the unique person he created us to be.

Challenge for today: Be myself and thank Him for something unique about me.

Yesterday we had a message on our phone saying our Visa Check Card had been suspended and were to call a certain number. It seemed strange to us as it came at night. When we called they wanted more information. Something didn't seem right to us so we called our credit card company and they told us right away that it was a scam. Isn't that just like the enemy? If we continue to go down the wrong path we can get in deeper and deeper trouble. But when things don't seem right in our spirit we need to stop and pay attention. We need to be in tune with the Holy Spirit so we are discerning and avoid the pitfalls the enemy puts before us. Paul says in Galatians 5:25b (Amplified) "If by the (Holy) Spirit we have our life in [God], let us go forward walking in line, our conduct controlled by the Spirit."

Challenge for today: Ask for the Holy Spirit's guidance today before making decisions.

Lately I noticed that our downstairs refrigerator/freezer was not working properly. Several of the items in the refrigerator were freezing and had to be discarded. Not long ago we had a wonderful Christian repair man out for our new stove and when I called him he told me some things to try. He could have charged us to come the 60 miles plus putting in a new thermostat but instead he had me use the hair dryer on two vents. That opened up an ice jam that was clogging things and bingo...it works fine now! I was so happy! Now the repair man could have made money on us but in the long run he will make more since I will gladly give out his name and also call him if we have any problems. God sees all our actions and motives, even when others are not aware. We need to do what is right and good even when others are not watching. It says in Ps. 44:2 (NIV) "...would not God have discovered it, since He knows the secrets of the heart?" How freeing it is when we live lives of integrity, in the realization that God is smiling as we listen to the Spirit and do what is right.

Challenge for today: Do something today that is selfless and will only be seen by God.

I love working for Share and Care (a shop for slightly used items). When I go through the bags and boxes that are donated, I never know what I will find! One big box I began going through had clothes that were torn and very used and dirty as if they had been discarded. My mind began thinking that I would probably have to dump the whole box. But, much to my surprise towards the bottom of the box there were some trendy, clean clothes and even name brand items. Not what I was expecting! Are we a lot like that in relationships as well? Maybe someone isn't dressed very well and doesn't come across very articulate or seems to have lots of problems. Do we expect God will use them in our lives? Surprisingly, God uses many different kinds of vessels and has messages to give us. Are we open to receive in whatever way He chooses to *talk* to us? Paul said in 1Corinthians1:27b& 29 (NIV) "But God chose the weak things of the world to shame the strong...so that no one may boast before Him."

Challenge for today: Be aware of and welcoming to someone who is poor in the eyes of the world.

Are there days that we catch ourselves in *people pleasing* and having a hard time to say "no"? I was asked to help serve at a funeral but had two other appointments already on that day so I had to say no. We are asked many things to do and often we end up doing more than we should to keep others around us happy. It is a quick way to *burn out* and we need to have personal boundaries. The Lord wants to direct our days and His Spirit leads in a way that is peace-filled rather than stress-filled. Saying "no" to others may be difficult but saying "yes" to the Spirit's leading will give us rest within, even when we may be outwardly busy. In Heb. 13:21b (NIV), Paul asks that the Lord "......equip you with everything good for doing His will, and may He work in us what is pleasing to Him, through Jesus Christ, to whom be glory for ever and ever." Let us remember that God will equip us with everything we need to carry out His will in our lives and bring glory to Him.

Challenge for today: Say "no" to anything you feel the Lord has not called you to do.

When our son's family went out Trick and Treating each one dressed in the jersey of their favorite player in basketball, soccer, volleyball and football. We all have favorite teams and players that often differ even in the same family. Al's mom was a big Lion fan and his dad was a Packer fan so game days could get intense. But I thought of how the Lord loves us all equally and each of us is #1 with Him. A relative once told me how her mom favored her and she was #1. When she got together with her sisters, each one felt the same, that they were there mom's favorite child. I applauded their mom that she had made each one of them feel so special and loved and favored. Let us remember that we are loved with the same love that the Father has for His Son. It can't get any better than that. He says in John 15:9 (Phillips) "I have loved you just as the Father has loved me. You must go on living in my love." Sometimes it may appear that He favors another more than us when we feel things are not going well and we are being exercised in our faith...but the truth is that He loves us all with an everlasting love. Let us live in the awareness of that love.

Challenge for today: Memorize a scripture that speaks of His love for you and carry it with you.

God at times asks us to do things that cause us to step out in faith and move beyond our comfort zone. I'm sure Abraham didn't find it easy to pick up and leave his home, not knowing where he was to go. We may also be asked to do something new that tests our faith and brings us into spiritual warfare. The enemy gets riled up and tries to discourage us from carrying through. Ever since I have been seeking to be obedient to the latest thing God has impressed on me to do, all kinds of things around the house have broken down and caused inconvenience....one thing after another! But when such things happen may it make us all the more determined to do His will. Let us not give up or give in but carry through until it is accomplished and He gets the glory. Paul says in Phil.3:15-16, (The Message) "So let's keep focused on the goal, those of us who want everything God has for us. If any of you have something else in mind, something less than total commitment, God will clear your blurred vision—You'll see it yet! Now that we're on the right track, let's stay on it."

Challenge for today: Carry through in doing something difficult you feel God has asked of you.

A while ago my husband and I helped clean out an older building so the work of renovation could begin for our new church. A wall had to be knocked out, carpet discarded, nails taken out of lumber, etc. During the process it didn't look like much and was a big mess. But the blueprint of the desired result was placed on the wall and today is now a welcoming space of worship. In so many ways we are like that mess and it's hard to imagine what we will be like some day. But the Lord is able to see what we are becoming and as it says in I John 3:2, (NIV) "Dear friends, now we are children of God, and what we will be has not yet been made known. But we know that when He appears, we shall be like Him, for we shall see Him as He is." Yes, we are already His children but one day, in eternity, we will be like Him without any weaknesses and imperfections. In the in between time, let us ask the Lord to help us visualize others and ourselves as He sees us... and may that change the way we live today.

Challenge for today: Ask the Lord to help you see others around you as He sees them.

We have a group of men that come to our house for retreat several times a year and they are called the Wildmen. (Men who are passionate for God) When I serve them lunch I always have a question for them to answer and one such question was: "If you can change one thing in your life what would it be?" I knew right away that for me it is to slow down and live in the present moment, enjoying God's presence more. I wake before dawn and spend time in the Word and prayer, but then I am eager to get on with my day rather than savoring the moment. Hurry can leave us feeling empty, and we may find ourselves rushing to get more, when we need to slow down and enjoy what is. We have enough time in a day to get done what the Lord has for us. I suspect we have enough time also to go out into the night air and look at the stars and give praise to our Creator. Let us give our full attention to what He has for us each day and not feel pressed and rush to do more! Like David in Ps. 23:2b-3a (Amplified) may we say, "He leads me beside the still and restful waters. He refreshes and restores my life (myself);" Let us live our one life well and refreshed!

Challenge for today: Spend 10 minutes quietly enjoying His presence in an ordinary setting.

Recently, I got my hair cut and told the gal to cut only an inch off as last time I got *sheared* by another beautician. She did as I asked her but when I got home I realized I needed at least another inch off. My request of her was a reaction from my last experience as I was afraid that I could get *sheared* again. I wonder if we do that in relation to the Lord. Maybe we have had a bad experience at a church and we tell the Lord that we are never going back there again. We may also refuse when He asks us to do something in an area we got *burned* in once a long time ago. Could we be limiting God's work in our lives when we put up roadblocks? We need to learn from the past but we also need to let go of the past and move on into all the new things God has for us. As it says in Isaiah 42:18 (The Message) "Forget about what's happened; don't keep going over old history. Be alert, be present. I'm about to do something brand-new. It's bursting out! Don't you see it?" Let us not miss what God has for us in the now.

Challenge for today: Ask God for a new way of seeing and responding to the opportunity He is giving you.

One night I made 3 different desserts and afterwards had a messy kitchen counter and sink full of dirty dishes. Often when we have retreatants here at Canaan's Rest, (our retreat's name) I just go to the freezer and pull out one or 2 desserts and give them a choice. It just seems to magically appear! It looks so easy, but they don't see the work of buying the ingredients, of putting it together, of baking, of doing dishes etc. Sometimes we may look at people in leadership as having an easy life as they are *just* leading. But there has been a cost to get there and they have surely endured years of God's preparation. On the surface it may look like a breeze but it has taken hard work, discipline, years of study and sacrifice. But leading is the best example of serving, and God chooses them; and it can't be earned! We need to rejoice in whatever position the Lord has placed us and honor those placed in leadership to carry such responsibility. In fact we are to treat everyone with honor and respect as it says in Rom 12:10-11 (NIV) "Be devoted to one another in brotherly love. Honor one another above yourselves. Never be lacking in zeal, but keep your spiritual fervor, serving the Lord."

Challenge for today: Show respect and honor to someone in a *seemly* lower position than you.

During the winter I am the first one out of bed to get the fire going in our wood stove. I often have to use a fire starter and it isn't long before there is a nice warm fire going! But one morning while I was making blueberry pancakes, I happened to look over at the stove and the fire was almost out. What happened? I opened the damper again and let the air in and soon the fire was blazing. In a spiritual sense, the fire of our love for the Lord can so quickly go out and we hardly notice when it happens. We need to be ever watchful and aware so that our love does not grow cold as we get caught up in other things....even good things! It is important to have open hearts continually and let the wind of His Spirit blow fresh winds of love upon us to keep the flame burning. Sometimes God uses another person in our lives to bring us encouragement, helping the flame to burn brightly. Other times He may use us to help others to be open to the Spirit's refreshing breeze. Paul told Timothy in II Tim. 1:6 (NIV) "For this reason I remind you to fan into flame the gift of God which is in you through the laying on my hands." May we not grow cold in our love for Him but give off the warmth of His love to others.

Challenge for today: Be open to the Spirit's movement in your life in a new way. Keep your *coals* glowing with His love.

All that we are and have belongs to God and what a difference that should make in how we live our lives. God has made us stewards and trusts us to manage and protect all He has made as He directs us. We are not the owners as David says in Ps. 24:1 (NIV) "The earth is the Lord's and all that is in it, the world and all who live in it." Everything we are and have we owe to God. If we truly believed that everything belongs to God, would we use our worldly treasures in a different way? Would we get excited as He directs us to give to people those things we may hold precious as He brings it to our attention? I love shopping for specific things others may need and often find such items when I work at "Share and Care" (a store for slightly used things) each week! I have also been the recipient of the generosity of others so many times. When we let God be in charge of our lives, and know that He will give to us all that we need there is no place for worry or grasping on to our possessions. And, like Paul, we can be content realizing He knows the amount for each of us to possess according to our faith. Let us live joyfully for we belong to God and He entrusts us to share in His heart of giving. May we be faithful stewards, knowing it is not our own strength or power that has given us wealth. Deut. 8:18a (NIV) says, "But remember the Lord your God, for it is He who gives you the ability to produce wealth."

Challenge for today: Put your faith into practice by giving something away to one who has need.

When we heard the weather prediction for more snow, below zero temperatures, and terrifically low wind chills we had to decide if we were going to prepare for what was coming. At the time the weather was comfortable and we were toasty warm. But nevertheless, we brought more wood to the back porch, put a shovel by the back door, and got plenty of food to have on hand. We also have *predictions* in the Word that there will be tough times ahead, and know, as Christians, we will need to be strong to stand. We can't wait until it gets bad and then prepare. We need to be in preparation mode now! That means spending time daily with Him in prayer and reading His Word, and storing up scriptures in our hearts. Also, we need to have a support base of Christian brothers and sisters to stand together and encourage one another. Yes, the time is coming when we will need to be able to stand firm in our faith. Paul said in Eph. 6:13-17 (The Message) "Be prepared. You're up against far more than you can handle on your own. Take all the help you can get, every weapon God has issued, so that when it's all over but the shouting you'll still be on your feet. Truth, righteousness, peace, faith, and salvation are more than words. Learn how to apply them. You'll need them throughout your life." Let each of us be alert, watchful and prepared!

Challenge for today: Memorize a scripture that will be strengthening when tough times come.

There are often things we want to change in our lives and we may have said to ourselves, "Oh, I wish I wasn't so undisciplined" or "I'd like to be more patient with my spouse!" etc. We can end up making resolutions and determinations to change. In fact, sometimes we'd like a whole transformation! But rather than trying hard and often failing, we need to relax into His grace and ask Him to do His work in us. As we open our hearts more to Him He will accomplish His work in us. Then our lives become more balanced, allowing us to live in simplicity and trust. We can't program our own hearts as we are dependent upon the Lord to untangle the mess and accomplish what is needed. He is able to help us discern the true from the false and we can ask Him to search our hearts and thoughts and to lead us in the right way. As it says in Ps. 139:23-24 (The Message) "Investigate my life, O God, find out everything about me: cross-examine and test me; get a clear picture of what I'm about; see for yourself whether I've done anything wrong—then guide me on the road to eternal life." Let us let go of the controls, surrender our hearts, and co-operate with Him so He can do His transformational work in our lives.

Challenge for today: Ask the Lord for His help in an area you have tried to change and failed!

I was awakened in the middle of the night to a grinding sound that went on for several hours. Since we live on a gravel road and no neighbors for several blocks, this was unusual! I finally figured out that it was the sound of a machine shredding the branches and left over logs of trees that had been cleared in the forest. I felt like the world had come right into my house and invaded my inner peace! As it says in Rom. 12:2a (Phillips) "Don't let the world around you squeeze you into its own mold, but let God remold your minds from within…." It's true that the world creeps in on us ever so gradually and we hardly notice at first. It's as if we are slumbering. We begin watching programs on TV that compromise our values, go places where the Lord is not welcomed, spend money on things that we are not proud of etc. Soon we are distracted and lose our focus on Him and His Kingdom. Much of my peace was robbed in the night by the sound of the machine. We may lose our peace in the same way as the world squeezes us into its mold. But the rest of verse 2 says, (The Message) "Readily recognize what He wants from you, and quickly respond to it. Unlike the culture around you, always dragging you down to its level of immaturity, God brings the best out of you, develops well-formed maturity in you."

Challenge for today: Ask the Lord to unveil one way the culture has crept into your heart and ask Him to work a change in you.

The other morning I had lots of things to do and thought that I really *need* to clean the house. Before I could start my work I had computer problems and wondered if I would be on the phone all morning with the tech and no other work would get done. But I figured out a way to bypass the problem and got into my day cleaning. While scrubbing the floor my heart was now saying, Yes! I *get* to clean my house! I had a different perspective and had such a heart of gratitude that I had the time and energy. I was also thinking of a friend with congestive heart failure and other health problems who is not able to do what I was doing. Sometimes we may complain at what the Lord is asking of us and think, why me?! Even His disciples wanted to be first, and to be served but Jesus way is just the opposite. He showed them by example of how to serve and put others first. He told the story of a servant who worked in the field and then came to the house to serve his master supper. The master wouldn't expect thanks for the servant was only doing his duty. It says in Luke 17:10 (NIV) "So you also, when you have done everything you were told to do, should say, 'We are unworthy servants; we have only done our duty.'" Let us have a servant attitude that feels honored to serve our master.

Challenge for today: Do a very menial task with a heart attitude to serve someone else.

My cousin is recovering from bunion surgery and I went to visit her and pray for her. She has the most wonderful scooter to rest that foot, permitting her to get around while pushing with her good foot. She will start putting weight on the foot that is healing in a month and will begin the process of walking on it again. She uses crutches and the scooter for support now but later will walk on her own. Perhaps that is not unlike us when we go through difficult or crippling times. The Lord may send people in His Body who will help hold us steady and give us strength and support. They share our load as it says in Gal. 6:4 (The Message) "Stoop down and reach out to those who are oppressed. Share their burdens, and so complete Christ's law." Then there will come a time when we are asked to give up our crutches and carry our own weight. It says in verse 5 of Gal. 6 (NIV) "for each one should carry his own load." My cousin will need to give up her scooter and crutches after a month goes by and start bearing her own weight, strengthening her foot. We also may need to let go of depending heavily on those around us, in His perfect timing. Then we are able sink deeply into the strength the Lord is offering us from Himself. As our faith gets exercised in this way, we seem to grow ever closer to Him.

Challenge for today: Ask the Lord to reveal to you someone who needs your unique help in bearing their burdens.

The other day when I went downstairs I noticed a strong odor coming from the cupboard under the sink. I checked out the bag of onions and sure enough in the bottom was a rotten one. It had already started to blacken the onions on either side of it and I quickly removed all that had been touched. Sometimes we get a whiff of something that is not quite right and we need to pay attention. Maybe something smells *fishy* or not quite right! As we look back on our lives were their times we had a sense that something didn't *feel* right but didn't quite know why? If we kept sniffing around would we have discovered why we had that uneasiness in our spirit that kept us from acting on something previously planned? We might have just chalked it up to being too cautious. We may have found out later that we should have listened to our spirit. Let us not underestimate the ways God speaks as it can not only affect us but also the people around us. If I had left that rotten onion in the bag, it would have ruined all the onions! May we be humble enough to admit we need His wisdom and discern His ways. It says in Rom. 11:33 (Amplified) "Oh, the depth of the riches and wisdom and knowledge of God! How unfathomable (inscrutable, unsearchable) are His judgments—His decisions! And how untraceable (mysterious, undiscoverable) are His ways-His methods, His paths!"

Challenge for today: Ask the Lord for His wisdom in discerning an area you lack His peace.

One day I walked to a friend's house and just before turning into her road, her Shih Tzu dog, Molli, began barking. She was outside at the time and saw me coming in the distance. Her master tried to restrain her but to no avail. She wanted to greet me and she persisted until he let her go into my waiting arms. She licked me and then frolicked around my legs to the extent I could hardly walk. What a greeting! I wonder sometimes if we are abandoned to the Lord or have we lost our zeal for Him. In Revelation 2 the church in Ephesus had endured patiently but sadly they had lost their first love. We also can be so busy serving the Lord but lose our zeal for Him. One has only to remember the ecstatic feelings experienced when finding the person of our dreams! No sacrifice was too great for that love. How much we need to persist and abandon ourselves daily to the Lord, so that nothing can keep us from Him. Let us not be held back by anything of this world but let ourselves go into the fullness of His love. May our prayer be like that of Ps.119:10, (Amplified) "With my whole heart have I sought You, inquiring for and of You and yearning for You; Oh, let me not wander or step aside (either in ignorance or willfully) from Your commandments."

Challenge for today: Find a new way today to express your love for the Lord.

When we arrived at our son's house we were greeted with hugs and kisses as soon as we stepped out of our car. Right away our grandson, who was 4 year old at the time, excitedly asked, "Grandma, do you have a prize for me?!" (We usually have a gift wrapped for each day we are there that the grandchildren open at breakfast time.) Now at age 4 it is understandable that our grandson would think of a gift immediately and ask for it, but if he were 14 that would be rude. Are we often that way with the Lord and have the attitude of "give me, give me!" Do we think more about what He gives us than who He is? Our two granddaughters are older and gave us hugs but never asked for a gift and simply waited. As we grow in the Lord we need to be more focused on Him than His gifts to us. I read from Ps. 48:1a & 9b (NIV) "Great is the Lord and most worthy of praise…..we meditate on your unfailing love." He is so worthy of our praise and desires that we come to Him, not just for what we can get from Him, but for Who He is. In the same way we like to hear a thank you from our grandkids, I'm sure the Lord loves when we praise and thank Him for all His gifts to us…especially for the gifts of His love, forgiveness, and life eternal.

Challenge for today: Spend time just thanking Him for who He and not asking for anything.

Have you ever prayed that God would help you to see another person through His eyes rather than yours? I'm sure what God sees is often very different from our short-sighted vision. Remember how Jesus saw Simon (who often put his foot in his mouth) and gave him a new name which meant, Rock. Even though Peter would deny Him, he became the leader and head of the apostles. Jesus saw in him what others did not see at the time. My dad lived to be 100 years old and when we knew the end was near, he was transferred from the hospital back to the nursing home. Hospice was called in and the nurse asked me many questions about my dad. I told her how content he was, so undemanding, accepted what is and didn't complain etc. I took her to his room so she could meet him. At the time I wondered what others would see...was he just a 100 year old man that needed lots of care? Perhaps that is what some of the staff thought. But I believe she saw him more as the Lord saw him for she treated him with such compassion and care. She knelt on the floor beside him and spoke into his ear and listened, for his speech was hard to understand. She helped him get comfortable and gave him reassurance and care. David said in Ps. 103:4b (NIV) that the Lord "crowns you with love and compassion" and isn't that what we all desire? May we see others as the Lord sees them and show His compassion and love!

Challenge for today: Ask the Lord for compassion in seeing a difficult person through His eyes.

When I went to a movie with a friend, we both refrained from having the popcorn and pop as she was just told by her Dr. to lose weight. Now being a friend I want to help and not hinder her goal to shed #10 or more. That means I won't bring her baked goods when I walk over to visit her as I usually do or encourage her to eat more when she comes to my house. We can help or hinder others in their walk with the Lord as well. When we are undisciplined and allow the world to creep into our lives, we are not good examples and mentors for others. But when we practice spiritual disciplines and walk in the grace He gives us, God can use us to bring encouragement to others and help them gain victory in their walk with Him. When we have a taste of who He is and how good He is, we will lose our appetite for worldly "junk food". It says in Ps. 34:8 (The Message) "Open your mouth and taste, open your eyes and see- how good God is. Blessed are you who run to him." May we develop more and more of a taste for the good things He offers and lose our appetite for what the world offers.

Challenge for today: Give up to the Lord an area of your life where you have been compromising.

Early one morning I sat in the recliner to have my devotions and as I looked up I was aghast to see the dirty vaulted ceiling and fan. I don't know how it escaped my notice before, but as I reflected, it had been awhile since I had cleaned there. It reminded me of how we need to deal with the sinful things the Lord reveals to us in our lives. We can't deal with everything all at once or it would be too much for us. Just like it say in Ex. 23:30a (NIV) "Little by little I will drive them out before you." But when our eyes are open to what needs changing, God's grace is already there to meet us and we need to act on it. I remember a friend asked me to pray for her as she wanted to get rid of a bad habit. She had had it for a long time and wanted to be set free in that area. We prayed and God's grace was upon her and she said she never had the desire for that bad habit again. Now, it is not always that easy, but His grace was there and we need to receive that grace when God is putting His finger on things in our lives. Maybe others can see what needs changing even before we do (like people who may have seen my dirty ceiling) but when we see we need to act. I went out to the garage and got the long extension pole and cleaned away and afterwards had to vacuum again. Sometimes our messes affect others too, but how wonderful when we get clean and are set free. It says in Ps. 51:10 and 12 (NIV) "Create in me a pure heart, O God, and renew a steadfast spirit within me...Restore to me the joy of your salvation and grant me a willing spirit, to sustain me."

Challenge for today: Open your heart to His whispers; give to the Lord a problem area in your life with a willingness to act on what He says.

One weekend we had a group of pastors here for a retreat and when Al (my husband) and I woke up the moon beams were streaming into our big windows. It seemed as if someone had left the light on and it was an awesome sight! We remarked how great it was that the pastors from the city would enjoy the beauty too, but at breakfast they all said they had missed it. Why? Because they had slept in and didn't come out of their room or even open their shades to see. Oh, I wonder how much we miss what the Lord has in store for us as we keep to ourselves with our personal blinds shut or we don't rise up early to seek Him! Every day He has new and wonderful things for us. But we will never know how much we miss if we remain behind shut blinds or closed doors. Let us seek Him early and not after the day is done or just when we are in a tight place and desperate for His help. Come to Him before your attention is on "your world"! What beauty Al and I saw and were awed by it, but what a shame if we would have missed out. Let us greet the dawn of new things He has for us. It says in Lam. 3:22-24 (NIV) "Because of the Lord's great love we are not consumed, for His compassions never fail. They are new every morning; great is your faithfulness. I say to myself, 'The Lord is my portion; therefore I will wait for Him.'"

Challenge for today: Open your eyes and see and experience the new thing the Lord has for you today!

I made a quick stop at our local supermarket for several food items and 2 special red garbage bags that when filled are picked up in our driveway. When I got home, much to my surprise there were 3 extra red bags in my sack and I had not paid for them. One of the cashiers must have put them in with my groceries by accident. Now, no one would know if I didn't pay the $16.50 that they were worth but I never questioned what I needed to do. The next day Al paid for them when he was in town and told the cashier what had happened! It brought to mind a memory about the time our granddaughter was running for Student Council president, (10 years old at the time) and she was asked what important thing she had learned. She responded with, "To do the right thing even when no one is looking!" Are we a person of integrity that does the right thing as His follower? Does the right thing even if there is not another soul that will find out? The Lord sees! When we do the right thing, we have a sense of deep peace within our hearts. We are reminded in Ps. 94:9b (NIV) "He who formed the eye does He not see?" The Lord sees everything and we are to do what is right before His eyes and also before others. As it says in Rom. 12:17 (Amplified) "Repay no one evil for evil, but take thought for what is honest and proper and noble (aiming to be above reproach) in the sight of everyone." Let us live lives that reflect we belong to Him!

Challenge for today: Go the second mile today to openly express you are a follower of Him!

One day a friend invited me over to her house and said she would get back to me about the time. I waited and waited and didn't hear from her. I proceeded to email her but still no response. A couple of hours later my husband was going to use the phone and realized there was a message on our answering machine for me. It doesn't beep! The message was there all the time but I missed it! It caused me to think of times we might think God has forgotten us and not heard or answered our prayers. We wait and wait and may wonder if He has abandoned us. But that is never the case. He is always there and speaking to us and leaving us messages. It is we who need to put ourselves in the position to receive those words from Him. We must tune our ear to "that still small voice!" Just as it was my fault for not checking the answering machine, God speaks and we need to listen to all of the many ways He may choose to answer us. My friend didn't use the mode of email that I was expecting but a phone message...so we need to be receptive for whatever mode He would speak to us! He also trains us to be aware of new ways He desires to communicate with us. Remember, our God is a very creative God! Sometimes He may even use another person to get His message to us. In Jer. 33:3 (NIV) it says, "Call to me and I will answer you and tell you great and unsearchable things you do not know."

Challenge for today: Become aware of God speaking in a new way to you.

W e all have probably listened to friends who have shared an experience of someone treating them hurtfully. Most likely we have been in this situation also and may not even know what we have done. Perhaps we remind them of someone who has mistreated them in the past. Maybe it is because we are follows of Christ that they want to shoot arrows at us. David certainly had that problem often and rehearses before God his dilemma. He says in Ps. 38:19 & 20 (NIV) "Many are those who are my vigorous enemies; those who hate me without reason are numerous. Those who repay my good with evil, slander me when I pursue what is good." At such times we need to be focused on the Lord and not what others think of us. It reminds me of our wood stove that radiates heat to the extent that we can comfortably go around in short sleeves. It may be freezing outside with way below zero temperatures, but we are warm as toast inside. Even so, when we get the cold shoulder from someone, a frigid remark, a cool stare, we can remain warmed within our hearts by the knowledge of whose child we are and His unconditional love for us! David must have known this as he expressed in Ps. 31:20-21 (NIV) "In the shelter of Your presence You hide them from the intrigues of men; in your dwelling You keep them safe from the strife of tongues. Praise be to the Lord, for He showed His wonderful love to me when I was in a besieged city."

Challenge for today: Show someone kindness and love that has been *cold* to you.

When we look through life from our own lens we can think it is good only if things are comfortable and enjoyable. But that is not necessarily how God views it. There are times we may find ourselves struggling to have a thankful heart in our present situation and may doubt that something good is going to come of it. Often it is easier to just complain, get negative and nearly give up! When we read about Queen Esther I wonder what we would do in her situation. She was brought into the palace against her own will, married to an old king and surrounded by idolatry and paganism She could have gotten depressed and wondered if God was punishing her. But instead of losing her faith she continued to believe God had placed her there for such a time as this. What about us? Do we look at each trial in a positive light and remain strong in our faith knowing God is in charge? Can we trust that sooner or later He will turn it around for our good? It says in Rom. 8:28 (Phillips) "Moreover we know that to those who love God, who are called according to His plan, everything that happens fits into a pattern of God." Let us willingly accept what God has for us and gratefully serve Him in all circumstances. He desires to teach us things that have eternal results so let us be strong and look from His perspective.

Challenge for today: Intently, thank the Lord for a difficult circumstance in your life.

Last night our granddaughter's soccer team won the championship and they were thrilled! At the start of the game they had to beat the other team by two goals in order to get the trophy they were dreaming of. The other team was also aware of that so they took 4 outstanding players that don't play on that team and played them in place of 4 regular players. Our granddaughter's coach told the other team what they were doing was probably illegal but they went on to play them anyway! Our granddaughter's team won by exactly 2 goals in the final few minutes!! Had the other team won, they would never have known if they were the true champions. When we know the Lord though, we don't have to be concerned about the ending for no matter what we go through in this life we have an amazingly happy ending! Though our faith may be severely exercised as we go through struggles we have a glorious "trophy" awaiting us. His finished work on the cross has reserved for us a place in heaven for all eternity. So even if we have tough battles let us finish well for we are a people of hope that know what awaits us! May we be like Paul who said in Acts 20:24 (Amplified) "But none of these things move me; neither do I esteem my life to myself, if only I may finish my course with joy and the ministry which I have obtained of (which was entrusted to me by) the Lord Jesus, faithfully to attest to the good news (Gospel) of God's grace—His unmerited favor, spiritual blessing and mercy."

Challenge for today: Keep your eyes on the goal and face your present battle with hope and joy!

Often we wish we had more hours in a day as life seems so rushed! When a person asked, "How are you?", the usual response is "Busy!" Wouldn't it be great if we could eliminate hurry from our lives and just live in the present, enjoying every moment? I try to go on a prayer walk each afternoon on our country gravel road where few cars pass by. I hear the sounds of nature and enjoy the beauty of what God has made. I notice the brilliant colors and the aroma of the woods, and things hidden from a quick view. Sometimes I sing to the Lord, sometimes I just whisper His name and enjoy His presence. Sometimes I stop and just listen in the quiet. God is a friend of silence and we need to be quiet so we can hear what He has to say to us in the stillness. When we live a life of hurry we miss the beauty of our surroundings, we miss hearing Him speak to our hearts. We miss coming face to face with ourselves. It's not so important what we say but what God speaks to us. His voice is hard to hear when the noise of the world and our own minds slips in and we are restless with decisions. When we slow down we get into the rhythm of God and we experience life at its fullest. Let us not miss Him but walk in step with Him. It says in Gal. 5:25 (NIV) "Since we live by the Spirit let us keep in step with the Spirit."

Challenge for today: Take a short prayer walk alone and open all your senses to the sights and sounds of God's beautiful creation.

Do you know someone who seems so Christ-like that you feel you are in the presence of the Lord when you are with him or her? A verse our whole Sunday School learned when I was growing up, and probably none of us will ever forget, is from Matt. 5:16 (NIV) "In the same way let your light shine before men that they may see your good deeds and praise your Father in Heaven." It was emphasized how important it is to be His light to others and represent Him wherever you go! That means our lives should be different than those of the world and when we enter a room we bring the aroma of Christ. All of us who know Him should be like a walking beacon that others can look at and get a glimpse of Him, His fragrance, and a taste of His love! I am in a group with women who are like that and I feel His presence just being among them. We don't spend our time gossiping but can share our prayer concerns and bring them to Him in prayer. They are available to serve and often found in the kitchen at church. Their lives are not centered on themselves but on building God's Kingdom. The object of our lives is to do His will and God wants to empower and equip us to do whatever it is He has for us each day. That makes life exciting and may the glory all go to Him.

Challenge for today: Be available today to listen or serve someone in need while being a vessel full of Him.

I felt very old and decrepit when I threw out my back bending over while vacuuming! Until that point I felt great and was running up and down stairs and doing everything with ease. But in one moment everything changed and I had to be so careful how I moved. Some positions were painful and it helped to support myself by leaning on something nearby or someone. I wondered how I was ever going to clean and get down on my knees to scrub since I was barely able to bend. We can get broadsided by the enemy or even a friend and our life changes in an instant. We are no longer sailing along smoothly but can feel a strong wind blowing against us. The enemy will whisper lies that we won't be able to complete or don't have what it takes to do what we feel God has asked of us! He is a liar!! I was able to get down on my knees after I walked around awhile. We walk out our faith in the same way. We are enabled to do things we never thought possible for He is doing it through us. It helps to stabilize ourselves by getting into the Word and rehearsing His promises to us. Sometimes he sends someone alongside us to help us stand against the force. May we remember the One who is most powerful to help is always present and will fight for us so we can stand our ground! We are told in Eph. 6:10 (NIV) "Finally, be strong in the Lord and in His mighty power."

Challenge for today: Find promises in scripture to refute a lie the enemy has told you.

One day I read from Luke 6:38 (NIV) when Jesus told His disciples, "Give, and it will be given to you. A good measure, pressed down, shaken together and running over, will be poured into your lap. For with the measure you use, it will be measured to you." Just before this Jesus said that we are not to judge or condemn others but forgive them and now He is saying we need to go beyond this and seek the best for others. The result is God will give to us generously, not meagerly PRESSED DOWN, (filling all the space in a container) SHAKEN, (so that grain will settle and fill the container even more fully) RUNNING OVER, (so that where there is no place for the extra to go that it has to run over the top). Just recently a woman came to Canaan (our retreat house) who has a very limited income. But she brought gifts for her time here...a big jar of honey, boxes of tea, and yummy cherries. I know how much she could really use these things herself and yet she had on her heart to give sacrificially! I was touched by this and imagined how the Lord feels when we give to Him not out of our abundance but sacrificially. I had the joy of taking her to get clothes for her large family at Share and Care (a place for almost new things). Just after we got home from town I heard a knock at our door. Someone handed me a plate of chocolates and a card with a check for Canaan that was far more than I had just spent. Truly, He gives us "good measure, pressed down and running over!" Let us listen to our hearts when we are prompted to give and give to Him generously.

Challenge for today: Open your heart and give to a need that may go overlooked by others.

How we respond to circumstances says a lot about us and our relationship to the Lord! When things get tough do we get bitter and complain or do we know that He is with us and will see us through them? I recall when a dear relative was in the hospital after she fell and had a deep gash in her head, a big black eye, and broken ribs. My husband and I went to see her and prayed for her. As we sat beside her bed she began to share how blessed she was! Now, if you saw how she looked, you would find that hard to believe! She was grateful her doctor had changed her meds and taken her off blood thinners a short time before the event or she could have fallen and bled to death. Then she was thankful that her pain had lessened, that her kids were there with her, that she had a caring nurse, that her daughter-in-law knew how to put the tourniquet in just the right place to stop the bleeding, and lastly, that a priest had come and given her communion and anointed her with oil. I think you get the picture! She had overflowing gratitude and the awareness that the Lord was with her though it all. I was reading from Phil. 4:4, 6, & 7 (NIV) "Rejoice in the Lord always. I will say it again: Rejoice! Do not be anxious about anything, but in everything, by prayer and petitions, with thanksgiving, present your requests to God. And the peace of God, which transcends all understanding, will guard your hearts and your minds in Christ Jesus." When we delight in Him we don't have to be worried about what happens to us, but just give it all to Him in thankful prayer. As we do this His peace will flood us and keep our hearts and our minds resting in Him!

Challenge for today: Live with a heart of thankfulness for everything that happens during your day!

When our son-in-law came home from Kuwait after his 6 month deployment there was a great celebration. When we saw the pictures and videos of his homecoming, each one of the family members radiated great happiness. They were finally all together as a family after so long! The 3 boys had been talking about dad, seeing him on Skype, writing to him etc. Nevertheless there is nothing like the actual being together. I think of that in relation to the Lord as we wait for His coming again! We love to talk to Him and read His "letters". We share about Him to others, but there is nothing like the reunion that is coming! We can't even imagine how we will feel in that moment. Even now as I write about it, joy floods me!! I John 3:2-3 (The Message) says, "But friends, that's exactly who we are: children of God. And that's only the beginning. Who knows how we'll end up! What we know is that when Christ is openly revealed, we'll see Him-and in seeing Him, become like Him. All of us who look forward to His Coming stay ready, with the glistening purity of Jesus' life as a model for our own." May we live each day as if it was the day of His arrival to take us to our real Home!

Challenge for today: Walk through this day with the awareness He is walking beside us the whole day!

One weekend three Sisters finally made it to Canaan's Rest (our retreat house) after trying to fit it into their schedules for several years. They were like calves released from the stall and came excited and thrilled, filling our house with a positive and joyful atmosphere. They had a childlike quality of wonderment as they enjoyed nature, quietness, exploring, listening, and sharing etc. They noticed the tall trees, the loons calling, the wild flowers, the lake gently shimmering and even that their rooms had a wooden cross on the wall. At meal times they asked many questions and even wanted to know how my husband and I had met and fell in love....... remember, they are nuns! They had so much contagious enthusiasm and were like "joy bulbs" that sparkle and give off light. Just like a single candle flame can give light to a room, they filled Canaan with their unique lights. They seem to bring Christ's presence wherever they go and as it says in II Tim. 2:21b (Phillips) they are a "vessel used for honorable purposes, dedicated and serviceable for the use of the master of the household, all ready, in fact, for any good purpose." Sometimes we forget that we are vessels and containers that He wants to use to bless others and bring His presence. Let us be empty of self so He can fill us and pour us out as He wills!

Challenge for today: Share your joy and excitement of being a child of God with someone He brings into your light!

Have you ever noticed in scripture how Jesus was so aware of His Father's timing? His disciples and others tried to get Him to act before the time but He was obedient to His Father. God's timing is perfect! A friend was getting ready to go to work at Share and Care at her usual time, but on one particular morning she got delayed. Most days she is there by 7:30 a. m. but that day she did not rush to get there. As a result she was home at the time her husband desperately needed her. Just before she was to leave he complained of a headache and then slumped over. She was able to get immediate help and he was rushed to the hospital by ambulance and later airlifted to a bigger hospital. He had a heart attack and 4 stints were put in. Timing was everything! Had she left the house at her usual time, he would not be here right now! It is important that we are sensitive to the Spirit and follow His leading, even at times when it may not make practical sense. We are reminded in Prov. 20:24 (NIV) "A man's steps are directed by the Lord. How can anyone understand his own way?" The Lord alone has the whole picture and our part is to listen and follow rather than rely on our own insight. It says in Prov. 4:11 (NIV) "I will guide you in the way of wisdom and lead you along straight paths."

Challenge for today: Listen to the Spirit and allow Him to direct each part of your day.

While out on my prayer walk I noticed many power lines lay along the side of the road. Every block or so there was another pole and they had pulleys and lots of wires attached. But they were not connected yet since the old poles were still in place. Now they look very nice as they are brand new but they are useless until they are connected to the power source. I wonder how much we are like that. We may stand out and do many good things outwardly but if the Lord hasn't asked us to do those things the power is lacking. Many activities in our church can keep us busy but the heart of the matter is what is God calling us to do? In Ps. 40:8 (Amplified) David says, "I delight to do Your will, O my God; yes, Your law is within my heart." God's will was his delight! The Lord is always speaking to us and His Spirit wants to direct each day's activities and anoint them with His love and power. But often we have selective hearing and then choose with our free will what things we will obey. We can end up getting stressed out, doing much more than He has asked of us, and missing what He has in store or us. Sometimes we have a hard time letting go of the old and continue doing things He asked of us in a different season. Paul prayed for the Colossians in 1:10b-11a (NIV) that they would live a life worthy of the Lord and please Him in every way; bearing fruit in every good work, growing in the knowledge of God, being strengthened with all POWER. May we live to please Him and be hooked up to the power source so we can bear much fruit and fruit that will remain!

Challenge for today: Seek to hear God's will for this day and follow Him with childlike faith and obedience.

Recently I visited The Little Portion Retreat House that is situated high on a hill. I sat in the chapel and watched a beautiful sunrise over the valley. There was a cross directly in front of the large chapel window that was made of colored glass and caught the sun's rays making it look "alive"! I was reminded of the love of the Lord that paid that ultimate price on the cross for each of us. It is hard to comprehend the depth of His love. Why do we often accept or believe what someone else thinks of us over how much He values us? All of us have experienced rejection as not everyone is going to love us or even like us! We can respond by trying to be perfect, trying to reach to the top to prove we are worthy, or maybe trying to have a multitude of friends etc. The bottom line is that love and acceptance is not based on what others think, or of our doing all the right things. God never rejects us! As we come to *know* that in our hearts, we will be free of what others think and realize it has no importance. Our value is based on His unconditional love and acceptance which enables us to endure the pain of rejection that comes from others, even His other children! It says in Jer. 31:3b (NIV) "I have loved you with an everlasting love; I have drawn you with loving- kindness." Let us live gratefully and freely in the awareness of His great love that He should care enough to suffer and give His life on the cross for us.

Challenge for today: Let the Lord lead you to someone and tell them how much they are loved!

Hope is powerful and we are to be people of hope. When I had back problems I thought at first that I would just ignore it and maybe it would go away. It became too painful for me to do that so I decided to take it easy and do more sitting around, but that didn't work either! Finally, I went for help to the chiropractor who saw the problem and did some adjustments on my back. She had a cancellation or would not have even been in town to help me...God sees all our needs and answers our prayers in the best possible way for each of us! Being worked on at the time didn't feel really great but it was necessary and I felt so much better afterwards. On my way home, I thought of how we say we desire change and growth in the Lord but do we really mean that? What if it means having some adjustments made in our lives or asking for help? Maybe we have lost hope somewhere along the way and think that things will always be the same and never get better. Remember it says in Ps. 147:11 (NIV) "The Lord takes pleasure in those who reverently and worshipfully fear Him, in those who hope in His mercy and loving-kindness." When we put things into God's hands, He will give us courage to let go of our fears and allow Him to do what is necessary in our lives to bring healing. Why would we rather live in the pain of our past or present when He is there to bring healing and hope? We may not have instant healing, as many times it seems to come gradually. Either way, may we be like David who cries out to the Lord in Ps. 39:7, (Amplified) "And now, Lord, what do I wait for and expect? My hope and expectation are in You."

Challenge for today: Trust God to bring healing in an area of your life that has brought you much pain.

Giving back to the Lord at least 10% was something we heard and saw practiced growing up in our home. My folks loved to give and gave far more than the tithe and wanted us to know the joy of giving also! When we had my dad's 100th birthday party he gave a little speech and encouraged all of us to give from our hearts at least the tithe. I believe our children and their grandchildren practice this as well, and at our granddaughter's school, the whole school is now aware! The teacher asked the class to draw a picture and tell what it meant to be a good citizen. Our 9 year old granddaughter drew a girl putting money in the offering box at church with the caption, "My family is a good citizen because every Sunday we give (She named the exact amount!) for offering in our church and it helps our church reach over 1,000 unchurched families and makes our church also help kids in Africa and India." One of the moms who saw the picture hanging on the hall wall at school took a picture of it on her phone and sent it to our daughter-in-law! Of course, the whole school can figure out our son's salary but maybe it will make others think about giving back to the Lord. As it says in II Cor. 9:6-7 (NIV) "Remember this: Whoever sows sparingly will also reap sparingly, and whoever sows generously will also reap generously. Each man should give what he has decided in is heart to give not reluctantly or under compulsion, for God loves a cheerful giver." Now our son never intended the school to know how much he gives, but his children are seeing by example, what it means to sow generously and learning about a wonderful blessing God offers each of us.

Challenge for today: Give in secret to someone or some cause the Lord puts on your heart.

Our church had a youth party and we all came dressed up in Biblical costumes. Our pastor met us at the door in a long tan robe with lettuce around his ears and white ash looking flakes on his face! Immediately I thought I knew who he was....the prodigal who went away from home and ended up eating what the pigs ate! But then he prayed 3 times in a row and I thought he must be Daniel and was on a vegetarian diet! I was wrong both times. He turned out to be Jonah who was swallowed up by a big fish and the lettuce was seaweed from being inside the fish for 3 days and nights. It made me realize how much we need to be discerning, even though we may think we already know. Things can change for each of life's situations. Just think of how many ways the children of Israel did battle. Sometimes they marched in silence and then shouted, sometimes they waited for the sound of the wind in the balsam trees, sometimes they set ambushes etc. Just because it was right one time didn't mean it was good for the next time. Let us ask the Lord for His discernment before we act and then follow His leading. Jer. 7:23b (Amplified) says, "Listen to and obey My voice, and I will be your God and you will be My people; and walk in the whole way I command you, that it may be well with you."

Challenge for today: Don't be quick to act but listen to the Lord first and follow in obedience.

The care of our bodies is really a spiritual practice and will give us strength for our life's journey! Too often we walk around tired, overworked, over committed, and stressed. We use caffeine to perk us up and keep us going. We are told in I Cor. 3:16 (NIV) "Don't you know that you yourselves are God's temple and that God's Spirit dwells in you?" That means our bodies are sacred and it is the place God's Spirit lives. So shouldn't we take excellent care of our bodies and get rest, eat better, drink more water, exercise, and keep it in good shape both mentally and physically? When we have retreatants here at our prayer home (Canaan's Rest) they usually go for walks and are rejuvenated by just being out in the beauty of creation with the Lord. It is a time they can pray and reflect on their lives, and get renewed. Paul writes in Rom. 12:1 (NIV) "Therefore, I urge you, brothers, in view of God's mercy to offer your bodies as living sacrifices, holy and pleasing to God—this is your spiritual act of worship." We come to the Lord not just on the soul level (mind, will and emotions) but with our bodies as well! Just knowing that God has chosen to make our bodies His dwelling place opens us up to be more aware of His presence so we can respond whole heartedly to Him!

Challenge for today: Do something special to care for your "temple" today! Remember, it is fearfully and wonderfully made by Him!

Our nephew's little boy was celebrating his 4th birthday and his dad was going to take him out on the lake to fish. He loves to fish but that day he said he couldn't go because Auntie Judy was coming over to see him. I should be very flattered that he wanted to wait for me, and even though he may like me, he had an ulterior motive....he knew I had a birthday present for him. When I went over to the cabin he came running out with a big smile and a hug. Of course, he was happier yet to open the gift I had hidden behind my back! It made me think of how often we go to the Lord with our hand out to receive something we want from Him. He loves to give to us but how sad if that is the only time we go to Him. Isn't it good that we come to Him just because we love Him and want to be with Him, even if we don't "need" something? It is more than enough already that He died for us and gives us new life. It is says in Isa. 61:10 (Amplified) "I will greatly rejoice in the Lord, my soul will exult in my God; for He has clothed me with the garments of salvation. He has covered me with the robe of righteousness, as a bridegroom decks himself with a garland, and as a bride adorns herself with her jewels." Let us love and delight in Him who gives us life abundant!

Challenge for today: Delight in the Lord and thank Him throughout the day for who He is!

Sometimes we are unaware of things in our life that need the Lord's corrective touch and he may choose to use someone in the Body of Christ to point it out! One day I put a new belt in our vacuum but placed it over three metal prongs that I shouldn't have. My son-in-law offered to vacuum for me and saw that the beaters were not going around and that the belt had slipped off. It could have taken me a while longer to detect it but in a few minutes he had the problem solved; and had it fixed and running perfectly. Sometimes we receive a word from a friend, our spouse, or even an *enemy* and we need to pay attention. Is it something we need to look at and take care of? Why haven't we seen it long ago? We grow as we are open to the Lord and others He sends to correct us. Even though the Lord loves us right where we are, it is good to take care of those things that hinder our relationship with Him and others. He is so ready to forgive us and strengthen us and we go on to gradually change and grow more like Him. Paul says in II Cor. 3:18 (Message) "And so we are transfigured much like the Messiah, our lives gradually becoming brighter and more beautiful as God enters our lives and we become like Him." Let us be willing to hear!

Challenge for today: Be willing to receive correction that will enable you to become more like Him.

Some days can get so busy it seems like we find more urgent things to do than to sit quietly before the Lord and be silent! During our last church service there was a time in the middle to just be quiet and listen to the Lord. At first there are often distractions of inner noises that seem louder than what God is saying. We can begin to hear God speak to our heart if we hang in there and simply wait upon Him. Soon we begin to hear His whispers. Silence opens the way of helping us be attentive to His Word and He speaks things that hit their mark in our hearts. We are meant to live in an ongoing conversation with Him; where He speaks to us and we speak to Him! He created us for intimate fellowship and we hear Him best when we set time aside to be with Him daily and listen. We are not wasting our time as we have this intimate time with Him! We can't go by what we always "feel". When it seems like nothing is happening on the surface, He may be filling us with Himself on a deeper level. Ps. 46:10 (Amplified) says, "Let be and be still, and know (recognize and understand) that I am God. I will be exalted among the nations! I will be exalted in the earth." As we are still and quiet before Him, listening to His voice, we may find we have the right words to give to others also.

Challenge for today: Find a special quiet place and spend a few minutes just listening to Him. You might even want to write down what He whispers to you!

When we were at the rodeo in San Antonio with our daughter's family there were many school buses full of children there. The children were in lines and care was given that they didn't get separated from their teacher and the rest of their class. We saw one man in a suit, probably the only man there in a suit, and he looked important as he wore a badge. While one class was lined up to pass we all had to wait. Then came another class and we waited some more. But this man thought has was too important to wait and tried to cross through the line of the children. A safety man put his hand out and made him step back and told him to wait like the rest! He did not look happy but did as he was told. Perhaps we could think that because of our position we are important and the rules don't apply to us. Maybe it's our looks, or our wealth, or our smooth speech that make us feel free to "break the rules"! James 2:10 (Amplified) tells us, "For whosoever keeps the Law (as a) whole but stumbles and offends in one (single instance) has become guilty of (breaking) all of it." We each have to give an account of our life before the Lord and let us be humble children who obey Him who sees, even when others may not! Jesus is the most perfect example for us as He was obedient to ALL His Father gave Him to do and say!

Challenge for today: Be conscientious to obey all the traffic laws, even if no one is looking!

I did it again! I had a reward coupon for a major store of $40.00 but forgot to use it when we shopped there yesterday....and also the previous time!! I will have another chance to use it but I blew it again and it escaped my memory. Have we also done that with God's promises? We go through a difficult time and completely forget His promises to us, and pay for it by being stressed or depressed; robbed of our peace. We say the Bible is a guide for our lives and we may even memorize many scriptures but then forget about them when we need to apply them the most! We may forget that He said in Ex. 33:14 (NIV) "My presence will go with you, and I will give you rest." Instead, we may feel all alone. The average person has 9 Bibles so it isn't that we don't have access to the promises but we need to let it be our "navigation system"! Too often the meaning of the Word can be informational and even up for debate. We can read the Bible from cover to cover many times but if it doesn't reach our hearts we remain unchanged. The important thing is that we have an intimate relationship with the One who this "love letter" is from. He has so much to say to us and give us, and as we receive from Him our lives become meaningful and rich. Also, when we really know Him we can cash in on the rewards as they are great and eternal!

Challenge for today: Take one of His promises and carry it with you in your heart today and let it change you forever!

Since I have been having back problems I have had more selfish thoughts. I wonder as I enter a room if I can find the most comfortable chair with a straight back....*or* if I drop something would someone pick it up for me....or if someone else would do my heavy work... or if I can sneak away for a few minutes to lie down etc. Right now I do have to be careful but if I continue this attitude when I am better; I could become one self-centered person! When we spend our time focusing on ourselves our world becomes very small. My husband and I live in the woods away from the city traffic and close to nature. We love it as we have the feeling of spaciousness and can enjoy the freedom to roam and explore. Not everyone can do this but we all can have that inner spaciousness in a spiritual sense. Paul says in Rom. 8:8 (The Message) "Obsession with self in these matters is a dead end; attention to God leads us out into the open, into a spacious free life. Focusing on the self is the opposite of focusing on God. Anyone completely absorbed in self ignores God, ends up thinking more about self than God." This is not pleasing to God and not the way to live! When we die to self our world opens up to God and others and our hearts expand. Paul exhorts the Corinthians to enter into a wide-open spacious life and not be fenced in or small. II Cor. 6:13 (The Message) says, "Open up your lives. Live openly and expansively." Doesn't it feel incredible to not be hemmed in but able to move freely in the Spirit?

Challenge for today: Find a way to serve someone else even if it means self-sacrifice on your part.

We were created for intimacy with God and how important it is to receive His love and then respond with love for Him and to others. Too often our Christian walk can get more mechanical and we miss the excitement of the journey and the constant communion with Him. Seeing two lovers so attentive to one another and aware of each other's presence is a reminder to us of the intimacy we are to have with the Lord. Even as they desire to spend every moment together, our lives were meant to be a continual communion with Him. It isn't about knowing just facts about Him but living connected to Him. Just as lovers can take one another for granted we can take Him for granted also and become ho-hum. He wants our hearts to be filled with thoughts of Him continually, and our ears open to His voice as He desires to speak with us all throughout the day. Even as we lay upon our beds at night, He is so close and embraces us with His peace. We are meant for Him! As it says in John 17:3 (NIV) "Now this is eternal life: that they may know you, the only true God, and Jesus Christ whom You have sent."

Challenge for today: Live connected to Him and listen to His whispers of love throughout the day.

Structure is good in our Christian walk and adds order and discipline to our lives. But can it be carried too far at times? Having daily devotions, a regular worship time, fasting, reading Scriptures, tithing etc. are all helpful for our spiritual growth, but if we get too focused on the method, we will miss the heart of our faith. Two seminarians from Kenya were staying for the summer at the home of a deacon's family. The American family was going to plant potatoes in their large garden one day and the seminarians insisted that they help. They laughed and sang and had a great time visiting as they worked. They, however, paid no attention to rows and just planted them all around, here and there, but in a general area! Since they weren't planted in neat rows it was hard for the ground to be tilled around them, but that didn't spoil the crop that resulted. The potatoes tasted just as good! Do we emphasize a certain way to pray; an exact way to worship Him; a certain time of day to have our quiet time, a particular version of the Bible to study? Let us not get so "stuck" in methods and rules but be free in the Spirit and enjoy the journey. It says in II Cor. 3:17 (Amplified) "Now the Lord is the Spirit, and where the Spirit of the Lord is there is liberty—emancipation from bondage, freedom."

Challenge for today: Be open for a new way of enjoying the Lord. Enjoy the refreshment of change!

The Lord has given out of His storehouse of riches and blessed us all so much. We are told in Matt. 10:8b (NIV) "Freely you have received, freely give." Giving back to Him brings incredible joy and often we do that by giving to others, not just in the offerings at church. Everyone cannot give a lot materially but there are many opportunities for giving in various ways. One dear friend has a heart to give but hasn't got a lot of means to do that since they have to watch carefully how they spend. There is very little left after they pay their monthly bills so every penny counts. I am amazed though at how the Lord blesses her that she may bless other! She stops at church on her way home from work to help the secretary and gets music ready for Sunday mornings. She is often found in the kitchen helping to serve meals or coffee on Sunday morning. She gives rides to people who have appointments and needs. I love to hear when she wins something as I feel the Lord is smiling on her. She recently won a TV in a drawing of 10,000 people and also received $100 from a local radio station to give away to others. The latter one she received for writing how she would bless others if she won that money. As she gives out to others I see God provides for her family as well. As it says in Phil. 4:19 (Amplified) "And my God will liberally supply (fill to the full) your every need according to His riches in glory in Christ Jesus." Let us give as He directs us and trust that He will meet all our needs and more!

Challenge for today: Be on the lookout for someone who has a need that could be overlooked and allow the Spirit to help you to respond with a portion of your "riches"!

In my private devotions I read from Ps. 102:1-2 (NIV) "Hear my prayer O Lord; let my cry for help come to you. Do not hide your face from me when I am in distress. Turn your ear to me; when I call, answer me quickly." We did call out to the Lord in our distress as we traveled to our son's home. It was 4:30 in the morning and still very dark out when two deer ran across the highway in front of us. My husband applied the brakes but hit the second deer, knocking out the front grill of our Highlander. After surveying the damage and calling the insurance company, we thanked the Lord that it wasn't worse! We were not hurt, the SUV could still run, and we would be able to continue our 11 hour journey to babysit our grandchildren. We all have a choice on what to focus on—we can be downhearted and wish negative things would never happen in our lives or we can see the Lord's hand and how He is present in all that happens to us. Let us react in faith and remember He is with us in everything that touches our lives 24/7! Just before Jesus ascended He spoke these words to His disciples and they are for us today: Matt. 28:20b (NIV) "And surely I am with you always, to the very end of the age."

Challenge for the day: Be aware of His presence in everything that happens today.

Since my cousin was on crutches she asked me to put a casserole dish into her car that was parked in her garage. She wanted to return it to a friend later. I had walked to her home and seen the car in her driveway so I told her that her car was outside and proceeded to take the dish out to the car. But the red Prius was locked and when I got her key it didn't work. I then put her dish on top of the car. Later she also went out there with her key and couldn't get it open. She called her husband, thinking the battery in the key needed replacing and tried to use the little emergency key also but with no success! When she asked her husband why he parked the car outside of the garage, he informed her that their car was still in the garage and that was the car of their guests! I mistakenly told her an untruth thinking I knew, but it was not right. I went by what I thought I saw with my eyes. We are not to be wise in our own eyes. (Prov.3:7) Sometimes we think we know by what we see with our eyes but it may not be so. As it says in II Cor. 4:18a, (NIV) "So we fix our eyes not on what is seen, but what is unseen." My cousin did hear a beep beep in her garage when pressing her key and also wondered about the little ding in her door but didn't realize it wasn't truly her car. Are we open to new information that goes contrary to what we think we know and have seen? Let us have eyes of faith and allow the new that He reveals to us.

Challenge for today: Ask God to open the eyes of your heart to consider a difficult situation from His perspective.

We are all getting older and from the time of our birth we are one step closer to our death. No matter where we are in our earthly journey we need to live well and hopefully be remembered by others as someone who loved and had wisdom. We may ask ourselves: Have we made choices along the way that have brought us closer to the Lord? Have we slowed down to make time for friends and ministry the Lord has gifted us to do? Maybe we have enjoyed our solitude and reading and the things we love to do a bit too much as well. As dear ones around us die we are more aware of the brevity of our lives. We may notice our bodies starting to wear out and long for the day we will receive a new one when we reach our heavenly home! May we use the time we have here on earth to proclaim Jesus to the next generation and mentor them when given the opportunity. We must not think we are ever too old for God to use as we have only to remember in scripture people like Moses, who led over a million people through the wilderness when he was 80 years old. Sarah was no spring chicken when she had Isaac or when Elizabeth had John. May we live out our older years with grace and be present to whatever God has for us. Just being in prayer for others is one of the most important ministries we can have. Each season of our lives has its unpredictable challenges and opportunities. May we pray with the Psalmist in Ps.71:18 (NIV) "Even when I am old and gray, do not forsake me, O God, till I declare your power to the next generation, your might to all who are to come." The Body of Christ desires the older and wiser saints to help guide them along their journey with encouragement; and light the way along the path of faith.

Challenge for today: Think about the story you want your life to tell and move in that direction. What do you want most to pass on to others?

While at the dentist office I noticed how the dental hygienist anticipated the needs of the dentist. She knew the procedure and what he needed next; he hardly had to ask for anything. They were synchronized and work on my tooth went very quickly and smoothly. I thought of how neat it is when we abide in the Lord and He in us, for there is beautiful and abundant fruit that results. John 15:5 (NIV) Jesus reminds us that we can't do anything if we are not vitally connected with Him, just like the branch is to the vine. He said, "I am the vine; you are the branches. If a man remains in Me and I in him, he will bear much fruit, apart from me you can do nothing." When we are His followers and desire to do His will above our will, there is no limit to what He can do through us. It is evident to others also, that we belong to Him and are His children when we obey Him. When we are in sync with Him,we can ask anything in His name and He will give it to us, for we will desire the same thing. What joy there is when we live deeply in Him! We become His presence to others and know that truly He loves and delights in us. Let us remain in that relationship with Him and practice what it means to truly dwell in the shelter of the Most High. It says in Psalm: 91:1-2 (NIV)"He who dwells in the shelter of the Most High will rest in the shadow of the Almighty. I will say of the Lord, 'He is my fortress, my God, in whom I trust.'"

Challenge for today: Experience God in ALL things today!

Sometimes it is the little things that are most appreciated and they seem to add up to something big in our hearts. While we were babysitting one weekend our granddaughter expressed a desire to have her own garden on the edge of their patio. We took her to the garden store so she could pick out some plants and bulbs and she was eager to get home to plant them. Her 6 year old brother decided he wanted to grow a pumpkin and begged to get some pumpkin seeds to grow his very own. Now the seeds only cost $1.69 but you would have thought it was the world as he was so excited. He planted several seeds and watered them, drew pictures of pumpkins and put them on the window, and went outside every little while to see if they had grown yet. It seemed more exciting to him than if we had taken him to an amusement park! Perhaps we don't realize how the little kindnesses we show to others can make such a difference in their lives. Just a card to say we are thinking of them and praying for them, or a check to tide them over when money is tight, or bringing supper to a family who is going through a time of grief etc. can make a difference. It may not be something big, but it gives others encouragement and faith to know God is with them and watching out for them. We need to be sensitive to the Spirit so that we act on his promptings when a need is present and He wants to use us to meet that need. It could be as simple as making a phone call and listening to their heart need. We are told in Col.3:17 (NIV) "And whatever you do; whether in word or deed, do it all in the name of the Lord Jesus, giving thanks to God the Father through Him." Whatever we do, may we do it in His name and for His glory!

Challenge for today: Do some "little thing" for someone you sense needs encouragement.

When Paul wrote to the Colossians in 12:12 (NIV) his exhortation to them was: "Therefore, as God's chosen people, holy and dearly loved, clothe your-selves with compassion, kindness, humility, gentleness and patience." These are qualities God wants to work in each of us but it doesn't happen overnight. Right now our 6 year old grandson is being trained in patience as he waits for his planted pumpkin seeds to show growth. He looks many, many times a day to see if some green sprout has appeared. He invited his friends to come and see his garden too and can only tell them what will soon happen. Right now something is happening under the soil but it is yet unseen to the eye, so patience and faith are needed. Likewise, we may be exercised on patience or humility, or any of these virtues mentioned but it may be impercep-tible to others at first. God knows just what is needed and has the exact circumstances to help produce these good qualities in us. We can therefore thank Him in all things, trusting Him that He knows best. Just like Grant, it may seem to take much longer than we would like but take heart! Also, remember He is working in those around us and those changes take time!

Challenge for today: Ask God to show you an area He is now at work in your life and welcome and cooperate with Him.

It is beautiful to observe how God's power has transformed someone's life when we haven't seen them for some time. It is almost like talking to a new person as he or she may respond so differently now because of God's work within their heart. We should all be making progress in our spiritual growth to become more like Jesus. No one is perfect or has arrived but that shouldn't keep us from surrendering to and receiving His grace to change and grow. How blessed we are to have His grace! Paul said in II Cor. 5:17 (NIV) "Therefore, if anyone is in Christ, he is a new creation; the old has gone, the new has come!" God cares more about our transformation than we do. He has a way of shining His light on our weak areas and character flaws that we may be blinded to. He may order up events and circumstances in our lives to help us face these things that need to change. His timing is always perfect! He gives us power to decrease that He may increase in our lives. Jesus told His disciples in Matt. 16:24-25 (NIV) "If anyone would come after me, he must deny himself and take up his cross and follow me. For whoever wants to save his life will lose it, but whoever loses his life for me will find it. " Let us lose our life to find it in Him.

Challenge for today: Ask the Lord to show you an area of your life not yet under His control.

It's good to celebrate Easter all year long for Christ's death, burial, and resurrection opened heaven's gates to us. Alleluia! Each time we partake of communion our hearts should overflow with gratitude for we are forgiven because of His sacrifice for us. The very word communion means thanksgiving, and our strength and power come from communion with Him. But, we still have to face our own personal cross. We must be willing to choose the will of our Father over that of our own, time and time again each and every day. Jesus said in Matt. 10:38 (NIV) "And anyone who does not take up his cross and follow me is not worthy of me." Our natural tendency is to use our own strength and mind to manage our lives; but as we give each situation over to Him, He works it out for His glory. The object of our life is to do God's will not to be successful or famous. His love and power flows through us to others as He has the freedom to live His life through us. Let us let go of our personal power and control and quit taking things into our own hands. Then we can tap into the energy and power of God and He can move freely through us! The most frustrated people are those that fight His will. True joy comes in surrendering to His perfect will and all that He has for us.

Challenge for today: Ask the Lord to equip you and enable you to do His will today as He gives you opportunities to choose between your will and His.

Our granddaughter plays soccer and had a grueling weekend as they battled it out for the championship in their tournament! They played in wind and rain and also had to delay games because of lightening. The last game was tied and went into two overtimes before her team was declared the winner. She was exhausted afterwards and had a long trip home but was it worth all that? Yes!! Yes!! Often we are in tough battles in our spiritual lives and get weary and worn down. It is strengthening to turn to His promises like Ps. 60:12 (Amplified) "Through God we shall do valiantly, for He it is Who shall tread down our adversaries." Yes, we can trust Him in the most adverse circumstance and we need to focus on His strength and power, not our own. We can get very weary and often the Lord brings someone alongside us to cheer us on. Time spent alone with Him also helps us to hear His voice of encouragement to our heart. We are told in I Cor. 15:58 (NIV) "Therefore, my dear brothers, stand firm. Let nothing move you.. Always give yourselves fully to the work of the Lord, because you know that your labor is not in vain." Let us not give up but fight the good fight of faith and not be moved!

Challenge for today: Persevere in something that you have wanted to give up!

We are always so amazed when we visit our grandchildren how utterly different they are from one another. Each has his own looks, personality, gifts, likes and dislikes etc. No two are alike and yet they belong to the same family. Isn't that what the Body of Christ is like? Paul says in Rom. 12:5 (NIV) "So in Christ we who are many form one body, and each member belongs to all the others." He goes on to talk about the different gifts and how we are to use them for the good of others and make the necessary adjustments. I think it is God's intention that we see our need for one another and how mutually dependent we are. Our differences are a cause for celebration and there is so much that is amazing about each person. Sometimes others that differ greatly from us may get on our nerves but instead of letting them get to us, we can ask what we are to learn. God often puts someone next to us to help us fill out in the places we are deficient. We grow as we are open to one another and share Christ together and inspire each other. Let us give our best as Jesus wants to build His church through us and together we can defeat the enemy.

Challenge for today: Think of the many things the Lord is trying to teach you through someone that is the opposite of you.

I think we all know what it is like to be judged and to have even our motives scrutinized. One day as we were traveling south we stopped at McDonalds for lunch. There was a short line and others were standing nearby, waiting around for their orders. I asked a man who was standing back a ways if he had been waited on and he pointed to a lady and mumbled something I couldn't hear. When she ordered I stepped up to place my order and the man quickly stepped in front of me and with a loud voice said, "I WAS HERE FIRST!" I told him how sorry I was and that I thought he was with this woman. People around me raised their eyebrows, surprised by his anger. When I picked up my order I apologized to him again but he still appeared angry. I was glad that the Lord knew my motive for I was not out to push him out of line, even if he didn't believe me. In Prov. 16:2 it says our motives are weighted by the Lord. Isn't it easy to judge others and think we know the motives of their hearts? In Matt. 7:1 -2 (Message) "Don't pick on people, jump on their failures, criticize their faults-unless, of course, you want the same treatment. That critical spirit has a way of boomeranging." Let us allow the Lord to be the judge and excuse ourselves from that position!

Challenge for today: Each time you are tempted to criticize another person, pray for them instead.

One day we were traveling on the freeway at a good speed and all of a sudden came to a dead stop. We thought there must have been an accident, but after bumper to bumper crawl speed for the next 45 minutes, we discovered that the problem was construction and a reduced lane. There were cars that "cheated" and drove on the shoulder and then tried to slyly ease their way back onto the freeway in front of others. Sometimes we might think we are making progress in our spiritual lives and all of a sudden we seem to come to a stand-still, feeling blocked and frustrated. It may be through no fault of our own or we may feel like others in our lives are impeding our progress. All we know is we are not in control and can only pray and wait, asking the Lord to teach us what He would have us learn. It does no good to try to get around it (as those drivers on the shoulder), or we will probably go through it later. May we be patient, trust, and use the time as it says in Rom. 12:12, (Amplified) "Rejoice and exult in hope; be steadfast and patient in suffering and tribulation; be constant in prayer." These can become some of our greatest times of growth in the Spirit as we realize His thoughts and plans for us are way beyond ours!

Challenge for today: Show extra patience towards others while behind of the wheel of your vehicle!

I went for a prayer walk on our hilly country road and there was a yellow road sign that showed several squiggly curves ahead. It is nice to know what to expect and when to slow down but life isn't always that way. Often something sudden and unexpected happens and we have a choice if we are going to call out to the Lord or if we are going to just tough it out on our own. Our culture applauds self-reliance but God's way is reliance on Him. There is a big difference! We get all worn out trying to figure things out and trying to control the circumstances. All the time the Lord is saying, lean into Me and My strength. Let Me give you wisdom from above and power for whatever curve may be ahead. I love to read the Psalms and David was an example of one who called out to the Lord and the Lord heard him, just as He does our cries and whispers. His answers are so much better than whatever we can figure out. Jeremiah 33:3 (The Message) says, "Call to me and I will answer you. I'll tell you marvelous and wondrous things that you could never figure out on your own."

Challenge for today: Ask God to take over an area in your life that you have tried to be in control.

Recently, about six inches of snow was predicted for our area. It turned out that we got only a dusting of snow but friends wrote that they got almost 20 inches of snow and were not able to get out! Since our lives went on as usual, it was hard to "walk in the shoes" of those that were not so fortunate. But we need to live our lives, not just focusing on what touches us but how others are affected. Both Al and I are on the Compassion Committee at our church. We have many scriptures about compassion and Paul gives us the command in Eph. 4:32 (NIV) "Be kind and compassionate to one another, forgiving each other, just as in Christ, God forgave you." Our church is involved in showing compassion to those in the community who have various needs. It may mean giving out a gas card, or taking them to the hospital for their chemo treatment, or sending a get well card, or making a visit and praying for healing etc. Isn't it interesting how when we hurt in some way, it makes us more sensitive to others who are hurting? Maybe we aren't going through the exact trial as someone else but let us be clothed with compassion for others.

Challenge for today: Do a compassionate act for someone who the Lord puts before you today.

One night I picked up two women for Bible Study and when one of them tried to put on her seat belt in the back seat it just wasn't working. She tried and tried, so I peeked back and said, "Perhaps you are trying to hook your belt up to the middle seat buckle instead of the side seat buckle." Sure enough once she did fasten it to the right one, it clicked right in. Sometimes things don't work out like we think they should and we can become disillusioned. We may read scriptures with promises and think, why am I not seeing results? But maybe we are not reading the conditions that go with the promise or maybe we are taking it out of context. God is always faithful to His promises as He says and He never changes! For example it says in James 4:8 that God will draw near to us, but it first says we are to draw near Him. It says in I John 1:7 (NIV) "But if we walk in the light, as He is in the light, we have fellowship with one another, and the blood of Jesus, His Son, purified us from every sin." Let each of us line up with His Word and make the right connections! Remember, He does not change!

Challenge for today: Ask Him to show you a place in your heart that is not filled with His light.

One day we were invited over to my cousin's cabin for dinner. He had just given his son a huge gift...a CAT with a 15 foot blade that was intended to make trails in the woods. This CAT that had been in Canada was delivered all the way to MN and was received with much joy. It reminded me of God's great gift to us when He sent His son, all the way from glory to earth to clear the way for our salvation. But we need to receive this gift just like Matt did when it was delivered. He was so thrilled and began at once to look it over and get it started. It was just the beginning for he used it to clear out the old logs and trees that were blocking the path they were making for walking and cross country skiing. We likewise need to receive the gift of God's grace for salvation and it is just the beginning of His work in our lives. He wants to clean out the things that hinder our walk with Him and give us a new path on which to walk. Now this is only one of the wonderful gifts He gives and other gifts often surprise us. Every day we are gifted by the Lord and as Paul says in II Cor. 9:15 (NIV) "Thanks be to God for His indescribable gift." May we give thanks and receive with open hearts all that He has for us!

Challenge for today: Give thanks for your salvation and share Him with someone else.

When I went to church, a mom next to me was holding her precious newborn baby who weighed only 6 1/2# and so wee. I thought back of our 3 children and how quickly they had grown up and now have children of their own. Where does the time go? Seems like our journey is so brief and before we know it, we are making necessary preparation for the next life. Our cultural tells us to go after what "we" want and it will make us happy. But we have only to look at the lives of celebrities that have everything to know that it is not so. When we are followers of Christ, we have a much bigger purpose and our joy comes in knowing Him deeply and being His servant to others. We need to prepare for the final journey and have things in order. Are there people we need to forgive? Are there things the Lord has for us to share with others? Do we need to slow down and enjoy the journey more? Are we listening to Him to order our days? We will all experience death and may each day be lived in preparation for that final Homecoming. It says in Ps. 90:12 (Amplified) "So teach us to number our days that we may get us a heart of wisdom."

Challenge for today: Take a few moments to ponder your Homecoming...have you finished all the things He called you to do?

Making prayer shawls with others at church is something I enjoy. One day I was using two big one pound balls of yarn and I crocheted the two strands together. One ball was unrolling nicely but the other one of brushed yarn got caught up on itself. It came out in tangled bunches and at first I had to stop to untangle before I could continue. I didn't get very far and it was very slow work. But two nice friends offered to help and did the untangling for me so I could keep going. It spoke to me of how we need others in our lives to help sort out things that seem difficult for us to do on our own. They often can see with more discernment what is "messing" us up. It was much easier when they helped me and I could continue. Yes, we need others! They are a gift to us from God, and when they have our best in mind, they are used as aids in our healing so we can be fruitful. Let us be vulnerable and accept those that God sends into our lives to help us in our walk with Him. It says in Ecc. 4:9-10 (The Message) "It's better to have a partner than to go it alone. Share the work, share the wealth. And if one falls down, the other helps. But if there's no one to help, tough!"

Challenge for today: Thank a friend who has walked beside you and helped you in the past.

When we lived in a parsonage that bordered the woods, our neighbor dog seemed to "adopt" me. He would lay by our back door and when he heard me get my shoes out of the closet, he would start barking with hopes that I was going for a prayer walk. I often walked on the prayer trail through the woods and climbed up into a deer stand to have a quiet time. The first few times I did this Spunky would bark and frantically circle the tree and bark some more. It was very distracting but in time he learned to just lie down at the foot of the tree and wait for me. It is rather like that when we go apart to spend time listening to the Lord. At first there are so many distractions going through our minds that it is hard to focus and really listen. But as we make it a habit, the distractions seem to get less and less and in the quiet we hear Him speak. Up high in the tree, I was able to see so much more and things looked different from that perspective. When we look from His higher view, those things that concerned us seem to fade away. Let us be faithful to go apart and quiet ourselves to listen to His voice. Often in the silence we can hear the whispers of God's love and sense being His beloved. In Zeph. 3:17 it says (NIV) "The Lord your God is with you, He is mighty to save. He will take great delight in you, He will quiet you with His love, He will rejoice over you with singing."

Challenge for today: Spend 10 minutes in a quiet place and listen to what He has to say to you.

I went back to Bone Builders (exercise class for seniors) after being gone for nearly a month. We had been traveling so I was not able to attend and felt quite out of shape. My #8 weights seemed to have grown heavier and I was barely able to finish the 12 reps of some of the exercises! Even though I had been walking most days, I had not been doing strength exercises and felt rather flabby! I wonder if we are like that in our spiritual lives too. We can get lazy and start skipping quiet times with the Lord, missing church, forgetting to pray about things that concern us, ignoring the Spirit's promptings etc. We may not realize it at the time but we are getting spiritually "flabby"! Then a trial comes along and it seems to wipe us out for we are not in good spiritual condition. As it says in Eph. 6:10b (Amplified) "Be strong in the Lord— Be empowered through your union with Him; draw your strength from Him—that strength which His boundless might provides." Our strength comes from a strong inner life with Jesus. Let us not be weak and go away from the Lord but draw close. Then we will gain our strength in Him so we can stand our ground!

Challenge for today: Spend quality time in fellowship with the Lord.

One day my husband and I went to work on the wood pile at the Point which is a peninsula property and cabin belonging to me and my siblings. The day was very cold and the wind was blustery so I took along a thermos of hot coffee. Before us was a huge pile of wood to split and we wondered if we could do it all in the allotted time we had. We worked for some time and it seemed like the pile grew but we purposed not to have a coffee break until we had half of the pile done. We sat in the car to get out of the wind and the coffee hit the spot. We started working again and didn't quit until the last piece of wood was split, which was just as it was getting dark. We had to preserver as it was tempting to leave part of the pile, but we knew we had a nice warm house to go home to. In our life here on earth, there are times we need to hang in there and persevere. No matter how hard it is now, no matter what we go through, we have an eternity with Him to look forward to. It helps to keep our focus on Him and as it says in Heb. 10:36, (The Message)... "But you need to stick it out, staying with God's plan so you'll be there for the promised completion." We are not to shrink back but persevere and move forward by faith.

Challenge for today: Complete something you have put off for a while.

When we arrived at our son's home in time for the Super Bowl, our 6 year old grandson, Grant, met us by the car with hugs and kisses. He was aware that I was bringing him a large wrapped prize and could hardly wait to open it. He quickly unwrapped it and I could see his disappointment over the football shoulder pads. He wouldn't even put them on. So later I gave him a second prize of Samurai swords that were in a holder to go on the back. He was ecstatic over them and used them right away! I thought I had missed the mark in choosing the first prize but later he put on the shoulder pads to protect himself in a sword fight with his sister. So what I thought was not a good gift later became the best gift. Now, are we like that when the Lord gives us a gift that is not what we were expecting and seems disappointing? At the time we may not realize what benefit if is for us, but later see the reason He planned this gift for our good. Let us not reject the gifts God gives us but be thankful and know that they will serve a good purpose in our future. It says in Ps. 33:20-22 (The Message) "We're depending on God; He's everything we need. What's more, our hearts brim with joy since we've taken for our own His holy name. Love us, God, with all you've got-that's what we're depending on." When we really know that He loves us we will know all His gifts are good too.

Challenge for today: Thank the Lord for a gift you have had trouble receiving.

W hen we go to see our grandkids and I tuck them in at night, they ask me to tell them stories from the past...especially ones when I was a nurse or about their daddy when he was little etc. When I share things that happened long ago, they always want more and don't mind if they have heard it before. As I rehearse things I also see God's hand in all of it and my faith is strengthened too. God told the Israelites to tell their children all about their release from bondage and the miracles the Lord did in their midst. He didn't want them to ever forget it and to know how God was with them and so powerful. The Psalmist says in Psalm 105:2 (NIV) "Sing to Him, sing praises to Him; tell of all His wonderful acts." We are to glory in Him and rejoice and as it says in verse 5, "Remember the wonders He has done." The Lord gave commands to the children of Israel to faithfully obey and to love the Lord with all their hearts and souls. He then said to fix those words in their hearts and in Deut.11:19 (NIV) "Teach them to your children, talking about them when you sit at home and when you walk along the road, and when you lie down and when you get up." I think that means all the time! May we be faithful to walk in His ways but also to share all that He has done for us.

Challenge for today: Ask the Lord to bring to your remembrance a situation when you experienced God's help and then give Him thanks and share with others.

We have two sons of our own but have also "adopted" a friend of our youngest son. He comes to our house and cleans out our chimney, helps put in our dock and lift, takes care of the biggest logs that are too heavy for Al etc. Since my husband had a hip replacement he no longer can go up on the roof and we are glad for Jeff's willingness to help. We may be used in the Body of Christ in a specific area but that doesn't mean we will always do what we are doing now. We may be teaching a Bible Study, helping with the youth, head of a committee etc. but the time may come when the Lord tells us to let someone else do it and moves us on to something else. One of the most important of all things is prayer and all of us can be people of prayer. When the day comes that we may not be able to serve physically in the Body, we can still pray anywhere and anytime. We need to be tuned into the Lord's voice to hear what He has for us at this season in our lives and do it with joy and for His pleasure. Col. 3:23-24 (NIV) Paul says," Whatever you do, work at it with all your heart, as working for the Lord, not for men, since you know that you will receive an inheritance from the Lord as a reward. It is the Lord Christ you are serving." Let us serve Him from our hearts and be exactly where He has us at this season of our lives!

Challenge for today: Ask the Lord to show you if you are obeying Him in this season of your life!

Isn't it wonderful when the Lord gives us friends that see the best in us, even when we fail? They are able to look past our weaknesses and failures and focus on our good points and strengths. One day I went for a walk in the spring of the year and came home and remarked to my husband about the wondrous beauty of the woods and lake. Now if you have never been up in the north woods you may only see all the fallen trees, stumps, brush, dying trees etc. But because I have lived through the seasons since I was a child, I have pictured in my mind's eye, the lush green forest that will soon come forth. I can imagine the wild ducks floating past on the lake even though right now the lake is still frozen. We can be so thankful that God sees us for what we will be and not for what we are now. He can look into the future and see His transforming Spirit at work in us and what the finished product will look like. Now others may look at us and see our many faults but He sees our intentions and our desire to become more like Him. He puts us in circumstances that will result in more of His character in our lives and result in precious fruit. Rather than trying to get out of difficult circumstance, we need to ask for insight into what He is trying to produce in us. May David's prayer also be ours from Ps. 86:11 (NIV) "Teach me your way, O Lord, and I will walk in your truth; give me an undivided heart, that I may fear your name."

Challenge for today: Ask myself, how do I see the image of God reflected in my life? Also see Him in another's life?

I am sure that we have all spoken words that we wish we could take back afterwards. Maybe we have received harsh words from someone that made us want to go away from them. Our tongues can get us in trouble and words have power for good or for evil. They can build up others or tear them down. What we say really reveals what is in our hearts. It is important to allow our tongues to be used by the Lord to speak His words to others. When we are obedient and speak what the Spirit gives us they become holy words. In Prov. 25:11 (Amplified) it says, "A word fitly spoken and in due season is like apples of gold in settings of silver." There may be times when we share a word that came unexpectedly to our mind. Later someone thanks us for that life changing word and we might not even remember what we said. Words can lift up, encourage, challenge, confront, sooth, instruct and God can use them to bring transformation. Words can change the very atmosphere of a room and put others at ease or create negativity. James warns us to keep a tight rein on our tongues or our religion is worthless. May we allow the Lord to use our tongues as instruments of His grace and love, bringing glory to Him.

Challenge for today: Speak an encouraging word to someone who appears discouraged.

After a long winter I love to do a deep cleaning throughout the whole house and open the windows and get fresh air. It feels good as I wash the linens down to the mattress, clean the blinds and windows, closets and drawers etc. It made me think of our hearts and how wonderful it feels when we are honest with the Lord and ask Him to cleanse us thoroughly. Sometimes we can just skip over things and think they are small or trivial, but He sees our hearts and knows when even our attitudes are not what they should be. The Lord is holy and sometimes we get careless in relation to His holiness. David sinned but when Nathan pointed out his sin, David repented and said in Ps. 51:4a (NIV), "Against you, you only, have I sinned and done what is evil in your sight." It was almost a year after his sin with Bathsheba before he asked for a clean heart and a right spirit. He first suffered the consequences and death of his son. Let us be quick to face the truth and be honest when we sin. Then as we repent we will receive His wonderful gift of forgiveness and restoration of joy! No better feeling than to be washed white as snow.

Challenge for today: Ask the Lord to search your heart and repent of anything He reveals to you that is not right.

When my husband retired from being a full time pastor we had to look for a church to become part of the Body. We prayed much and felt led to join a small church in our town. The Sunday we joined our new church, we each got a yellow corsage pinned on us as we arrived. There were lots of hugs but when people tried to hug me, I stepped back and told them I was just getting over a cold. It was hard to do that but I didn't want them to catch my "bug". Ordinarily I welcome hugs and can't even get into church without receiving several. It made me wonder how people who have been wounded by others feel and is their expectation one of rejection? Do they step back and feel others are cool towards them, even though people may be trying to reach out to them? After a few times of trying to get to know them, others may give up. We can blame others for many things that may be of our own doing. Sometimes our body language gives out the message that shows what is really going on in our hearts. We all need to know in a deep way how loved we are first by Him who is Love and then share that love to others...especially those that need to know that most. In I John 4:7 (The Message) it says, "Beloved friends, let us continue to love each other since love comes from God. Everyone who loves is born of God and experiences a relationship with God."

Challenge for today: Reach out with God's love to someone who seems to feel unloved.

I love to go on a prayer walk each day and seems like the Lord speaks to me in my surroundings. I go up and down several steep hills on our gravel road and one would think it is much better to be going down the hill than up. But I am more sure footed going up the steep grade, especially if it is icy. Going down, I tend to go faster and faster and would be rather easy for my feet to slip out from under me. We may choose in our spiritual lives the easier way of having everything go smoothly and life without problems while we quickly sail along. But it is in our hard times that we discover how dependent on the Lord we really are. Yes, I may have to puff a bit going up a hill but I dig my shoes in and am more stable on my feet. The times we have to suffer and persevere may be the very times we feel closest to Him. He has promised us strength to go through whatever is ahead of us and will get us up the steepest places. It can be a time we can also face ourselves more honestly and connect with others. We may not prefer the hard times but they add to the picture of our whole life, helping us enter in more deeply. We read in II Chron. 16:9a (NIV) "For the eyes of the Lord range throughout the earth to strengthen those whose hearts are fully committed to Him." Let us gain our strength in Him for whatever comes to us each day.

Challenge for today: Don't take the easy way out but persevere in a difficult circumstance.

Our son, Kurt, has a friend Bo who is a gourmet cook and we love when he comes to the Lake as we get the left-overs. Sometimes it is steak with cilantro Chimichurri sauce, or Jambalaya or Tequila Lime BBQ Spare ribs etc., but it is always fantastic! When I go down to the cabin refrigerator to get the delicious gourmet dishes left behind, it causes me think of what we leave behind spiritually for others to feed on. Hopefully, we leave behind lasting good fruit. We realize the importance of this as we think of the riches we have received by the many people who have touched our lives! The Spirit may bring to our remembrance instructive words given to us by our parents or scriptures that others have spoken to us in difficult times. Also, the many words of wisdom given at the right time or thoughts by authors we respect. But what do we leave behind? Each of us can become as a tree constantly bearing fruit to feed others. The Lord wants our lives to reflect Him and to bear lasting fruit. Jesus said in John 15:16 (Amplified) "You have not chosen Me, but I have chosen you and I have appointed you (I have planted you), that you might go and bear fruit and keep on bearing, and that your fruit may be lasting (that it may remain, abide), so that whatever you ask the Father in My name (as presenting all that I AM), He may give it to you."

Challenge for today: When you go through your day, do a deed that could bear fruit for the future!

My dear friend Hazel has gone Home to be with the Lord, but she taught me so much in the time I got to know her. She was 92 years old, blind, lived in a trailer that had no hot water when the weather got cold. She had two sons that did not live nearby and seldom came. She could have thought, poor me! Why has all this happened to me? But that was not her question or her outlook on life. Instead, she was so grateful for whatever someone did for her. I often brought our left-overs and it was received like a banquet. When I brought her cake with cherries and whipped cream, her response was, "I can't think of a better way to start the day! How lucky I am!" When I got her a part for her wash machine and put it on, she got tears and would have danced if she could. It makes one think of how the Lord must love it when we tell Him how grateful we are for His blessings. Do we get to dancing and praising or do we think He should have given us a "new wash machine" instead. Maybe He can't give us more because of our attitude of ingratitude. It is easy to give to someone like Hazel who showed so much appreciation but not as easy to give to those who demand and think they should get more. May we be more like Hazel and believe our Father knows just what we need and what is good for us. Most of all may we give thanks to Him as it says in II Cor. 9:15 (NIV) "Thanks be to God for His indescribable gift."

Challenge for today: Show appreciation for a gift that you have taken for granted.

It was late one night as Al and I returned home from a weekend in Duluth, and there on our back steps was a big box from Fed-Ex. We didn't know when it had been left there but I was concerned as we had 4 bottles of expensive juice we had ordered. Sure enough, when I opened the box all 4 bottles were broken and juice all over. What a mess! I wonder what we do when things get challenging and stressful and the pressure is on. Do we fall apart of do we go to the hidden place with God and let Him give us stability and peace? Things seem to be getting worse around us, and as His children we have a place to go that is a solid place and one of great peace. He has given us promises to help us to stand when the times get tough and even hinds' feet to walk on those high difficult places. In Hab. 3:19 (Amplified) it says, "The Lord is my Strength, my personal bravery, and my invincible army: He makes my feet like hinds' feet and will make me to walk (not stand still in terror, but to walk) and make (spiritual) progress upon my high places (of trouble, suffering, or responsibility)!" Let us not be crushed and fall apart but let us become stronger and leap on those high places when the going gets rough! In fact, those very things can make us stronger.

Challenge for today: Go to that secret place and spend some time with Him.

I should have seen the warning signs about my computer not letting my e-mails through! Some friends write me daily and I thought it was unusual that I hadn't heard from any of them. I wish I would have investigated sooner. It resulted with a backlog of messages and only a few getting through. The others messages went to my i-Pad which later got deleted by the tech person I use. What about us in our spiritual lives? Are we missing out on the many things the Lord is trying to get through to us? We may have warning signs also that we are going off on our own and only partially hearing what He is saying. We may not feel free and something doesn't seem quite right. We need to pay attention and ask for His help to stay on course. He is to be our primary focus and the voice we listen to. When we are divided within, we do not hear as we should or see things as they are. Joshua told the people they had to choose whom they would serve and the choice is also up to us. Let us not be "double-minded Christians" that have one eye on the world and one eye on Him! But let us give Him our whole selves as it says in Ps.119:10 (NIV) "I seek you with all my heart; do not let me stray from your commands."

Challenge for today: Pay attention to whatever is not peaceful within and ask the Lord for discernment.

I was not looking forward to the first of the month since I had to put an ointment on my face and chest to kill off the pre-cancer cells. That meant no makeup at all! The first 21 days I kept looking worse each day as this destruction was taking place! During this time others shared how they had been through this process also and the results were wonderful which brought me encouragement. It wasn't long afterwards that my skin began to peel off and new skin was being formed. What a picture of how it is to die to our old self. It can get messy looking at the time as the old gets killed off. Others may think we are quite a mess! But then comes the resurrection in Christ. It is spoken of in II Cor. 5:17-18 (NIV) "Therefore, if anyone is in Christ, he is a new creation; the old has gone, the new has come! All this is from God, who reconciled us to Himself through Christ and gave us the ministry of reconciliation." Aren't you glad the Lord removes our past sins, cancers, things we are not proud of, and makes us to be more like Him? Daily may we be willing to die to ourselves and go through this process! Let us also share with others along the way that it is worth it all!

Challenge for today: Show by your life that His will comes first and not your own!

Our granddaughter, Lily, is so focused when she plays soccer that she is not distracted by other things going on around her. She is totally into the game! How about us? Do we get our focus off the Lord and on our problems, our busy schedules, possibility of losing a job, worries of the future etc.? I hear older people express concern about what will happen when they can no longer live in their homes or take care of themselves. Whatever the concern we have can overwhelm us and cause our lives to get fragmented and our focus taken off of the Lord. Jesus tells us not to be anxious but to set our hearts on His kingdom. In Matt. 6:33 (NIV) He said, "But seek first His kingdom and His righteousness, and all these things will be given to you as well. Therefore do not worry about tomorrow, for tomorrow will worry about itself. Each day has enough trouble of its own." We are to look to the Lord's faithfulness to provide all that we need, and our part is to trust. We can voice every concern, large or small, to Him and He hears and answers according to His perfect will. Why do we worry when we can pray and give each concern to Him? Let us not live scattered lives but ones that are focused on Him and His provision for every need.

Challenge for today: Think of a concern you have and find a verse from the Word to stay your thoughts.

I'm sure we have all heard that our lives are some-times the only Bible others may read. They may not go to church or ever open a Bible but when they see a life lived in love may want to know more. The church today is often trying to engage our culture and wants to find the latest trend to get people to come through its doors. But a life lived for Him can be the biggest advertisement! Maybe we have had the awesome experience of being with a "holy person" and we feel like we have been in the presence of the Lord! When God lives in us and we have surrendered ourselves to Him, His love is able to shine through and touch others in deep ways. I have been reading about the early church that grew quickly as the Holy Spirit was poured out on them. Others saw His presence manifested in the lives of the believers by the way they lived and treated others and by the power of the Spirit operating through them. More came to faith because of them and were added to the number of His followers. What about us? Are others drawn to Him because they see His presence in our lives? May Paul's prayer for the Ephesians be our prayer in Eph. 3:19 (NIV) "and to know this love that surpasses knowledge—that you may be filled to the measure of all the fullness of God."

Challenge for today: Tell another Christian that has touched your life how you see the Lord in him or her.

One Saturday night we were at a wedding reception and a friend motioned for us to join her at a table near the front. I asked her if we should really sit there as it was so close to the bridal table. She assured us and another couple with us, that it was fine so we sat there and enjoyed the appetizers...that is, until the bride's mother came and asked us to move! She said they had forgotten to put a reserve sign on the table but it was for the parents. So we got up and went to the "lowest" table in the very back by the door with a stroller parked by it! Immediately it came to mind the story in Luke 14 where Jesus told the parable of the wedding feast and how people scrambled to take the places of honor. But He encourages us all to take the lowest place instead, lest we be humiliated when our place is given to someone else. He said in Luke 14:11 (NIV) "For everyone who exalts himself will be humbled and he who humbles himself will be exalted." Let us be humble before Him and before others! We told our pastor the lesson we had just learned! He was calling off the numbers of the tables to go through the buffet line. He must have thought we had learned our lesson, as he called our table before the parent's table, when it should have been the last one!!

Challenge for today: Do a humble deed for someone today and don't broadcast it!

I went to hear a talk on Lyme disease that was given by an RN/pastor's wife who had suffered many years with undiagnosed Lyme disease. I can't imagine how she must have been misunderstood as she had so many unexplained symptoms that seemed to travel around her body. She knew something was wrong but doctors said everything was fine and prescribed antidepressants. But one day it was discovered that she had neurological Lyme disease and then treatment could begin! Think of how she must have been misjudged by many and others probably thought it was all in her mind. But there was a reason. How many times do we judge others and think we know and see accurately. We are told in Scripture that one day Jesus will judge men's secrets and he does not judge by appearance... why do we? We are warned in Matt. 7:1-2 (Amplified) about what happens when we judge. "Do not judge and criticize and condemn others, so that you may not be judged and criticized and condemned yourselves. For just as you judge and criticize and condemn others, you will be judged and criticized and condemned, and in accordance with the measure you (use to) deal out to others, it will be dealt out again to you." Let us not focus on the faults of others but deal with those things in ourselves that need to change. We owe everyone the debt of love so may we resist criticizing and judging others around us.

Challenge for today: Repent of others you have judged and ask God to help see them through His eyes.

In St. George, Utah, there is a bronze sculpture of an old woman going through the veil of death into the open arms of her Savior. Leaving her old life behind, she is entering into the wonder of life forever in Glory! I am reminded on the day of my dad's "homecoming" and how blessed I felt that God gave me an earthly father whose arms were always open to me with unconditional love. The last time I was with him, I tucked a prayer shawl around him to keep him warm. His speech was getting hard to understand but he mentioned the picture on his wall of our lake cabin. We talked about the wonderful memories there and oh how he loved nature and the beauty of the woods. His bed was low so I just knelt by his bed and prayed for him. The last words I said to him were, "I love you" and those were his last words to me. I didn't realize that it would be the final time I would see him alive here on earth. But even if I did know, that would be the message I would want him to give him. How important it is to tell the people around us how we feel about them, and not take for granted that they know. God can use our words to bring encouragement, comfort, love, peace, hope, and joy. Let us be led by His Spirit to speak words of love and life to others. In Col. 4:6a (NIV) Paul encourages us to "let your conversation be always full of grace, seasoned with salt" and full of love!

Challenge for today; Give an encouraging word to someone you meet today.

It was a very exciting day, October 7th when our grandson, John Mark, arrived from Korea! The wait had been so long for Mark and Andrea and it was the answer to many prayers from people everywhere. They took videos of John Mark's arrival and there were tears of joy and thanksgiving. He was just 13 months old when they got him but he seemed to take comfort in them right away. We waited a month for his adjustment time and then drove 19 hours to see him! What an awesome experience! We took him for walks and played with him and got to know our new grandson. Later the adoption became final and irreversible, which gives great security to John Mark. He was chosen by Mark and Andrea and he belongs to them. I often hear Mark calling him, "son". We also have been adopted into God's family, not because we are so good and have kept all his commandments, but because He loves us and paid the price for us to be His. We are chosen and we belong! We have brothers and sisters who also belong and we are all part of the family of God. We are loved beyond our comprehension even when we fail and yet He forgives us and loves us just the same. Aren't you glad the transaction is sealed and we can now live as His beloved adopted children until we see Him face- to- face. Eph. 1:5-6 (NIV) says, " He predestined us to be adopted as His sons through Jesus Christ, in accordance with His pleasure and will—to the praise of His glorious grace, which He has freely given us in the One he loves."

Challenge for today: Thank the Lord for adopting you and reach out to another sister or brother.

I was watering my plants one day and noticed a most unusual sight. I have a four tier plant stand and a plant on the upper level had also planted part of itself in the soil of a pot on the second level. It was trying to take over not only its own pot but that of another. God has given each of us a pot or a special place to flourish and it is not like anyone else's. He is the one that places us and we are to "bloom where we are planted." But we are not to let anyone else take over our life as we are each responsible for ourselves before the Lord. It says so in Rom. 14:12 (Amplified) "And so each of us shall give and account of himself (give and answer in reference to judgment) to God." We all will have to answer to God alone someday. We hear so much about enabling others or being controlled by someone else but neither one is good. God wants us to be free to be ourselves and to grow in the way He has ordained for us. He is watchful over us for as it says in Heb. 4:13 (Amplified) "And not a creature exists that is concealed from His sight, but all things are open and exposed, naked and defenseless to the eyes of Him with whom we have to do."

Challenge for today: Do something that is uniquely the 'you' that God created, not like anyone else.

I just finished making maple syrup and the sound of the ping of the jars as they sealed was music to my ears. The process of making syrup is quite long and before it comes to me the trees have been tapped, the sap gathered daily, plus partially boiling it down on an outdoor stove. Patience is still needed for standing at the stove a long time and stirring while waiting for the temperature to get to 216 F before putting the syrup into jars. I would love to shorten the process and fill the jars before reaching that temperature but it would not turn out nearly as thick and good. That is not unlike our spiritual lives as we go through challenging times that test our faith. We would love to escape out of the circumstances when we feel we've had enough. Many times it seems forever that we have been in a difficult situation that is beyond our control and we want to be done with it all. But the Lord sees and knows just what it takes in each of our individual lives to perfect us and make us more like Him. We however, do not always discern that, and may complain or question Him as to why this doesn't come to an end now! But let us be like David in Ps. 40:1 (Amplified) "I waited patiently and expectantly for the Lord; and He inclined to me and heard my cry." Yes, He heard David and set his feet on a rock and put a new song in his heart! No matter how long we may have to wait, let us not lose heart or grow faint for we will reap if we do not lose courage.

Challenge for today: Thank the Lord for taking you through hard times in the past and trust Him right where He has you now!

When we were in our second church, a parishioner took Al fishing along the Manitou River amongst thick woods. I was at home with our three small children and later that day the Deputy Sheriff came to our door to tell me Al was lost and I needed to organize a search party! At first I couldn't believe it, but he was serious and I called a member from the church. There was a whole group of men from church looking for Al in a very short time. One had a big bullhorn and Al heard it and started walking towards the sound, "Reverend Hendrickson!! Reverend Hendrickson!" Al had eaten wild berries and was a little sick and hot and had thoughts that he may have to spend the whole night in the dark woods. The story ends well as there was cheering and prayers of thanks when Al came out into the clearing and had reunion time. We have all been lost our way in a sense and need to be found by the Lord. We are in darkness and hungry for that which will satisfy the thirst of our souls. The Lord uses many ways to reach us and not everyone responds to the 'bullhorn' but continues going their own way. His voice of love continues to call us and He awaits our response to rescue us. When we come out of the darkness of wandering about, we can look into His Word for directions to apply to our lives. It says in Ps. 119:105 (Amplified) "Your word is a lamp to my feet and a light to my path." Let each one of us respond and come out of the darkness and into His light!

Challenge for today: Share with someone else today how you were found!

A friend was having trouble with a computer program so I offered to bring my computer to church to see if I could be of help. She had questions about this particular program and I told her that it worked just fine on my computer. But when we got together we discovered that what worked on my mine did not work on hers at all. Isn't that the way life is? We are all so individual and what helps me may not help you at all. It is easy to tell someone else what should work for them, but it doesn't always accomplish good results for them. Even medically speaking, what can be the answer for what seems like the same symptoms may turn out to be different for another. The Lord created each one of us and deals with us individually. It says in Isaiah 43:1b (NIV) "Fear not, for I have redeemed you; I have summoned you by name; you are mine." Later in the chapter He says He has created us for His glory and He loves us and says we are precious in His sight. Wow! There is not another person exactly like us and each of us is loved unconditionally by our Father. Let us remember that as we relate to others and ask for His wisdom and words before giving them advice.

Challenge for today: Really listen with your heart to another person without interrupting them to give advice.

My sister and I like to play scrabble together and are quite evenly matched. One day in the first game we played I was leading as she couldn't seem to get a vowel. Time after time when she drew her letters, it was another consonant. I felt a little bad for her and refrained from gloating over my big lead. I was sure it would end with me beating her but before long things changed! She was getting good letters and I was not. By the end of the game she beat me by 44 points. The next game she was leading me most of the way through, but in the end I beat her by 22 points. I think we have all experienced feelings that life is not fair. Why is so and so getting a better deal and look what is happening in my life? If we think about it, often things are going our way but it doesn't stay that way. Many times we may be certain we know how things will end, but it turns out far differently. Sometimes people who have more and have things going their way really lose in the end. Let us be humble to accept what is given us and what is given to others. We have a loving Father who knows just what we need at the time and will give according to His purposes in our lives. It says in Jer.10:23, (NIV) "I know, O Lord, that a man's life is not his own; it is not for man to direct his steps." Let us trust Him in all things!

Challenge for today: Thank the Lord for how He is directing your life, especially the things you may not understand.

We all need the Lord! The more we grow the more we come to realize how much we need His mercy and grace. Often when we mess up, we know this in a much deeper way. The other day I went to the Co-op that is usually crowded with very little aisle space. A gal was standing in front of the lentils that I wanted to grab on the bottom shelf. I leaned down to reach them, and when I did the bag of flax seeds I was carrying in my arms dropped to the floor. It was almost like an "explosion" for the contents spilled everywhere, oh my!! A very nice man who volunteers there kindly said, "I will take care of that, just go about your shopping." Those were just the words I needed to hear! How often are we in need of God's mercy as we blow it in so many more ways than we can possibly realize! David was aware of this as he says in Ps. 103:8 (NIV) "The Lord is compassionate and gracious, slow to anger, abounding in love." When we really know that in the depth of our being, we will be most gracious in extending mercy to others. It says in James 2:13 (Amplified) "For to him who has shown no mercy the judgment (will be) merciless, but mercy (full of glad confidence) exults victoriously over judgment." I am so glad the Lord doesn't give us what we deserve but is merciful towards us. How blessed we are to have such a loving Father.

Challenge for today: Show mercy to someone as you go about your day but also to yourself!

It is always exciting to prepare for our trip to San Antonio to see our daughter's family, but one time we ran into some glitches. In order to get into the Air Force Base we needed proof of our car insurance and since we got a brand new car it hadn't come in the mail in time. We called our insurance agent to have him give us another extension to last while we were there. Then our license plate didn't come and it had to be sent by Fed Ex Express. Finally we were packed and set to go! All this made me think of our journey to glory and how we are making preparations for that each day here on earth. Some things are very important as we prepare and we must first of all trust and have faith in the One we will spend eternity with. The Holy Spirit has been given us as our guarantee (our insurance). Importantly our lives are to be lived for Him (much like our license plate) showing others who we belong to. We need to be heedful of the road He has us on for if we go our own way, we will be taking lots of detours. In fact we may go many miles out of our way. God wants us to enjoy the journey and also to pay attention to the road signs along the way and follow the highway of holiness. Let us be like Abraham of whom it is said in Heb. 11:10 (NIV) "For he was looking forward to the city with foundations, whose architect and builder is God. " May we travel light and safe travels!!

Challenge for today: Be aware of any excess baggage you have and release to the Lord.

When I go for a prayer walk, I often see a man sitting in his garage facing the gravel road and a swamp. I wondered why he looks in that direction when the peaceful lake, beautiful trees, and blossoming flowers are the other direction. Why not just go down to the lake and sit on the dock and enjoy the beauty of creation. I don't know him well enough to ask him why but it did make me think of how much we can be like him. The Lord has so much for us and we settle for so little. We may look to others to bring satisfaction rather than Him. There is a good chance we have all discovered that people very close to us cannot give us what we need all the time. We are not to put that expectation on others to do for us what only God can do. If we practice that we will always be disappointed. God is our source and we need to have our expectations in the right place. If our eyes are on others rather than Him, then we need to change our focus! He won't disappoint us and will always be there for us, even when others are not. Let us be like David in Ps. 27:8 (NIV) when he prays, "My heart says of you, 'Seek His face!' Your face Lord I will seek." Look to the Lord first and keep your eyes on Him.

Challenge for today: Put God first and express what is in your heart to Him.

I am convinced we are surrounded by saints in disguise more than we are aware! I am in a Bible study on Tuesday mornings with gals from our church and it is the highlight of my week! I am one of the youngest there and my eyes have been opened to see that I am sitting amongst strong women of faith and older warriors. We answer the questions from our lesson book, and one by one they share things they have risked and gone through. Some have lost their mates and are carrying on serving the Lord with zeal. One gal and her husband left their home and traveled for 5 years in a camper to help build churches all over the country. Another has been on missions to Africa and other faraway places. I realize as they share how blessed I am to be amongst women of faith who find their strength in the Lord. We may not always recognize these saints on the surface, but if we take time to get to know them and listen to their stories, we will be encouraged in our own spiritual journeys. Paul's prayer for the Ephesians in Eph. 1: 17-18 (Amplified) can be for us too, "(For I always pray to) the God of our Lord Jesus Christ, the Father of glory, that He may grant you a spirit of wisdom and revelation (of insight into mysteries and secrets) in the (deep and intimate) knowledge of Him. By having the eyes of your heart flooded with light, so that you can know and understand the hope to which He has called you, and how rich His glorious inheritance in the saints (His set-apart ones)." May we live as His saints today in all we do and say and think.

Challenge for today: Share with a saint how you see Jesus in him or her.

During the summer we have several campfires with all the relatives that are at the lake. One night after we had our wiener roast and had eaten to our fill, we played Gossip. Our niece volunteered to be the first one to go apart while we talked about her. None of the things said were true and we all found outlandish things to make up about her! When she came back to the group she had to guess who said such an awful things. There was lots of laughter and it took some time to guess what each person had said. If this were "real", just imagine the damage that could be done to someone's reputation. Careless and thoughtless words are wounding. Sometimes we don't even know who started the untruths but our part should be to stop it immediately before it goes any farther. We are told in scripture that our speech is to be gracious and seasoned with salt. If we are the one being talked about, we have to make the choice to forgive them and not keep rehearsing in our minds what they said about us. In Psalm 19:14 (NIV) the people sang these words to the Lord: "Let the words of my mouth and the meditation of my heart be pleasing in your sight, O Lord, my Rock and my Redeemer." Let this also be our song and practice daily in our lives.

Challenge for today: Speak what is loving to others and will build them up.

One evening I got a telephone call while I was busy making supper. The person said it showed up that there were many things wrong with my computer and proceeded to transfer me to a "tech". I had a hard time understanding him as he had a foreign accent. I asked our daughter, Ann, after a short time to come and take over this call while I finished making supper. She listened for a while and had a caution in her spirit. When he requested again to take over my computer, she asked for their number and said we would think about it and would call back. But when she looked up the number she discovered it was a scam and we were so glad he didn't gain control. Someone else who didn't catch on ended up paying $300 to fix their computer that was already working properly. Spiritually speaking, the enemy comes so slyly and tries to gain entrance with half-truths and familiar things to trip us up. He seems to know just what buttons to press. But we need to pray for discernment and ask for help from the Lord and other members in the Body. Once we knew we had been saved from a scam, we rejoiced and were so thankful. In I Peter 5:8 -9 (The Message) we are given a warning, "Keep a cool head. Stay alert. The Devil is poised to pounce, and would like nothing better than to catch you napping. Keep your guard up. You're not the only one plunged into these hard times. It's the same with Christians all over the world. So keep a firm grip on the faith." Let us be alert to the enemy's tactics and not caught off guard.

Challenge for today: Ask the Lord for discernment in any area of your life that you sense the enemy is trying to gain access.

Have you ever noticed how one size does not fit all? I remember when my mother-in-law (who was quite large at the time) went shopping with her friend (who was just a little slip of a thing), were tempted to test that label with a pair of tights. The tights would be stretched out to the limit for one and for the other they would definitely sag. Likewise, even though Al and I are close on the spiritual journey, what works for him may not work for me! He recently got a new office chair and told me I could use it any time I desired. So one fine day I sat in it to do some studying and I felt like a little girl sitting up to a table that was too high. It was not the correct setting at all for me! Also, whenever I get in the car after Al has been driving, I have to move the seat forward and adjust the mirrors or I would not be able to see what is around me. It doesn't mean he is wrong or I am right but it just isn't the same "fit" for me. This may apply to us in our spiritual disciplines and many things on our spiritual journeys. We are all unique and have to be where the Lord would have us individually and not the place where someone else is. We likewise, need to give others the freedom to be in the place God has for them without judging them. It says in Ps. 86:11-12 (Amplified) "Teach me YOUR way, O Lord, that I may walk and live in Your truth; direct and unite my heart (solely, reverently) to fear and honor Your name. I will confess and praise You, O Lord my God, with my whole (united) heart; and I will glorify Your name forevermore." Our Heavenly father desires that we learn His way that is exactly right for us. Since He knows us best, inside and out, can we not trust Him?

Challenge for today: Practice spiritual disciplines that seem to befit you and rejoice in the joy and comfort of it!

How we treat one another reveals what is in our heart. Eph. 4:32 (Amplified) exhorts us, "And become useful and helpful and kind to one another, tenderhearted (compassionate, understanding, loving-hearted), forgiving one another (readily and freely), as God in Christ forgave you." This is often easier to quote than to practice, even for little ones. While we were at a soccer game, our 4 year old grandson, Grant, was playing and accidently hit a little red headed girl with a stone he was throwing into a culvert. The girl's daddy comforted her and then moved her to a little chair and gave her a snack. Grant didn't try to defend himself but immediately went over to her and bent down to look into her eyes and asked if she was alright. He stayed around to make sure she was okay and was so sweet. Don't we have a lot to learn from this example? Since we are human we hurt others even when we don't mean to. Rather than rationalizing or defending ourselves, how much better to just go to the other person and ask them to forgive us and then show we care. It's not about who is right and who is wrong, but rather about allowing God's love to flow through us. Let us walk in love and forgiveness!

Challenge for today: Ask the Lord for a tender heart and show his love to someone you meet today.

I was reminded recently of how important it is to welcome the gift of the Holy Spirit into our lives. He gives life and power and counsel and even prays for us! It says in Rom 8:26-27 (Phillips) "The Spirit also helps us in our present limitations. For example, we do not know how to pray worthily, but His Spirit within us is actually praying for us in those agonizing longings which cannot find words. He who knows the heart's secrets understands the Spirit's intention as He prays according to God's will for those who love Him." How vital it is not to quench the Spirit and sometimes we do that little by little until we lose our spiritual power. One night I was all set to do things around the house and to work on my computer when all of a sudden the lights flickered and went out. There was no storm but in one moment, we had no power at all. Everything changed and we were in the shadows. When we keep resisting the Spirit and going our own way, He may not feel welcome and our spiritual power diminishes little by little. Sometimes we do things repeatedly that we know are not in alignment of His will, and He is grieved. But when we repent and let Him have free reign what a difference it makes... just like when the power came on again and there was light in our house! I felt like dancing! Everything was right again. May we not resist the Spirit but allow Him to lead us and guide us into the fullness of all that God has planned for our lives! All of us need His comfort and tenderness in our lives.

Challenge for today: Ask the Holy Spirit to reveal to you any area of your life that is grieving Him.

My husband said to me one morning how different we are as I hit the floor running when I awaken and it takes him a while to get going. That is true and although I can get a lot done before morning coffee break, I need to slow down and just enjoy each moment. I read an article about how we live too fast, drive too fast, and talk too fast etc. When we eat too fast we are robbed of the sensory pleasure of our food, proper digestion is inhibited, and we also eat more than we should. Rushing triggers the body's stress response, digestive enzymes dry up, and nutrients are not absorbed. Instead, we need to slow down, take 10 deep breaths even before we eat and allow our body to relax. If we skip eating and tune out our body's hunger signals it sets us up for uncontrolled eating later and usually for carbohydrates. It made me think of our spiritual lives and how we need to take time to slow down and quiet ourselves so we can receive the nurturance the Lord has for us this day and this time. He wants us to feed on His word and to let it sink deeply into us. When we hurry and rush off for the day we can't absorb our spiritual nutrients... just like rushing lessens our body's ability to digest properly what we eat. When we eat on the run, we usually just munch on junk food and don't eat those foods that would nourish us and satisfy us for the long haul. We need to slow down, enjoy time with Him and savor what Holy Spirit desires to feed us. When we do this we will find we are left full and satisfied with the richness of what He pours out to us. Psalm 147:14 (Amplified) says, "He makes peace in your borders; He fills you with the finest of the wheat."

Challenge for today: Spend quality time absorbing the spiritual nutrients you are fed by Holy Spirit.

Taking a prayer walk each afternoon is my favorite time of day. I noticed a tree one day that was dead and had not one leaf on it. Soon it would either fall down by weather or my husband would end up chopping it down. Sometimes it is difficult to tell which trees are dead or simply which ones have just lost their leaves in the fall season. But in the summer it is easy to know for all the live ones have an abundance of leaves. One day we will be known for our leaves (fruit) or lack of it! Matt. 12:33 (The Message) says "If you grow a healthy tree, you'll pick healthy fruit. If you grow a diseased tree, you'll pick worm-eaten fruit. The fruit tells you about the tree." The same is true with us as others will know us by what they see in our lives, our attitudes, our works, and our acts of kindness. In fact, one day we will receive rewards for the deeds we have done. It says in Ecc. 12:14 (The Message) "And that's it. Eventually God will bring everything that we do out into the open and judge it according to its hidden intend, whether it's good or evil." What will He find on our trees? Those things that we did to be seen of others will be like leaves that have fallen to the ground. But those things done in His name will be rewarded...even a cup of cold water. Let us remember when we sow righteousness we will reap a sure reward! (Prov. 11:18)

Challenge for today: Do an act of kindness for another, simply out of love for the Lord.

There are wonderful words found in Jer. 29:11 (Amplified) "For I know the thoughts and plans that I have for you, says the Lord, thoughts and plans for welfare and peace and not for evil, to give you hope in the final outcome." When I read this I began to wonder just how God's blueprint for our lives must look. He has a perfect plan set out for each of us but how many times do we take detours or plan B? I'm quite certain there must be lots of detours just like the children of Israel who took a very long one! When my sister-in-law was here she told us about a chipmunk that was in her backyard in Upper Michigan. She put 3 kernels of popcorn out on a cement ledge for him and the chipmunk was only 5 feet away from it! Did he take the direct route for his snack? No! Instead, he went up and down a fence, up and down a tree, over here and there, and finally after about 75 feet of zigzagging, he got his prized snack. I wonder what our map looks like in regard to God's plan. Ideally ours would be directly in line with His, but how often do we take detours because we insist on our own way and think our way is better? But let us submit daily to what He has for us and then, as it says in Is. 30:21 (The Message) "Your teacher will be right there, local and on the job, urging you on whenever you wander left or right, 'This is right road. Walk down this road.'"

Challenge for today: Any place you feel you have missed God's path and gone off to the right or left, ask Him to put you back on the right path!

It is such a blessing and so peaceful to have unity and harmony in one's family and in the Body of Christ. David said in Ps. 133:1&3 (NIV), "How good and pleasant it is when brothers live together in unity!...It is as if the dew of Hermon were falling on Mount Zion. For there the Lord bestows His blessing, even life forevermore." Each week I try to get to Line Dancing for exercise, but since I never grew up dancing I have to pay particular attention and focus on the various steps. There are times I have to look to those around me to make sure I am doing the right dance steps and in the right timing. It is so neat to see each one in perfect harmony although occasionally one of us can get off. The gal in the line just behind me knows all the dances and I look to her if I am in question. Occasionally she has her mind elsewhere and gets off also. Most of the time I can catch it right away and will continue the dance, in sync with the rest of the group. In the Body of Christ any one of us can get off at times and our eyes have to be on the Lord and listening to Him. When we feel disharmony we need to ask the Lord for help and readjust. He may give us mentors but we still have to discern for ourselves and seek to be in step with Him. Now there are a couple dances I would rather not do as they are more complicated but I have no say in what the leader chooses. Just like the Lord is in charge and we have to make a special effort to seek for peace in the Body of Christ. Paul says in Eph. 4:3 (Amplified) "Be eager and strive earnestly to guard and keep the harmony and oneness of (and produced by) the Spirit in the binding power of peace."

Challenge for today: Seek peace in your family and be willing to change where needed.

I was reading from one of my favorite Psalms, and verse 8 of Psalm 32 (Amplified) says, " I (the Lord) will instruct you and teach you in the way you should go; I will counsel you with My eye upon you." How open are we to the Lord's instruction throughout our day? Do we cling to our own plans or are we receptive to His Spirit? Sometimes we have our day so carefully planned out that we are closed to any changes He might make or any directive He might give us. It's important to be flexible and open! One day when the relatives were all at the Lake, we planned a picnic for Saturday evening. My sister-in-law was visiting us and she and I had just come home from a movie when we found out no picnic! It was canceled due to high winds and some of the men were still out fishing. We had prepared the food but had to change plans. Instead Al and his sister and I found a little hollow clearing behind our sauna and had a wiener roast, just the 3 of us. It was such a neat time of sharing and we knew then it was just part of His plan for us. He has such good things in store for us, but we can miss them if we won't receive His instructions and counsel. When we barrel through, insisting on our own plan we can mess up other people's lives too. It is a freeing thing to hold things loosely and be ready for any changes God might make. His eye is always upon us."

Challenge for today: Be sensitive to Spirit as you go about your day and follow His leading.

While our son Kurt and his buddies were here at the lake we had a mishap on the night they prepared a feast for us. There was a hot bubbling carrot soufflé being carried to the table along with Beef Wellington etc. All of a sudden I heard a big splat and the soufflé was upside down on the floor, still bubbling! We were able to salvage the part not touching the floor and Kurt helped me clean up the rest of it. His friend didn't say how it happened or that it wasn't his fault or rationalize it away. The handle on the dish carrier had broken and it would have happened to whoever carried it. We all have mishaps in the routine of our days. Some are messier than others but it just happens. Why are we surprised when we stumble or others around us make mistakes? Why do we spend so much time defending ourselves or rationalizing? Let us instead ask God to help us see even the good He can work out of it. I was filled with gratitude in this instance as I became aware that the hot soufflé could have spilled on the person sitting only inches away; and he would have been severely burned! The familiar verse in Rom. 8:28 (Amplified) says, "We are assured and know that (God being a partner in their labor) all things work together and are (fitting into a plan) for good to and for those who love God and are called according to (His) design and purpose." Let us accept our mistakes and mis- haps and not be hard on ourselves. The enemy wants to send us into a tailspin but the Lord wants to weave them all together and bring good out of it.

Challenge for today: Forgive yourself for a mistake you made and ask God to weave it into a blessing!

Springtime is a wonderful time in the North woods as the winters can get long. It seems like everyone rejoices when the snow has melted, the loons return, the trees start to bud and flowers peek out of the soil. Each day the woods become more "alive" and green and soon nests begin appearing in the branches. A beautiful sight! It is also beautiful to see new Christians bud and grow and become more alive in Christ. Even those that are very old and still seeking to grow and become more like Him are awe-inspiring. Why would we want to stay put and stagnate and not blossom? Maybe it is because we are holding on to our own ways and not desiring His. When I taught a Bible Study class a woman came who was rather depressed and said she felt like she was stuck in a deep dark hole. I offered to help her and pray for her to come out of it but she said, "No!" She didn't want to as it was familiar and she wanted to stay where she was; so sad! The Lord invites us out into the light, to walk with us, nourish us, speak to us, and guide us. It says in I Peter 2:9 (NIV) "But you are a chosen people, a royal priesthood, a holy nation, a people belonging to God, that you may declare the praises of Him who called you out of darkness into His wonderful light." Let us expose ourselves more and more to the warmth of His love and walk in the light of the Lord.

Challenge for today: Notice where you are in the shadows and come into the light.

Since we run a retreat house I keep food frozen in two chest freezers in our garage. Before the weather gets too warm, I like to defrost them and clean them out. I spent part of my time one day, almost upside down as I had to bend over and dig deep all the way to the bottom. I did not remember all that was stored in there and was surprised by the food that needed to be used up. It caused me to think of our hearts and how much has been put into them throughout our life time...teachings, sermons, devotional thoughts, words from friends etc. It is easy to forget what was put into us so long ago. Cleansing and airing is vital so that new things can be put in. The former things were good but need to be used and put into practice. Then the new can come in and we can build on that. If they are only just nice things we heard and do not influence our lives for change then they are like old food in the freezer, where the flavor and taste is compromised. When we are overloaded with only with the old, we will miss the new the Lord has for us. It says in Matt. 13:52 (The Message) "Then you see how every student well-trained in God's Kingdom is like the owner of a general store who can put his hands on anything you need, old or new, exactly when you need it." Let us welcome Holy Spirit to take both the old and familiar and the new fresh to work in us and through us.

Challenge for today: Thank the Lord for the old but be open to the new, letting it produce change.

I went to see the movie, Heaven is for Real, and it filled my heart with joy and anticipation for what awaits us some day. Just think, we will get to spend eternity with those saints that we have read about in scripture and can hear their stories first hand! Can you imagine the diversity of color and cultures? We will be surrounded by people from every tribe, tongue, and nation....but with no divisions, just all One Body. We have also been given the promise that whatever disappointments, whatever pain, whatever sorrows we had on earth will one day all disappear. We will experience life at its best and find fulfillment of our dreams. It is recorded in John 17:3 (NIV) that Jesus said, "Now this is eternal life that they may know you, the only true God, and Jesus Christ, whom you have sent." Our anticipation doesn't eliminate pain that we may be going through right now but it may give us a new perspective and that can lessen our suffering. None of us knows how many days we will have on earth so let us live life to the fullest. It says in Ps. 90:12 (NIV) "Teach us to number our days aright, that we may gain a heart of wisdom." God's timing to take us Home is perfect and our last day on earth is really the best day of our lives since all eternity awaits us. What a difference it should make in our daily lives! May we spend each day drawing closer to our heavenly Father and loving and serving our brothers and sisters with whom we will spend eternity. The day is coming when our loved ones who have gone before us, will be waiting to welcome us! Yes!

Challenge for today: Live this day as if it were your last day on earth!

My husband asked me to help him with the firewood and gave me the easy job of running the splitter. He, on the other hand, had to handle large chunks of wood and after they were split would put them into a well stacked pile. Each time he put a stump on the block we couldn't tell exactly what was on the inside...if it was hard or if it would just crumble away. Sometimes it was quite surprising. Often huge pieces looked so good but were soft and rotten on the inside. Other smaller pieces were nice and hard and would burn a long time in our stove. It made me think of our hearts and how only the Lord knows what is inside each of them. We may look good on the outside but full of unforgiveness, hatred, anger, bitterness etc. on the inside. We are warned not to judge others as only He knows the hearts of all. In II Chron. 6:30-31 (Amplified) Solomon had a beautiful prayer at the dedication of the temple and asked God to hear the prayers of the people. He prayed, "Then hear from heaven, Your dwelling place, and forgive, and render to every man according to all his ways, whose heart You know; for You, You only, know men's hearts, That they may fear You and walk in Your ways as long as they live in the land which You gave to our fathers." May the Lord continually cleanse our hearts of all that is "rotten" and help us to walk in His ways all the days of our lives!

Challenge for today: Ask the Lord to judge and cleanse your heart and help you to refrain from judging others.

God is so creative and designed every atom in our bodies. Just like Michelangelo, He can see the image of Himself buried inside of us. He uses His chisel of grace to hew away our rough walls so that more of His image will be seen. When my husband and I were in South Padre we saw the world's largest sand castle and were amazed at the detail by the artist. He started with 15 tons of sand and gradually made a beautiful sculpture for others to admire and enjoy. I thought of our lives and how we enter the world, not knowing the shape our lives will take. One thing we know is that it won't be exactly like any other, so we don't need to compare it. We get in trouble when we try to force our own way and plan, ignoring what God has in mind for us. When we try to be someone else or try to hurry up what He is forming in us, we only mess things up. God has a time table and a plan and we will be filled with His peace when we follow that. It says in Ps. 25:12-13 (NIV) "Who, then, is the man that fears he Lord? He will instruct him in the way chosen for him. He will spend his days in prosperity and his descendants will inherit the land." Let us fit into God's purposes for each of our lives and thank Him for His creation in us.

Challenge for today: Take time to be creative today and do something that is life-giving.

My neighbor and I recently planted a garden with rows of carrots, lettuce, radishes, spinach, kohlrabi, green beans, onions, and beets. By faith I believe these seeds will produce, but for now they are in good soil and being exposed to the sun and rain as we patiently wait. Each seed has the potential to become something very specific and good but takes time to develop and grow. It's just like the Body of Christ. We are to be just what He created us to be to add flavor, color, and nourishment to the Body. If we are an onion we will not be like a carrot or beet for we were never meant to be! People with the same gifting will have some similarities, much like the seeds in the same row but still individual. The danger is that we try to be what God never intended us to be. We must practice patience with others as they grow and become more of what He intended, but we also need patience with ourselves. Don't we wish we were spiritual giants with great faith all the time? But we seem to grow little by little as we are exposed to the Sonshine of His presence, the daily reading of His word, and openness to His Spirit etc. I marvel at His patience with our slow progress. II Peter 3:9 (NIV) Peter says, "The Lord is not slow in keeping His promise, as some understand slowness. He is patient with you, not wanting anyone to perish, but everyone to come to repentance." May we be persevering in our faith and patient with others and ourselves, but also live with the expectation of what He created each of us to become!

Challenge for today: Celebrate what He planted you to be and share with another how their gift has blessed you.

One Tuesday morning in our Bible Study we were in Romans 8 and talked about living the Spirit-filled life. Verses 16 & 17 (The Message) say, "God's Spirit touches our spirits and confirms who we really are. We know who He is and we know who we are: Father and children. And we know where we are going to get what's coming to us—an unbelievable inheritance!" We shared instances when we just knew it was the Lord and felt led by His Spirit. Later that very day, Kurt, our youngest son, called asking for wisdom and prayer to help someone who was severely depressed. We talked about things that may help, including scriptures of hope and encouragement. I suggested possibly starting a men's group so he could have an army of men to stand with this troubled man. When we got off the phone he asked the Lord what scriptures to give and just then a vehicle passed him with the bumper sticker that read Ps. 91:1. Wow! 911 Emergency! That was also the very word God used in my life when we were going through a difficult time in our church. I memorized the whole chapter and would quote it over and over again as I was driving places, swimming laps etc. "He who dwells in the shelter of the Most High will rest in the shadow of the Almighty. I will say of the Lord, 'He is my refuge and my fortress, my God, in whom I trust.'" Ps. 91:1&2 (NIV) Two days later Kurt began a men's group for men he knows in the area and they were able to be the army that surrounded this discouraged man. Isn't it astounding how His Spirit is at work to guide us in even the smallest details of our lives?

Challenge for today: Listen closely today for promptings by His Spirit and obey His gentle whispers!

I love light and the first thing I do each day is to open the blinds and let the light in. My aunt, who is very special in my life, has macular degeneration and lives with only peripheral vision. She is legally blind and welcomes all the light she can get. How about us? Do we welcome the light? We are told in Isaiah 2:5 (The Message) "Come, family of Jacob, let's live in the light of God." God is light and He wants to shine in the darkness of our lives and bring dawn. His desire is to bring us out of the shadows and expose us to His light so that we may walk in the light of His presence. He also says we are to be a light in the world and not to hide our lights. Matt. 5:14-15 (The Message) says it well, "Here's another way to put it: You're here to be a light, bringing out the God-colors in the world. God is not a secret to be kept. We're going public with this, as public as a city on a hill. If I make you light-bearers, you don't think I'm going to hide you under a bucket, do You? I'm putting you on a light stand. Now that I've put you there on a hilltop, on a light stand— shine!" How do we do this? We can start by praying for others to come into His light and that the darkness may be scattered. Our lives should be a witness, even without words as we are His light-bearers. Today and each day may we open the blinds of our hearts and live as children carrying His light!!

Challenge for today: Share with someone, He sends your way, when you first awakened to God.

I'm sure we have all said, "He is so nice and doesn't deserve that!" I have thought many times what if God gave us what we actually deserved. Oh my! It would not be all the wonderful blessings we have been given; but rather our due for every unkind thought and action. Early one morning our son Kurt was on the road to come up to the lake at 3:30 am. While he was traveling he was praying and asking the Lord to just bless his time. He was so excited to get here that he was speeding as he went through Kansas City. Before very long he was stopped by a patrol man and quickly admitted that he was going much faster than he should have been going. The officer asked him where in MN was his destination. Kurt showed him pictures on his I-Phone of the cabin, sauna, and the big fish he had caught. Fortunately, the officer was also a fisherman and had fished on a lake only 25 minutes away from here. Kurt didn't get a ticket or warning, even though he deserved it! I'm sure he was full of gratitude. What about us? Do we realize all the grace given us? How blessed we are that God doesn't give us what we deserve. Paul says in II Cor.9:8 (Amplified) "And God is able to make all grace (every favor and earthly blessing) come to you in abundance, so that you may always and under all circumstances and whatever the need be self-sufficient (possessing enough to require no aid or support and furnished in abundance for every good work and charitable donation)." Let us remember His grace toward us and in gratitude to the Lord express grace to others.

Challenge for today: Express God's grace to all those around you today.

One evening when we had a group from church over, an Elder asked us the question, "What do you feel God is saying to you at this time in your life?" The first thought that came immediately to my mind was that I am to be attentive to Him. I often rush through my day rather than being fully present in the moment. When I am doing one thing I am already thinking of what needs to be done next. Instead, I want to be mindful and aware of what is happening right now and attentive to the Lord's voice as He speaks to me. Perhaps we all miss so much when we rush about and our lives get so busy. How can we come home to our hearts when we do this? Do we even bring our real self before the Lord or do we hide who that is? Sometimes we can be inattentive because we are afraid of being known for who we really are. But if we slow down we will hear His voice to our hearts telling us we belong and are loved. I believe we will also feel more spiritually alive and experience Him in new ways as we pay particular attention to what is happening in our lives in the present. It is likely we will find our lives changed and even what is familiar to us will become fresh and new. May our inner and outer life come together so we may see Him in everything and experience His gift of life in its depth. It says in Prov. 5:1 (Amplified) "My Son, be attentive to my wisdom (godly Wisdom learned by actual and costly experience), and incline your ear to my understanding (of what is becoming prudent for you)." He gives His undivided attention to us; let us be attentive to Him.

Challenge for today: Slow down and see God in each event of your life, and welcome Him to help you see all things through His eyes!

Have you ever experienced the joy of the lost lamb whom was found or the woman in scripture who found her lost coin after lighting her lamp and sweeping the floor? While at our daughter's house we took our three grandsons to the Charleston Aquarium. We saw so many interesting things and had a fun time but when we got in the car to go back home, my husband said he didn't have his billfold! Oh my! We all felt stressed and began praying. We went back to the aquarium and searched the whole place as best we could. We began thinking of the possible consequences since we were only on the first leg of our journey and needed those credit cards, and our driver's license to get into the Air Force Base etc. The boys were very cooperative and retraced their steps, feeling bad for grandpa. We had planned to stop to eat on the way home but went right home instead. But to the joy of us all, Ann met us at the door to tell us she had grandpa's billfold. Al had left his billfold on the table after putting in the paper with directions, and never put it in his pocket. We started cheering and thanking the Lord with all of our hearts and went out to celebrate. We felt like the woman described in Luke 15:9-10 (NIV) "And when she finds it, she calls her friends and neighbors together and says, 'Rejoice with me; I have found my lost coin.' In the same way, I tell you there is rejoicing in the presence of the angels of God over one sinner who repents." What we found was significant to us, but not like the magnitude of the lost soul who was found. Nothing compares with the joy in Heaven over one sinner that repents!

Challenge for today: Pray for someone who is lost and if His Spirit prompts you, make use of an opportunity to share the Lord.

Wild berry picking is something I have done since childhood and our freezer is usually full of berries all winter long. One day I invited a friend to go with me and we were welcomed to the "vineyard" of the owner and told it was all free...in other words, all GRACE! We were shown where the berries were especially big but given the freedom to pick where we desired. We had to work harder to get the big berries since they were more hidden but worth the extra effort. Soon some strangers came to pick too, but we were not worried that there would be enough berries for all of us. We knew from experience that there was plenty for all. It did surprise us though that some pickers came right to where we were picking since there was such a large field of berries before us. At first I wondered if they would snatch "our berries" from under our nose that were waiting to be picked by us!! But we had no right to get uptight since it wasn't our vineyard in the first place. It belongs to Him. We picked side by side for some time and talked together. When they departed our spirit was uplifted by our sharing together. It could be that the Lord was saying to be open to whatever He has and who He brings into our lives and not to be fearful or territorial. Our little section is only part of the larger Vineyard that doesn't belong to us but to God. It is important to see the bigger picture and remember whose Vineyard it is. In Isaiah 27:2-3 (NIV) it says, "In that day—'Sing about a fruitful vineyard: I, the Lord, watch over it; I water it continually. I guard it day and night so that no one may harm it.'" Let us enjoy working together in His Vineyard.

Challenge for today: Help and encourage others in the ministry (land) the Lord has given them.

When we were babysitting our grandkids, Lily went upstairs carrying her cat like a baby in her arms. I made a comment that maybe her cat was getting a little pudgy and her response was, "Oh no, grandma, she is just fluffy!" I smiled at that and thought of how we can look at people in our lives in different ways. We can view them as children who God loves so much that He gave His life for them, even while they are still in process of becoming. Or, we can regard them as children with many flaws and negative traits that can cause us irritation. But in order to see them in the light of His love, all we have to do is remember God's patience with us! He loves us: even when we are little stinkers, even when we blow it, even when we make messes, even when we say hurtful words, even when we have bad attitudes and do the wrong things. God is so merciful to us and we need to remember to show that same mercy to others. In Heb. 10:24-25 (Amplified) we are told how to see others: "And let us consider and give attentive, continuous care to watching over one another, studying how we may stir up (stimulate and incite) to love and helpful deeds and noble activities. Not forsaking or neglecting to assemble together (as believers), as is the habit of some people, but admonishing (warning, urging, and encouraging) one another, and all the more faithfully as you see the day approaching." We are to bring encouragement to others, love them, and spur them on and not tear them down.

Challenge for today: Show patience to others and bring a word of encouragement.

While we were at our son Mark's home we enjoyed time with our grandson, John Mark, who was 2 years old at the time. It was a joy to see his obedience at his young age, contrary to many children entering "the terrible twos"! He had learned that there are consequences if he chooses not to obey and occasionally he did try to test the waters. But when we babysat him he was an angel and promptly obeyed us, so we actually had more time to just have fun. We took him on a walk to the park, the fountain etc. We had his best in mind but didn't let him get by with things. When it came time for bed we had him help clean up his toys and put them away etc. It must give the Lord such joy when we obey His voice and heed His word to our hearts instead of throwing a temper tantrum when we don't get our way. If we think about it, He knows what is best and is looking at the big picture and foresees what is going to happen in the future. Too often we test Him as we may try to get by with things. But when I was reading from Ps. 94 it tells us that God knows our very thoughts and it is to our advantage if we are disciplined by Him. Verses 12-13 (NIV) say, "Blessed is the man you discipline, O Lord, the man you teach from your law; you grant him relief from days of trouble, till a pit is dug for the wicked." Let us bring joy to the Lord and give Him obedience from our hearts.

Challenge for today: Ask for the Lord's help to obey promptly and accept His discipline when needed.

One time when we were visiting our youngest son, Kurt, he made physical motions to us with excitement as he was on the phone. We could tell by his smile that he was getting some good news on the other end of the line. We knew he had the possibility of winning a trip to Paris through his work and thought maybe he had won the trip for him and his wife, Brenda. But when he put down his phone he gave the breathtaking news to all of us—His MRI came out clean and he didn't have a return of his brain cancer! The Doctors were quite astounded at the success of treating his Hemangeopericytoma and that he was not left with any side-effects. Now that news was far better than a trip to Paris! Sometimes we get so excited over worldly things and feel like we have arrived because we obtained some earthly treasure. But that is peanuts! We can have far greater riches in the Lord that last more than this life time. We have a glorious future with Him that lasts for eternity. It tells us in I Peter 1:3-5 (NIV) "Praise be to the God and Father of our Lord Jesus Christ! In His great mercy He has given us new birth into a living hope through the resurrection of Jesus Christ from the dead, and not an inheritance that can never perish, spoil or fade-kept in heaven for you, who through faith are shielded by God's power until the coming of the salvation that is ready to be revealed in the last time." Now that is awesome news! Kurt didn't win the trip to Paris, although it was very close, but he is thrilled with the good news he received and also his inheritance that awaits him.

Challenge for today: Share with someone else today of how the Lord has rescued or blessed you!

We can get wounded as followers of Christ. Well, the fact is we WILL get wounded! Sometimes it happens so unexpectedly that it catches us by surprise. While in the berry patch I often sing and enjoy being with the Lord as I pick those nice big berries and soak in the sunshine. But unforeseen to me at times I can get in poison ivy without recognizing it at the time as I truck through thick tall brush. But when I get home and start itching and seeing those red bumps, I know I need to put on the CalaGel. We can also get bumps and bruises as we serve Him and since He has been through it all, He fully understands what we are experiencing. He was in every way like us and knows what it is like to be hurt, betrayed, spoken against, physically wounded etc. He has promised to be with us and to give us soothing balm to heal the places where we hurt. Our part is to pour out our hearts to Him who hears and sympathizes with us. He understands for He has suffered ever so much more and just for you and me! He does not condemn us but desires to anoint us with healing oil of gladness. Let us, as it says in Heb. 4:16 (NIV) "Let us then approach the throne of grace with confidence, so that we may receive mercy and find grace to help us in our time of need." May we not give up or give in for His grace is waiting to be poured out upon us and it is enough!

Challenge for today: Forgive anyone who has hurt you (or ask the Lord to reveal it to you) and ask for His healing oil to be poured into your wounds.

I sat on the dock one warm day and dangled my feet in the refreshing lake as I wrote letters. A horsefly bit me on my leg and I slapped it and threw it in the water thinking it was dead. But a short time later it revived and came back and tried to bite me again. I squashed it harder this time and threw it back in the water but once more it came back. The third time I made sure it was a "goner" and back in the water it went. I think it is similar to bad habits and attitudes that we assume we are finished. We may have different behavior for a while but then all of a sudden we get tripped up again and revert to the old ways. It is not easy to have a clean break with old habits, and we have to be aware that we constantly need His help lest we fall back into behavior and attitudes that don't bring honor to Him. We also have to acknowledge that we need to change and allow Him to work that change in us. May our daily prayer be as Paul's prayer for the Colossians in 1:10 (Amplified) "That you may walk (live and conduct yourselves) in a manner worthy of the Lord, fully pleasing to Him and desiring to please Him in all things, bearing fruit in every good work and steadily growing and increasing in 'and by' the knowledge of God—with fuller, deeper, and clearer insight, acquaintance and recognition."

Challenge for today: Admit you need the Lord's help to overcome a long standing habit and ask Him to bring about a change in you.

Wouldn't it be great if life was all forward and upward? Al and I love the mountains of Colorado and when we walk the trails they wind around, go up and down and anywhere but straight. Isn't that what life is like? Certainly not a straight line! There are many ups and downs but the good thing is that our failures and humiliations can actually help us to see in a new way. I'm sure we have all had difficult situations in our lives that we could not control or understand. But those times of failing or undergoing suffering can open up new spaces within us in which we learn and love in new ways. Even our addictions can later bring us to thank the Lord for our former patterns as it breaks down our false self and opens us to grace and love. When we allow Him the controls of our lives and grow spiritually we can get to the place where we actually see down as up. Such times teach us things we would not know otherwise. When we fall, we recover from the fall and may experience His mercy! Let us be open and learn from our failures and know He doesn't love us any less but just the same. We can cast every care and even our failures on Him. It says in Ps. 55:22a (The Message) "Pile your troubles on God's shoulders—He'll carry your load, He'll help you out. He'll never let good people topple into ruin."

Challenge for today: Remember a past failure and thank Him for being there and helping you through.

When our grandson, John Mark, turned 4 we went on Skype and sang Happy Birthday and watched him open the gifts we had sent him. He was a little shy and would tell mommy or daddy what he wanted to say and then let them tell us. But we could see by his expression if he liked his gifts! I had a piece of cake that I put a candle on top and held it up for John Mark to see as we sang to him. But the reality is that he never got to taste the cake since he was 1100 miles away. The scripture came to mind from Ps. 34:8 (The Message) "Open your mouth and taste, open your eyes and see—how good God is. Blessed are you who run to Him." The Lord wants us to partake of all that He has for us but often we do not draw close and we miss out. Just as we were sad that John Mark couldn't taste the cake, it must make the Lord disappointed when we fail to receive the many blessings He wants to give us; or sadness when we neglect to spend time talking to Him. He tells us to come to Him! It is His desire that we delight in Him and as we do we will know in our hearts that HE IS GOOD! Let us draw near to Him and taste His goodness!

Challenge for today: Spend time enjoying the Lord in a new way and sharing your heart with Him.

God is concerned with every detail of our lives and has promised to take care of us. We need to put everything into His hands, from the big things to the small things, and not keep reaching for the controls. The other day I said to Al, "You know that since we got all our appliances when we built our new house they will probably all wear out at once. I must pray that the washer and dryer don't break down when all our family is gathered here this summer." (We do tons of wash when they are here!) Only a couple days later my washer broke down and my dryer was making too much noise for a healthy one. We happened to be going to a bigger town to shop the next morning so I put in a call to our repair man who can fix most anything. No answer! We proceeded to look at new washers and dryers and just when we had to make the decision, the repair man called and said it was time for new ones as they had exceeded their life expectancy. God's timing is perfect down to the fine details, and the appliances happened to be on sale too! These are just mundane things but God can use them to strengthen our faith and confirm that we are hearing Him. He wants to guide our footsteps and speaks to us in a variety of ways. We need to have openness and trust and let Him order our day. He is sovereign and may we be like David who said in Ps. 13:5-6 (Amplified) "But I have trusted, leaned on, and been confident in Your mercy and loving-kindness; my heart shall rejoice and be in high spirits in Your salvation. I will sing to the Lord, because He has dealt bountifully with me."

Challenge for today: Ask the Lord to take over an area of concern in your life and wait for His leading.

Have you ever had company that seemed to just flood your home with light and joy? We had a visit from gracious friends who filled our house with rays of sunshine. We met them while Al was interim pastor in a church nearby and it seemed like the Lord connected us in fellowship right away. Often one of the ladies' youthful 90 year old mother would come to visit and she would accompany her to our church. While having coffee they asked to receive the devotionals I sent out by e-mail each day. Then one Sunday the dear soul expressed a desire to see the places I wrote about so we invited them both over for coffee. We sat on the deck overlooking the lake, visited our very rustic cabin, examined the sauna, went out on the dock, and went to the Point where we often swam etc. They had such enthusiasm, and when they asked many questions and wanted to know more, it gave both Al and I deep joy. It made me aware of how the heart of the Lord rejoices when we get excited about His Words and ask questions because we are interested to know more! When we want to experience the things we have read about in the Word! When we want to give back to Him, just as these two ladies came bearing gifts! When we want to discuss what we read in His word and it gives us new ways of seeing things. Other times we just enjoy the present moment with Him. The mother could have said, "I am 90 years old and I'm tired so I will just look from my lounge chair." But no, she wanted to see and experience everything. Al and I were so blessed and we can still savor the sweet aroma they left behind. It says in II Cor. 2:15 (NIV) "For we are to God the aroma of Christ among those who are being saved and those who are perishing."

Challenge for today: Spread the aroma of Christ and purpose to recognize it in others also.

Our lives get so busy and I am reminded often how important it is to take time to be quiet and go apart as Jesus did. He would engage the crowds but then He always made time to rejuvenate by time alone with His Father. Luke describes one day in Jesus' life that is a good pattern for us. First it involves solitude, then community where what happens in our solitude is shared, and then work that is given out of a full heart to a needy world. We can't give without times to receive or give what we don't have. Many times we try and pour out of an empty vessel. When we are quiet and still it is easier to hear Him and our souls are nourished and refilled with Him. We need to be attentive to what is going on in our inner world as well as our outer world. One day I just sat on the dock in quiet and took in my world around me and in me. For the first time I noticed that the Lilies that had been forming underwater the day before were now showing above the water. The Lady Slippers were blooming nearby but I hadn't noticed them. I wonder how much escapes our attention. When we catch sight of the need for quiet, the Lord will draw each of us into a unique healthy rhythm, perfect for us that is life-giving. A place where we are not empty and stressed out; but a life that is lived fully and brings glory to Him and fulfillment to us! The kind of life that is from being filled to overflowing! It says in Matt. 11:28-30 (The Message) "Get away with Me and you'll recover your life. I'll show you how to take a real rest. Walk with Me and work with Me—watch how I do it. Learn the unforced rhythms of grace. I won't lay anything heavy or ill-fitting on you. Keep company with Me and you'll learn to live freely and lightly."

Challenge for today: Allow Him to draw you to Himself 10 minutes of your day; and just sit in the quiet, enjoying Him and listening to Him.

I have always thought that hospitality is important and saw it being practiced in my own home while growing up. There was hardly a Sunday we didn't have company for dinner and often during the week. When I was about 4 years old mom invited 2 missionaries to stay with us for 6 months and offered them her and dad's bedroom. Mom would ask people on the spur of the moment if she thought there was a need and didn't stop to think if the house was perfect. She wasn't out to impress! We are all called to hospitality and to provide space for another. Hospitality is merely giving something that is alive in us for the good of another. It can be simple things such as making a phone call, sending a note, inviting someone for a meal or overnight, or simply listening to another. I have been reading in Romans 1 as Paul expresses his longing to see the saints in Rome that they be mutually encouraged and comforted by each other's faith. When we get together as brothers and sisters in Christ, isn't that what it is about...to encourage one another in our faith? We are also witnesses of the love of Christ to share with those that do not know him! First of all we need to know how much we are beloved and have a sense of self so we can give to others. As we are open to being hospitable God's love can overflow into the lives of those around us. Let us have a welcoming spirit and genuinely receive others so they may be encouraged and comforted. I think we will find our hearts strengthened as well when we do it as unto Him. In Matt. 25:40b (Amplified) Jesus says, ..."Truly, I tell you, in so far as you did it for one of the least (in the estimation of men) of these My brethren, you did it for me."

Challenge for today: Show hospitality in a new way today to someone who has a need.

When we visit our grandkids we usually play lots of games and try to see the places they frequent. Our son-in-law was stationed at the Air Force Base in Charleston at the time. One day we went with our three tall handsome grandsons to the blacktop basketball and tennis courts. Paul and I had a couple games of tennis and then I suggested we join grandpa and Joe and Lars in playing Horse. I could see the look in the boy's eyes that they thought that grandma would be no competition at all! Grandpa is quite good on the basketball court and Joe is 6'3" and Paul almost 6'. Lars, though shorter, has a very competitive edge so you understand what I was up against. But I told them from the start they might be surprised since I grew up with brothers! Well, it wasn't long before I had eliminated three of them and it was down to Lars and me. He felt confident he would beat me, but shock of shocks, I beat him! They couldn't believe it! It made me think of how it is in our weaknesses that God's power is seen even more! Scripture is full of examples of this and we need only to think of David taking down the giant Goliath with just one small stone. God uses the most unlikely people in our weaknesses to shame the wise. It is freeing to realize how weak we are but how strong He is, and desirous to shine forth in our weaknesses. It says in I Cor. 1:27 & 29 (Phillips) "But God has chosen what the world calls foolish to shame the wise; He has chosen what the world calls weak to shame the strong...that no man may boast in the presence of God." Aren't you glad God uses weak, imperfect people that others may see God at work in and through us? Let us surrender our weaknesses to Him so He may be free to move in His power to make us strong in Him.

Challenge for today: Notice God at work in an area of normal weakness in another vessel and lovingly tell that person how you see Christ flowing in that area.

It's hard to be patient and wait and sometimes it seems to take forever. When a mother is pregnant 9 months is a long time to wait for the birth of her baby, or a patient waiting for the biopsy results, or a farmer waiting for the harvest. When Al and I were unofficially engaged we knew we had 3 long years to wait until marriage as I was in nurses training and you couldn't be married back then. God never rushes and His timing often seems slower than our own, but is always perfect! We have many instances in the Bible of how those that had to wait were being prepared for something great. Moses thought God would use him at 40 but He didn't' call him to lead the people out of bondage until he was 80. He used the time in the wilderness to develop him into the most humble man on the face of the earth. David's character was formed and he learned to become a humble king as he waited for his time to come. He said in Ps. 40:1 (NIV) "I waited patiently for the Lord; He turned to me and heard my cry." God moves on His timeline not ours. I suspect we would think we are ready before His time. Jesus Himself was totally submitted to His Father's timing, and was not persuaded by those around him. He knew what things to teach His disciples and when. We should not act before God's time for if we ignore God's timing we will have to suffer the consequences. God wants to complete in us what He is setting out for us to become. While we wait we can pray and grow closer to Him and live in anticipation of all that He has planned.

Challenge for today: Give to the Lord something you are anxious about and wait patiently for His timing.

One day Al's cell phone not only went through the wash but was in the dryer for a short time before it was discovered. I remembered hearing about putting wet cell phones in rice and went on line to find out exactly how to do it. If I had not recalled hearing about the rice solution, I think we would have been out shopping for a new cell phone. Spiritually we sometime hear or read a word and it barely registers on the screen of our heart at the time. The person who spoke it or preached it may feel the words were wasted. But someday, in the right timing and circumstances it comes to light! In fact, the Holy Spirit may bring it to our remembrance in the exact moment needed. God is always speaking to us, and often we hear only faintly or may even try to block it out. The Lord tells us again and again to listen to Him. And He says in John 18:37b (Amplified), "Everyone who is of the Truth (who is a friend of the Truth, who belongs to the Truth) hears and listens to my voice." Just like the message I heard some time ago about using rice; the Holy Spirit can bring to light what we have read and heard... that means even things we gave only our partial attention. Also, there are times it seems like our words were not readily heard by another; yet we can trust that someday the Lord may use those very words to bring change or direction. As we go about our day, let us do as it says in James 1:19 (Phillips) "Knowing this, then, dear brothers, let every man be quick to listen but slow to use his tongue and slow to lose his temper."

Challenge for today: Ask the Lord to help you to listen more attentively to Him and others in your life.

Yesterday my cousin, Scott, and his family came over for coffee and we had a time of sharing, laughter, tears, and prayer. Scott is battling brain cancer and has already outlived the doctor's estimated time he has left. Another cousin, Mary, and friends I know, are living in pain and the darkness of the unknown. So many prayers have been given for them and we see God at the center of their trials even though they have not experienced healing of their bodies. We notice how they are becoming stronger in their faith and experiencing God's mercies in fresh and new ways. It isn't what they would have chosen but there is an acceptance of what is. Their peace comes knowing God is more aware of their situation than the doctors and they can take comfort in that hope. Whatever we go through, He is always with us and it can be a time of awakening to His life and love in deeper ways. We need to hang on tightly and say we totally trust Him, even though we may not understand. He will walk with each of us in such a perfect way that we won't desire to give up! Life is truly a gift from God and He desires to give each of us life more abundantly. Our Father is love, and there is no darkness in Him at all. Our faith is fastened to His goodness and we all need to let go and allow God to be God! All of us, at times, are running parts of our lives and think we know best! It says in Is. 49:16a (Amplified) "Behold, I have indelibly imprinted (tattooed a picture of) you on the palm of each of My hands." He will not forget us! One thing we know and that is that He is faithful and with us no matter what we go through. He is our source for each moment and shares in our sufferings. Let us surrender to His love and ask for His will to be done in our lives.

Challenge for today: Thank God for your life as it is right now; and release any areas He shows you that you have not allowed Him to rule.

Often things are not as they seem on the surface and we need to look deeper. When we go to a public pool the water may look very clean and inviting. But studies have shown how many contaminates there are in the pool water. But our lake that has weeds, fish, crabs, small branches etc. actually tests much cleaner. One day as I sat on the dock and looked deep into the water, I thought of how this water could appear "dangerous" but actually it is far safer and cleaner than many public pools! Isn't that how it often is spiritually for we need to look beyond the surface to know what things are good for our spirit and which things are not healthy? Too often we look at the outward appearance and make a judgment but we need to look deeper and discern. When Samuel anointed David to be king, he had to by-pass all his brothers that looked perfect to his natural eye. He waited for God to show him as He knows the hearts of all men. These are the words found in I Sam. 16:7 (Amplified) that the Lord told Samuel about the son He would choose rather than his first born. "But the Lord said to Samuel, Look not on his appearance or at the height of his statue, for I have rejected him. For the Lord sees not as man sees; for man looks on the outward appearance, but the Lord looks on the heart." Let us not quickly judge a situation but seek the Lord and ask for His discernment.

Challenge for today: Seek discernment over a question-able situation or relationship in your life.

One night when I went to my computer there was an e-mail from a former parishioner thanking me for the devotional on healing that I had sent to her. She was astounded that it came at that particular time as she was preparing a Power Point presentation. It was for her pastor who was going to use it for the healing service he was giving on physical healing and healing from inner hurts. She talked about the timing being absolutely perfect and said chills went down her spine when my e-mail came. But the strange thing was that I never meant that e-mail for her. She has the same first name as another friend and it got sent to her by mistake. But isn't it neat how the Lord uses our "mistakes" and uses them to bring good? I can almost picture the Lord smiling and saying, "You didn't mean that e-mail for her, Judy, but I did!" I have been reading in the book of Romans and the familiar 28th verse of Romans 8 (Phillips) stood out to me: "Moreover we know that to those who love God, who are called according to His plan, everything that happens fits into a pattern for good." We don't always get it right when we are trying to hear and discern God's voice. But He knows our hearts and even when the decision is wrong, He can take that blunder and somehow fit it into a plan that is good. Let us not be afraid of making a mistake but be like trusting children who know our Father can make it come out alright in the end.

Challenge for today: Act in faith on something you feel God has been asking you to do and simply trust He will work it for good.

Our grandson, Grant, is into Superheroes and loves the action figures, movies and books about them. At one of his soccer games he went running down the field slightly bowed over and his arm straight out before him... just like he was Batman flying through the air! Now Kurt and Brenda, his parents, looked and knew exactly who he was imitating even though others may not have caught on. I thought of how we are to be imitators of Christ and are to be other worldly. This is not our home and we are His followers that are just passing through. We recognize others who also belong to the family of God just as Kurt and Brenda recognized Grant's actions. Jesus told his followers that His kingdom was not of this world and He said in John 15:18 & 19 (NIV) "If the world hates you, keep in mind that it hated Me first. If you belonged to the world, it would love you as its own. As it is, you do not belong to the world, but I have chosen you out of the world. That is why the world hates you." We should be different from the world for our Superhero is Christ and we are His followers. At times, we will be hated and misunderstood and spoken against, but let us remember Whose we are and Whom we are imitating. Paul says in Eph. 5:1 (The Message) "Watch what God does and then you do it, like children who learn proper behavior from their parents. Mostly what God does is love you."

Challenge for today: Let His light so shine through you that others notice you are different and may even inquire about it.

Lately I have been picking raspberries and that often means getting pricked, getting stung by a bee, stepping into holes and pressing into a thicket to get the big ones! It also means many times sweating in the sun etc. Now is it worth it? When we eat warm raspberry muffins from the oven, have raspberry pie, raspberry sundaes, or jam on our pancakes, it is so worth it! But often it means pressing past obstacles to reach the goal. Isn't that how it is in a spiritual sense? Sometimes we may be tempted to give up when the going gets rough; but the Lord wants us to press on. It may take sacrifice, discipline, and hard work but we need to press through and reach the goal He has for each of us. In fact we grow the most in the challenging times when we refuse to give up. It says in Heb. 12:11 (Phillips) "At the time, discipline isn't much fun. It always feels like it's going against the grain. Later, of course, it pays off handsomely, for it's the well-trained who find themselves mature in their relationship with God." Let us not hold back or give up but go on to be fruitful in everything God has for us. He will give us the needed strength and encouragement for each task He puts before us.

Challenge for today: Ask for the Lord's help to press on and overcome an area that has been difficult for you.

Our Lord desires to be our focus and the center of our lives. All the other things are really periphery and we can give even the smallest, as well as the biggest, concerns over to Him. Sometimes He just surprises us and we realize He is showing His involvement in even the mundane things in our everyday lives. Yesterday was such a day as Al and I made a trip to the nursery to get 5 new shrubs to improve our landscaping. My husband and I do not have a green thumb so we were hoping for help from someone at the gardening center. But much to our delight while we were there our neighbor, who is a landscaper, showed up and helped us pick out what we needed! But not only that, he stopped by our house and helped us plant them! We had no idea the size holes we needed to dig, or the cutting of the fabric around the root ball, or the spreading out of the roots etc. His timing couldn't have been more perfect and we whole-heartedly thanked him and the Lord! Isn't it awesome how the Lord shows up in the most unexpected places and times when we need Him? We must be alert or we will miss Him. We need to purposefully arrange our lives in a way that always leaves an open door for Him to enter our days! He wants to pervade all the times of our lives throughout the day and deepen our relationship with Him. His heart calls us from the time we get up in the morning until we go to bed. He wants us to connect with Him and to be our focus. He has given us so many ways to do that and they can be varied. We can start the day with a grateful spirit, thanking Him for His presence, power, and love. John 15:4 (NIV) says it so well, "Remain in me, and I will remain in you. No branch can bear fruit by itself; it must remain in the vine. Neither can you bear fruit unless you remain in me." May we find ourselves sensing Him and responding to His presence within us.

Challenge for today: Watch for the hidden ways the Lord comes to you and openly invite Him into that area of your life!

We live in the North woods and have to be on guard for a dangerous type of tick when we come in from outdoors. We practice daily inspections! One day I was feeling rather sick and when Al took me to the doctor I was hoping for a quick miracle pill. It didn't take the doctor very long to diagnose from my symptoms and tests that I had Anaplasmosis and Lyme disease. Sure enough she gave me the miracle drug and told me I would feel better the next day. That was hard to believe since I felt so crummy at the time. But I did feel much better in 24 hours and was amazed. Even so, I still had lingering symptoms of headaches, nausea and lack of full energy. It made me think of what it is like before we really know the Lord. We are all "sin sick" and need the Great Physician! People might even say, "Come to the Lord and He will take care of all of your problems!" The step of inviting Him into our hearts may seem small (like the pill) and yet it is powerful! He comes into our lives and gradually many things change. Many times our whole outlook is vastly different. But all those changes don't happen overnight. Although I was on the mend, for quite some time my liver and other tests showed I was still recovering. It takes time for our bodies to be healed, just as it takes time for changes to happen in our spiritual lives. We need to trust the Great Physician and follow His advice. Just like with my earthly doctor I have to allow Him to take care of me. He even gives us a manual to follow, the Bible. May we receive the word that Jesus gave the leper in Luke 17:19 (NIV) "Rise and go, your faith has made you well."

Challenge for today: Share with another person how your spiritual healing began and something that drastically changed in your life over time.

We just received a letter from a "special" friend from our former church. While we were in that church we had several "special people" that attended, and they usually sat with me in the pew. When we moved away, this dear woman of God wrote letters to us and 23 years later she continues to write often! She can only print and usually the letters say the same thing each time. She always includes; "I love Jesus...I go to church...I love you... You are good to me...you are my friend...write to me back soon." Now this appears very simplistic but doesn't it say it all? Most importantly she loves Jesus first and spends time each week in church. Then she expresses love for us and lets us know we are important to her. She also wants a response and asks that we write back and share with her. Our lives are filled with so many words, but when you remove the 'fluff' what is important? First, that we receive God's love and love Him in return. Secondly, that we reach out to others and show them His love. Thirdly, we receive from others what God gives to us through them. Everything else is secondary when we get down to the basics. Let us get our priorities straight that He is first, others second, and ourselves third. Jesus said it simply in reply to the Pharisees in Matt. 22:37-39 (NIV) "Love the Lord your God with all your heart and with all your soul and with all your mind. This is the first and greatest commandment. And the second is like it. Love your neighbor as yourself."

Challenge for today: Ask the Lord to show you where you are not putting Him first in your life and allow Him to change it.

When we go visit our son's family, often the grand-kids put on a show for us. One such time they dressed up and Paige (10 years old at the time) put on her mommy's dress and 4" heels and carefully walked down the stairs. Eight year old Lily had on her mommy's blouse and scarf and frilly skirt. Four year old Grant had on a Superman outfit and all three of them performed for us. They were interviewed and asked such questions as, their favorite color to the meaning of life. We laughed at their antics until we ached since we knew they were just children and not the adults they were portraying. Sometimes we may think we are more spiritually mature than we actually are. We want God to give us meat (a big steak) when we are ready for only milk. There are times we may show our immaturity by our hurtful and care-less words. Or we may refuse to persevere in trials and want to get out of them as quickly as possible. Our faith is proved in our trials and James says in James 1:2-4 (NIV) "Consider it pure joy, my brothers, whenever you face trials of many kinds, because you now that the testing of your faith develops perseverance. Perseverance must finish its work so that you may be *mature* and complete, not lacking anything." We may fool others but the Lord sees us as we truly are and knows what we are ready for. He is desirous that we grow in His grace and mature to become more like Him.

Challenge for today: Rejoice in a present trial you are going through and learn well and with patience what He is trying to teach you.

One Sunday morning a man came up to me after the service and tucked in a tag that was showing on the back of my blouse. He said it bothered him the whole service and he could hardly hear the sermon. (I think he was kidding!) I'm sure we all would love to be perfect but the fact is we all have imperfections that others see; and we fail many times. But if we live our lives so that everyone will approve of us all the time, we will feel like we are walking on eggshells. The most important thing is to know that God loves us and is for us. If we have not experienced it yet, the chances are we will, that someone in our life will not like us and be against us. That is not a comfortable situation but the Lord can teach us through it. He patiently teaches us to find our worth and our confidence in Him. Rather than feeling rejection because of another's opinion of us, we need to remember how the Lord looks at us. Paul says in Rom 8:31 (Amplified) "What then shall we say to (all) this: If God is for us, who (can be) against us?—Who can be our foe, if God is on our side?" When the creator of the universe is for us, what does it matter what man thinks? That is not to say if we have some obnoxious behavior we shouldn't be willing to let Him change us. But, He loves and accepts us right where we are now, and is for us. We don't have to go around worrying what others may think and if we are behaving perfectly. We can rest In His love and approval and go about our day with our confidence resting in Him.

Challenge for today: Think of someone who may not approve of you, and put them to rest in God's hands.

A gal in my Bone Builder exercise class told about her recent 16 mile bike trip. She is quite physically fit and although she can usually make that without any problem, this time she was extremely exhausted and could barely finish. She decided to check out her bike and discovered that one of the brake pads was on which slowed her down the entire way. Now she understood why she was impeded in her progress and had it repaired right away! Do we get bogged down on our spiritual journey and get worn out as we carry so much baggage with us? Many things can hinder us and slow us down just like the brake pad: things like unforgiveness, resentment, pride, selfishness, envy, hatred etc. But we need to lay every hindrance aside that slows us down, and focus on Jesus. It says in Heb. 12:1-2a (Amplified) "Therefore then, since we are surrounded by so great a cloud of witnesses (who have borne testimony to the Truth), let us strip off and throw aside every encumbrance (unnecessary weight) and sin which so readily (deftly and cleverly) clings to and entangles us, and let us run with patient endurance and steady and active persistence the appointed course of the race set before us. Looking away (from all that will distract) to Jesus, Who is the Leader and the Source of our faith (giving the first incentive for our belief) and is also its Finisher (bringing it to maturity and perfection)." Let us get rid of all of our entanglements and distractions that slow us down and focus on Him!

Challenge for today: Ask the Lord to show you any excess baggage that you have been carrying and give it to Him.

Our times are in His hands and each day we need to give the day to the Lord. I'm sure we have all had days when we wondered how we could fit everything in, and it is so freeing to just ask Him to orchestrate every detail. Yesterday was such a day for me and at the end of the day I could so clearly see His hand directing it all. I got up early and made a rhubarb cake and two dishes to serve at our potluck. I was just finishing when relatives came to our door with 3 little ones for a visit and coffee. While they were here I got a phone call that our garden was ready to plant! When they left I had just enough time do the planting with my gardening partner. I came home and just got cleaned up and it was time to get to a graduation party! I then returned home in time for someone who stopped by for prayer. When he left we had the family picnic and time of games and finally time for bed. I looked back and thanked the Lord as He fit everything in so perfectly. The Lord wants to direct our steps and our life is exciting as we follow how He directs us moment by moment. We can make tentative plans but with the mindset to be open to change if He should lead us in a different way. It says in Prov. 16:9 (Amplified) "A man's mind plans his way, but the Lord directs his steps and makes them sure." Our plans do not always fit God's plan and we need to willingly put our plans aside for His. If our life belongs to Him then we can say like Jeremiah in his prayer in Jer. 10:23 (NIV) "I know, O Lord, that a man's life is not his own; it is not for man to direct his steps." Releasing our plans to Him allows us to remain in His peace and rest and results in a heart of gratitude toward Him!

Challenge for today: Tell the Lord the day is His and ask Him to help you follow His leading.

When our landscaper stopped by he told us how our shrubs were not very healthy because the plastic fabric around them had prevented them from their natural growth. He was right for as we raked back the rocks we saw that the plastic was so tight around them, protecting them from weeds, they couldn't get the moisture they needed. The very thing we thought was protecting them was hindering them! What came to my mind as I was cutting back the fabric was how we can get so uptight with rules and the *right* behavior that we see life from a very narrow window. We can think we know how everyone should live and act and what things are proper for a Christian. In fact, we may find we are trying to be the Holy Spirit in someone else's life rather than letting the Lord deal with them in His right timing and way. Each person needs nutrients, water, and space to grow just like our shrubs, and each one is different as it matures. Others will not be attracted to the Christian life by hard-shelled people that are rule orientated and lacking in love and joy. They will feel like the shrubs that are restricted and not able to branch out and be who Christ made them to be. We all need the soil of grace, the warmth of His love, space to absorb the water of His Spirit, and the nutrients from His word. Let us be flexible with ourselves and others and not demand that we all grow in the same way and bloom at the same time. Let us be free in grace as it says in Eph. 2:8 (NIV) "For it is by grace you have been saved, through faith-and this is not from yourselves, it is the gift of God-not by works, so that no one can boast."

Challenge for today: Get rid of the "shoulds" in your life and walk in grace.

Isn't it neat to observe someone doing something kind when they are unaware that anyone sees them? Today I read from Jer. 17:10 (NIV) that, "I the Lord search the heart and examine the mind, to reward a man according to his conduct, according to what his deeds deserve." The Lord sees it all and knows when our motives are good and also when we try to hide what is in our hearts. That is so humbling for He sees what others may not see...the good and the bad! A young woman was waitressing and a couple came in, both in wheelchairs, and she gave them a lot of special attention. She felt badly that the couple in the booth next to them probably didn't get as much service as she would have liked to have given them. When the handicapped couple left they gave her a very small tip but she had a surprise waiting at the next table! This couple gave her a check for $100 with a personal encouraging note as they had seen how she had so graciously served the handicapped couple. They were impressed but that is not why she did it. How amazing that she was rewarded. May we do everything for the Lord and His glory whether others see or not...and when He shows us the hidden negative things, may we be willing to also let Him change us.

Challenge for today: Do a good deed just for Him and don't tell a soul!

Yesterday Al said the mosquitoes were fierce in his office and I told him to check the screen. There is a blind on the window and even though it is mostly up, you can't see the top of the screen. I went outside where I could see it better and sure enough the screen was slightly out in one corner. We had to work hard to get it snuggly into the groove because it was a little bent. All this time more mosquitoes were getting in and we were busy slapping them. It made me think of the enemy and how he tries so hard to get into our lives! He wants to get into any crack, opening, or weakness he can find into our lives. It can be so small but he wants to gain entrance and take over as much ground as he can. It often affects not only our life but the lives of those around us, just like I had to deal with the mosquitoes! It says in Prov. 10:17b (Amplified) "And he who neglects or refuses reproof (not only himself) goes astray (but also) causes to err and is a path toward ruin for others." Every day we have spiritual battles and we need to be alert for the enemy's tactics. We are warned in I Peter 5:8-9 (The Message) "Keep a cool head. Stay alert. The Devil is poised to pounce, and would like nothing better than to catch you napping. Keep your guard up. You're not the only ones plunged into these hard times. It's the same with Christians all over the world. So keep a firm grip on the faith." Let us be alert, and put up our shield of faith to put out any flaming arrows sent at us!

Challenge for today: Ask for the Lord to show you any area the enemy has gained or is trying to access your life, and allow Him to reveal, clear, and occupy it!

The other day my cousin's family was going to hunt for morel mushrooms. As they were leaving their daughter had in her hand a travel mug of hot tea and with the other held her daughter's hand. They aren't sure what happened but possibly the cover popped off the tea; and some spilt down on 7 year old Abby's chest. She began screaming in pain and they tore off her clothes and got her to the tub where they began pouring cold water on her. While her skin was peeling off, she cried out, "God help me, God help me!" Her mommy kept saying "I'm so sorry!" and Abby responded with, "I forgive you, mom, I forgive you." Her daddy made the decision to call 911 and while in the ambulance Abby got an IV with pain medication. It turned out she had second degree burns and is recovering with blisters but no infection. I thought of how Jesus told us to be like little children and in Matt 18:3-4 (Amplified) He said, "Truly, I say to you, unless you repent (change, turn about) and become like little children (trusting, lowly, loving, forgiving), you can never enter the Kingdom of Heaven (at all). And whoever receives and accepts and welcomes one little child (trusting, lowly loving, forgiving) is greatest in the Kingdom of Heaven." Little Abby has much to teach us as the first thing she did was to call upon the Lord and ask for His help. "God help me!" Isn't that simple but the most important? Then secondly, she affirmed forgiveness for the unintentional mishap. No matter what is done to us, as His children we are to forgive. Sometimes it takes time for us to work things through; but it is so healing and freeing when we can forgive others, even as we have been forgiven. Let us be childlike and live in awareness of how totally dependent we are on Him!

Challenge for today: Tell the Lord how much you need Him in every aspect of your life and trust Him in childlike faith. (Like Abby, it is good sometimes to speak to Father *out loud*!)

I meet with a group of gals on the surrounding lakes once a month called, "Ladies of the Lake". As it was my turn to have them, I asked each of them to do a random act of kindness and then share it when we met. I prayed for a situation where I could show kindness; but wondered how it would happen since we were going on a trip. But not long after, while in Kentucky, Al was filling up our tank with gas and I walked next door to McDonalds to get us coffee. There was only one lady before me in line and she had a baby in the highchair, a boy beside her, and a toddler crying. She had her billfold opened and was searching and searching through it. She had already ordered and couldn't find the $20 bill she thought she put in at home and had only six one dollar bills. I asked the man who was taking her order how much she was short and he said it was $16. I gave him the money and she seemed overwhelmed. I told her, "God bless you" and she thanked me profusely and said, "God bless you too!" Just then her friends showed up with their kids and they were all going to have lunch together. How sad it would have been for her if she and her kids had to go without food in front of their friends. I just knew what God wanted me to do and she was also an answer to my prayer to show an act of kindness. In Acts 20:35 (Amplified) Paul said, "In everything I have pointed out to you (by example) that, by working diligently in this manner we ought to assist the weak, being mindful for the words of the Lord Jesus; how He Himself said, 'It is more blessed (makes one happier and more to be envied) to give than to receive.'"

Challenge for today: Do an act of kindness as you are led by the Spirit.

Recently I took out a burned out bulb from our ceiling fan; and attempted to put in a new one. I tried several times and wasn't making any progress. All of a sudden I noticed that only part of the old bulb had come out and the silver screw part was still left in the socket. I could have tried all day to put in a new bulb and it would have never fit. Sometimes we try to force something that isn't at all in God's plan! We can get stressed and waste so much time and energy; when we could be at peace if we just surrendered everything to Him! He *always* has the best plan. Why do we think we need to figure out everything when He has asked us to trust Him; even when we may not know the "whys"? I tried to remove the stem part of the bulb but needed Al's help. Sometimes we require help also as something in our lives needs to be removed in order to make room for what He has for us. It says in Prov. 3:5-7 (The Message) "Trust God from the bottom of your heart; don't try to figure out everything on your own. Listen for God's voice in everything you do, everywhere you go; He's the one who will keep you on track. Don't assume that you know it all. Run to God! Run from evil!" Let us trust the Master Planner and not think we have to reason everything out. Instead, get out of the way and let Him direct our lives!

Challenge for today: Trust God in an area of your life that you may not understand what He is doing.

Sometimes we think something is a mistake when all along the Lord has something else planned for us. When we were adding on a Prayer Porch to our house we ordered windows for three sides. But when they arrived the back window didn't open as we had put in our order. We were disappointed and wondered about the cross breeze on warm days. But a short time later we were presented with a cut glass picture of Jesus in the Garden of Gethsemane that fit perfectly in that window. One of our members made it as a gift for Canaan's Rest. People walking on the road can see it too and the light shines through to illuminate the picture of Jesus. We can't have that window open since the picture has found a permanent place in that window, and what was once thought to be a mistake was really just what was needed! Maybe there are things in our lives that appear to be "mistakes" and it is best not to complain or have a pity party, but wait for Him to give us the rest of the picture. One day we may see the purpose but for now we might just have to trust. He has said in Prov. 4:11 (NIV) "I guide you in the way of wisdom and lead you along straight paths." We have such limited perspective but He sees the big picture and wants to guide us. So let us hold on in faith to see the blessings that await us.

Challenge for today: Trust Him in your present circumstances and anticipate what He has in store for you.

While we with our daughter's family on the Air Force base, at 5 p.m. the bugle would sound followed by a pause. Then the National Anthem would be played loudly over a speaker. Everyone on base must stop what they are doing and stand at attention and face towards the flag. You can salute or put your had over your heart and if you are in your car you must stop. In the morning at 7 a.m. there is also revelry. Wouldn't it be great if we had reminders like the sound of the bugle throughout the day to pray and be mindful of the Lord? Some people think of the Him each time they go through a door, or may pause for a time of reflection on the hour. When we were at the monastery, bells would ring out when it was time for prayer and the monks would assemble. There are many ways to be more conscious of the Lord and when we forget Him during our day, we feel fragmented and empty. He wants to be included in our thoughts and actions and in every circumstance. He desires that we be conscious of Him in all things, not just a fleeting thought at the end of our day. David says in Ps. 139 that he is never out of the Lord's sight and there is no place he can go that He is not there. Verses 5 -7 (Amplified) says "You have beset me and shut me in-behind and before, and You have laid Your hand upon me. Your (infinite) knowledge is too wonderful for me; it is high above me, I cannot reach it. Where could I go from Your Spirit? Or where could I flee from Your presence?" We are never in a place that He is not. Let us become more conscious of Him in all things!

Challenge for today: On the hour, pause and think of the Lord and thank Him for His presence with you.

Our small church was just painted by a dozen or more willing workers who were well fed during the process. The building changed from being 2 or 3 colors to being one nice cream color that more reflects a lighthouse, after its name. Churches are made up of many people with many ideas of what a church should look like. But the important thing is to have harmony and oneness and not everyone doing their own thing without regard for the whole. My husband used to say to our congregation, "We are a rag tag bunch. Look around you as it isn't going to get any better than this!" Prior to the painting there was siding that was white, mixed in with siding of bluish gray, and it was quite an eye sore as we waited for the renovating to be finished. It says in Rom. 14:17 & 19 (Amplified) "(After all) the kingdom of God is not a matter of (getting the) food and drink (one likes), but instead is righteousness (that state which makes a person acceptable to God) and (heart) peace, and joy in the Holy Spirit. So let us then definitely aim for and eagerly pursue what makes for harmony and for mutual upbuilding (edification and development) of one another." It took some time for the renovating process to be completed and in the meantime it looked more like a mess to the world outside. But the Holy Spirit was at work and bringing things together and creating harmony and unity. We are all being nourished but finding our places and fitting together takes time. It's like the rubbing together of stones, but in the end they are smooth and well fitted.

Challenge for today: Give up your personal preferences for the whole and ask God to show you what He is creating from the individual pieces.

The Lord has promised us perfect peace as we trust Him. When we depend on ourselves rather than Him we can easily get stressed and worried and lose our peace. There are times we wonder how things are going to turn out; will we get the job, will the MRI come out good, will we have enough money for the incoming bills, will we live to see our grandkids etc. But peace is not dependent on our circumstances! We can have everything going well in our lives and have all the world's goods and yet be full of anxiety. What we really need to do is to pray and keep our eyes on Him with full trust. If we do this we can grow in faith and gain strength even through uncertain and difficult times. We all have concerns but worry is concern that has gotten out of control and we lose the big picture. Paul tells the Philippians in Phil 4:6-7 (The Message) "Don't fret or worry. Instead of worrying, pray. Let petitions and praises shape your worries into prayers, letting God know your concerns. Before you know it, a sense of God's wholeness and everything coming together for good, will come and settle you down. It's wonderful what happens when Christ displaces worry at the center of your life." May His peace that transcends our understanding, guard our hearts and our minds in Christ Jesus.

Challenge for today: Give Him a worry you have and thank Him that this is an opportunity to trust Him in a deeper way. Sprinkle praise and gratitude over your prayer if your peace starts slipping away!

Al and I went to an open house at our local bank and we spied a nearby table with cookies and coffee. I proceeded to take a cup and when I poured the coffee it started coming out a hole in the bottom of my cup. Not just a little but a lot! I didn't take time to stop and examine why this was happening but quickly took another cup and put under it so it wouldn't spray all over. The teller came over and helped clean up as the coffee had gone on the table and napkins. Have you ever had a similar experience of something suddenly happening to you that was no fault of your own? You may wonder who was behind it or why it was happening but at the time you just have to react and deal with it. Sometimes we find out later what it was all about, but not always. We just have to put it into God's hands and know that He is our safely net, our sure tower, our shield, our rock! He will deal with those who mean us harm. (In my case, I'm sure no one did it intentionally.) Jesus says in Matt. 5 in verses 11-12 (The Message) "Count yourselves blessed every time people put you down or throw you out or speak lies about you to discredit me. What it means is that the truth is too close for comfort and they are uncomfortable. You can be glad when that happens—give a cheer, even!—for though they don't like it, I do! And all heaven applauds. And know that you are in good company. My prophets and witnesses have always gotten into this kind of trouble." How wonderful that we can put our trust in Him for everything that happens in our daily lives!

Challenge for today: Respond in love and forgiveness to someone who makes life difficult for you!

Have you ever wondered what it would be like to be Peter, James or John when they were with Jesus on the mountain top? They must have been filled with awe as they saw Jesus transfigured before their very eyes...His blazing whiteness, the appearance of Moses and Elijah, and the voice that spoke of His belovedness. Wouldn't you have wanted to be there too? I read about this in Mark 9, the day before Al and went to get our eyes checked. We had our eyes dilated and when we came out of the office we could hardly see. Everything shown so brightly and it was hard to just focus .Usually they give us sunglasses but none were offered that day. I thought of Jesus and how His brilliance reflects light from within Him and we can't take it all in. He comes to us in many different ways and reveals His glory and purity and power but we only receive a portion of it. Sometimes He gives us those mountain top experiences like the 3 disciples and we would really like to stay there and not come down. But there is much to be learned in the valleys and the ordinariness of our lives too. Let us praise Him in whatever way He reveals Himself to us, whether it is a mountain top experience, or grace in the valley, or His presence in the mundane of our lives. He is always present with us. It says in Deut. 31:6 (The Message) "Be strong. Take courage. Don't be intimidated. Don't give them a second thought because God, your God, is striding ahead of you. He's right there with you. He won't let you down; He won't leave you."

Challenge for today: Thank the Lord for the valleys in your life as well as the mountain top experiences.

I just finished making Gluten-free Chocolate Cookie Rounds that have peanut butter balls in the middle. It gave my heart much joy to make them for we are anticipating the arrival of our 3 grandsons for 11 days. Since our grandsons must have gluten-free food I love to make special meals and treats for them. They have big smiles on their faces when they come to the table to enjoy gluten free pizza or lasagna or have chocolate chip cookies on a stick for dessert. When I was baking I thought, if I have joy preparing for our grandkids, it must give the Lord even more pleasure when He prepares gifts for us. I wonder how often He has something special ready to give and then we ruin it by refusing to be in the right place to receive. Sometimes we can even blame Him when all along we are in the wrong position. Or maybe our hearts are so ungrateful that how can He give us more? I love the words from Zeph. 3:17 (NIV) "The Lord your God is with you, He is mighty to save. He will take great delight in you, He will quiet you with His love, He will rejoice over you with singing." He delights in us and even sings songs over us. Wow! It's almost too good to be true but it is! I delight in our grandchildren and we have an unwritten policy that says you can brag all you want about your grandkids! (not exactly scriptural!) What would the Lord say about each of us?

Challenge for today: Thank Him for His delight in you and spend time quietly listening to His song over you.

So often in scripture we are told to remember what the Lord has done and how He has been present throughout our lives. Deut. 8:2 (Amplified) says, "And you shall (earnestly) remember all the way which the Lord your God led you these forty years in the wilderness, to humble you and to prove you, to know what was in your (mind and) heart, whether you would keep His commandments or not." I thought back to the mission trips to Mexico that we took with others from our church. We felt so dependent on God and experienced His presence and power in new ways. I prayed often before we went that He would give me love for the people and an opportunity to share Him with them. I was surprised at their great hunger for God and their faith to apply scriptures to their everyday lives. My Spanish was so limited but the Spirit seemed to bridge the language barrier and we communicated in ways of the heart. I remember at one service a woman asked me to pray for her knee as she could barely walk. I didn't even know the Spanish word for knee but laid my hands on it and prayed mostly in English. The next night when I went to the service she was dancing around the church and totally healed. It was the faith of that dear woman (not mine) for she believed God would do it right then. We also made house visits and I had money given to me by our church members to use. I felt led to give some of it to a little woman in an adobe hut. She began to cry and raise her hands in praise as she and her husband had been praying for God to send them money. Her husband needed his heart medication and they had no money for it. We all gave thanks and praise. Tears flowed when we left these dear brothers and sisters.

Challenge for today: Recall a time you saw a demonstration of God's power and knew it was Him! Return gratitude to Him for those times as He brings them to mind!

We just came in from having a sizzling hot Finnish sauna... one that burns wood and warms up the rocks on top. We read how it helps people with Lyme disease and all of us who need to get rid of the toxins in our bodies. Now some people wonder why anyone would subject themselves to such heat. But what a wonderful feeling afterwards of being deeply cleansed and totally relaxed! Now, doesn't that sound a lot like the times we go through intense adversity and wonder how long we can take it? We may even say, "Lord, get me out of this tight painful situation soon!" Job went through so much and stated his case before the Lord as he looked for Him in all that was happening to him. Job says in 23:10 (NIV) "But He knows the way that I take; when He has tested me, I will come forth as gold." God allows us to go through hard times of testing and often dry times when we can't sense His presence. But He is all the while teaching us and "killing off" the things in our lives that need to go to death. It is a time to learn to trust Him in deeper ways and not depend on our changeable emotions. The Psalmist said in Ps. 66:10 & 12a (Amplified) "For You, O God, have proved us; You have tried us as silver is tried, refined *and* purified. You brought us out into a broad, moist place—to abundance and refreshment and the open air." The Lord tests us; we should not attempt to by-pass those trying times but learn all that God is teaching us through them!

Challenge for today: Ask the Lord what He is teaching you through a circumstance that is out of your control.

We are warned in II Cor. 10:12 (Amplified) to not compare ourselves with others or we are without understanding. Paul says, "Not that we (have the audacity to) venture to class or (even to) compare ourselves with some who exult *and* furnish testimonials for themselves! However, when they measure themselves with themselves and compare themselves with one another, they are without understanding *and* behave unwisely." Isn't it easy to compare ourselves, our possessions, our looks, our families, and our professions etc. with others? When I went for my prayer walk, I counted 17 mailboxes all in a row near the T in the road. It would be easy for those people who owned those mailboxes to make comparisons with the one next to them. It would be wonderful to go to our box and find checks every day or letters from loved ones. But, some days there is no mail or there may be bills or unwanted letters. We might love to have what is in our neighbor's box instead. Remember, it is the Lord who determines what goes in our box each day! We can receive all things coming from His hand as He knows the heart of each one of us so well. When we get all checks or gifts we may begin to think we are entitled to more and deserve more than others. Sometimes we get bills and unwanted situations in our lives and we may think God is mad at us or loves others more. We need to allow the Lord to determine what is best for us each day and not look to see what our neighbor received. He deals with us individually and we can trust Him with everything that concerns our lives for He is our Father of love.

Challenge for today: Receive whatever comes into your box (heart) today and thank Him.

Our daughter, Ann, took our 3 grandsons to Germany and traveled 10 hours on a military plane with the temperature of 40 degrees. (I would have been frozen!) They "sacrificed" by going on a military plane in order to go to a faraway land to take in the beauty and sights. Their trip was simply for home school learning and pleasure, but it made me think of the missionaries that leave everything behind to go to a foreign country to share the Gospel. They have sacrificed everything for the kingdom. Jesus said in Mark 10:29-30 (Amplified) "… Truly I tell you, there is no one who has given up *and* left house or brothers or sisters or mother or father or children or lands for my sake and for the Gospel, Who will not receive a hundred times as much now and in this time, houses and brothers and sisters and mothers and children and lands, with persecutions, and in the age to come, eternal life." Are we willing to sacrifice for whatever He may call us to do? When we are in His will there is a deep joy that bubbles in our heart. I remember being at a missionary camp and seeing each missionary light up like a candle whenever they talked about *their country*. God had put His plan and purposes in their hearts and it seemed like no sacrifice was too great. Jesus made the ultimate sacrifice for us, and may we be so open to Him that whatever He asks of us, we respond with YES!

Challenge for today: Ask Holy Spirit to show you any area of your life that you are in disobedience and request His help and willingness to obey.

One morning I woke up and felt so weak that I didn't even have the energy to make breakfast. Al prayed for me and that the doctor would have wisdom to know how to help me. I never dreamed I would be put in the hospital; but I had double pneumonia with a high fever and low oxygen level. The first day I had IV's and just slept the entire time. But the second day the curtains were opened and I felt better and watched little children playing in the courtyard. I noticed on my wall was a beautiful picture of the woods with bright light shining through the trees. God had used a similar picture years ago in my life to make me more aware of His presence. I just relaxed quietly in His arms and felt His healing light come into my body. Later I thought of how we all want to be whole and transformed more like Christ. Sometimes it takes a crises but in our heart of hearts, isn't that what we all want? I wish it happened instantaneously or at least that the transformation would take place overnight. But more often it is a long journey of many mountains and valleys. I wished that the doctor could have given me a powerful antibiotic and sent me home, (actually that is what I was expecting) but I could see this was going to be a longer process. Let us not be impatient with the Lord as He has so many ways to strengthen us in our faith and help us grow to be more Christ-like. May Moses' song be our song in Ex. 15:2 (NIV) "The Lord is my strength and my song; He has become my salvation. He is my God and I will praise Him, my father's God, and I will exalt Him."

Challenge for today: Totally lean on the Lord in an area where you have been strong in your own strength.

Nature can speak to us if we are looking and listening and will help us to see the Lord. Some mornings when I wake up the moon is streaming in our window and the heavens are filled with bright stars. Just think He determines the number of the stars and even knows them by name. Certainly, even more so, He knows each of us in a most personal way. It says in Ps. 103:11 (Amplified) "For as the heavens are high above the earth, so great are His mercy and loving-kindness towards those who reverently worshipfully fear Him." If we are paying attention we will notice that all nature is invited to make a joyful noise to the Lord and break into song. Ps. 98:7-8 (NIV) says, "Let the sea resound and all that is in it, the world, and all who live in it. Let the rivers clap their hands, let the mountains sing together for joy;" While living in Brunswick one day I walked the prayer trail to the river. Just as I arrived at the water's edge, an otter popped his head up and proceeded to splash and put on a performance. He would look at me, plunge down and about in the water and pop up again and again. Nature can speak of His love in new ways that we don't want to miss. May we draw closer to the Lord as we take in His beautiful creation and know that our Father delights in displaying His love to us in a myriad of ways.

Challenge for today: Let nature teach you something you have not been aware of before and give praise to our Creator.

Waiting is not easy and we probably all struggle with having patience as we wait. I read today from James 5:7-8 (The Message) "Meanwhile, friends, wait patiently for the Master's arrival. You see farmers do this all the time, waiting for their valuable crops to mature, patiently letting the rain do its slow but sure work. Be patient like that. Stay steady and strong. The Master could arrive at any time." We are waiting for His coming and we also spend a lot of time waiting for many other things in our lives. I recall in one of our former churches; I was the one who always put the coffee pot on, set the table and put the food out for the quilters. One day I plugged the coffee in and I was going to call the gals to eat when I noticed the big coffee pot hadn't even started to perk. We discovered the receptacle was faulty and had to find another outlet for it but in the meantime we had to wait and wait. By the time we finally had our coffee it tasted far better than usual. The wait had only increased our desire and anticipation for it. I have been thinking of all that God does in us as we wait. He alone sees what is necessary in our lives! David was anointed King by Samuel 14 years before he was actually inaugurated as King. During that time God was preparing a shepherd boy to become a king and lead a nation. Who knows what God is preparing us for as we wait? Let us be patient in the waiting and trust He is forming in us what is needful.

Challenge for today: Rejoice and have deep heartfelt thanksgiving for what God is doing in you as you wait!

I was coming back from my prayer walk and almost home when I saw a bright light shining at our neighbor's house. I thought it was unusual as I had never seen one there before and it looked almost like a city street light. (We have none here...only the moon!) Since I was curious, I walked almost a block to her house and discovered it was the sun shining through the trees on an old metal post. It made me think of how there are things in our lives that are difficult and painful but how the Lord wants to take those very things and shine through them. We may ask the Lord why someone we love has to experience so much pain; or go through such a terrible trial or tragedy. But when we give it all to Him, He can shine through any circumstance and the light of His caring presence can be seen. The scripture from Malachi 4:2-3 (NIV) comes to mind: "But for you who revere my name, the sun of righteousness will rise with healing in its wings. And you will go out and leap like calves released from the stall. Then you will trample down the wicked; they will be ashes under the soles of your feet on the day when I do these things, says the Lord Almighty." What a difference when we don't blame God for things we can't understand but trust that He is good and will arise with healing in His wings.

Challenge for today: Rely on God in a difficult situation and trust Him for the healing or resolution that is on its way.

When we lived in Iowa we had special meetings for pastors and wives to receive prayer and ministry. It was then that God put in our hearts to have a retreat house where weary clergy couples could come away and be in a quiet place to hear the Lord and get prayer. We sought the Lord when and where this would happen and waited and waited with each move to a new church to hear if this was the place. God has His timing and it wasn't until our last church that we were led to build on the hill overlooking the Lake where we had property and a cabin. When it is God's plan He provides exactly what is needed. Since we had always lived in parsonages, we had no equity in a house so had to build in faith and trust for the full provision. God so generously provided all our needs even in times where we didn't know where it would come from. One day we received a large check from a former church that had money given in their offerings by members who shared our vision. We wept when this surprise came in the mail. After the house was completed, we felt it would be good to have a prayer porch added where retreatants could spend time alone if there were multiple couples here at the time. God answered and sent the exact amount. Some retreatants expressed a desire for a sauna and we did not have the money at the time. Many prayed and God sent us to the penny what it cost to have one built. If it is in His will He has promised, as it says in Phil. 4:19 (Amplified), "And my God will liberally supply (fill to the full) every need according to His riches in glory in Christ Jesus." All the praise goes to Him.

Challenge for today: If God asks you to do something in faith, respond and trust Him to reveal the perfect timing and provision!

Our three grandsons had 2 very tiny adorable kittens that brought much joy to them but they also demanded a lot of work. When they first got Nermal and Cookie they made many trips to the vet for medications and shots and they had to feed them with a dropper. The kitties demanded lots of attention and daily care, feeding, changing of the litter box, Lyme sulfur dips etc. Even though they were cute they also interrupted the schedules of others to provide the needed care for them. Sometimes they just wanted to be held and other times they ran around, teasing and hitting each other. I wonder how much we are like Nermal and Cookie. Sometimes we are content and easy to be around. Other times we are "mean spirited" with others and they have to exercise patience with us. Every now and then, perhaps a "spiritual spanking" is needed and we reap what we have sown. Others may choose to hang in there with us and perhaps wonder if we are ever going to grow up in various areas of our lives! Isn't it wonderful that the Lord doesn't give up on us but is as Moses said in Exodus 34:6b-7a (The Message) "... God, God, a God of mercy and grace, endlessly patient—so much love, so deeply true—loyal in love for a thousand generations, forgiving iniquity, rebellion, and sin." Even as He is so patient with us, let us also exercise love and patience with one another.

Challenge for today: Ask the Lord for patience with others and also for yourself!

The Lord is sovereign and as it says in Eph. 3:20 (NIV) "Now to Him who is able to do immeasurably more than all we ask or imagine, according to the power that is at work within us, to Him be glory in the church and in Christ Jesus throughout all generations, for ever and ever! Amen!" The Lord is able to carry out His purposes in ways that are beyond our thoughts and prayers. We often had special meetings in our church in Des Moines, Iowa. One such time A.G. Dornfeld, a father of one of our members, came. After his message he asked where the pastor's wife was and called me from the back of the church to come up front and help him pray for people. When we were through praying for the many people that came forward, I asked him if he would pray for my sinuses. I was having some sinus headaches. He prayed over me and later I noticed I couldn't see well when I was wearing my contact lenses. I went to get my eyes checked out and found that my eyes were healed and I no longer needed contacts or glasses! Later, when Dornfeld came back for more meetings, I told him what had happened. He chuckled and praised the Lord and then said he would pray for my sinus problem again. My sinuses weren't healed immediately but now I can say that I no longer am bothered by them. What I discovered was that it is all up to the Lord. We can ask Him but His will stands and also His timing!

Challenge for today: Tell the Lord something you may be wrestling with and then leave it *all* with Him.

L ast night a dear friend e-mailed that on top of her fibromyalgia and congestive heart failure, low blood pressure, and diverticulitis, she has spots on her bones that may be cancer. My heart hurts for her and I thought, don't give up hope. Don't ever give up hope for you have the Lord. I had just read in my devotions the verse from Micah 7:7 (The Message) "But me, I'm not giving up. I'm sticking around to see what God will do. I'm waiting for God to make things right. I'm counting on God to listen to me." No matter what we go through; God listens to our cry and is with us in the midst of our circumstances. We may be facing health issues as well as broken relationships. We might be grieving for the loss of someone we loved. Perhaps we are wondering how we can solve our financial difficulties. Whatever it is, He is with us and even when we get old he has promised to carry us. He says in Is. 46:3b-4 (The Message) "I've been carrying you on my back from the day you were born, and I'll keep on carrying you when you're old. I'll be there, bearing you and when you're old and gray. I've done it and will keep on doing it, carrying you on my back, saving you." We don't have to lose hope or go through things alone for we have a loving Father who is with us and gives us His peace.

Challenge for today: Tell the Lord you are trusting Him to bring you through whatever is ahead that is yet unknown.

L ast night I found out that we had been "robbed"! My gardening partner went out to our fenced in garden and discovered some sneaky critter found his way under the fence somewhere and ate all our cabbage plants. We will have to look carefully around the whole enclosure to find where he found an entrance and reinforce it. What we were robbed of was so insignificant compared to how we get spiritually robbed so often in our lives. Just living in the past or heavily in the future can rob us of living in the present. That causes us to miss out on that close intimate fellowship with Him. We often get robbed when we live in unforgiveness for our hearts will lack His wonderful peace. When we refuse to obey the Spirit's promptings and go our own way we are robbed of His perfect plan for our lives and settle for less. When we moan about our circumstances instead of seeking His face we lose hope. The enemy wants to seek entrance into our lives in whatever crack he can find. Let us not get robbed for we have One that is stronger; that is with us and will always help us. We have the wonderful promise in Ps. 73:23-24 (NIV) that He is right here with us until the very end. "Yet I am always with you; you hold me by my right hand. You guide me with your counsel, and afterwards you will take me into glory."

Challenge for today: Refuse to allow entrance to the enemy and ask the Lord for His protection in any area that you are vulnerable.

I don't know if I have ever known a father that is so engaged in the lives of his children as our son, Kurt. While their family is at Canaan he is doing everything he can to help his kids have a wonderful time from dawn until dusk. When they first arrived after supper the grandkids were full of anticipation of everything they wanted to do and by the time we roasted marshmallows by the campfire they had already been for a boat ride, fished in the boat and off the dock, made torches, built sand castles, rode on the four-wheeler, and built individual campfires. Wouldn't the Lord be so pleased if we would be fully engaged in the things of the Spirit....full of anticipation and excited over whatever He has for us? Too often we miss out on so much as we sit on the sidelines as observers and don't fully enter in. We were made to be vitally connected and walk closely with Him and not just when we are in desperate circumstances and need His help. Energy is given when we enter in and we will find joy welling up in our souls. He will not withhold good things from us and even ordinary things will be seen in new light. Ps. 86:11-12 (NIV) says, "Teach me your way, O Lord, and I will walk in your truth; give me an undivided heart, that I may fear your name, I will praise you, O Lord my God, with *all* my heart; I will glorify your name forever." Let us not be onlookers but enter into life with all our hearts.

Challenge for today: Don't hold back but experience life fully!

When we are with our grandkids, often it is a time to learn from them! Grandpa can be a tease and Grant, who is in kindergarten, likes to tease him back. Often when Grant wants to get even with grandpa he asks me to spank grandpa and even brings me a wooden spoon. It is all in jest but sometimes maybe our heart rejoices when we see others get what they "deserve"; especially when they have done something hurtful. Humm! Do we hope that we won't get what we "deserve"? Sometimes instead of spanking grandpa I go over and give him a huge long noisy kiss and Grant just giggles and thinks it so funny! I am so glad that God doesn't give us what we deserve or He would have a spanking stick out all the time. When we are dealing with others also, there are times it is better to give a kiss (loving acts) that can turn them around, when a "spanking" wouldn't work! We need wisdom to know when to do that. God may let us suffer the consequences of our hurtful actions, but there are also times He just covers us over with His merciful love and gives us what we totally don't deserve. David Says in Ps. 25:6 &7b (NIV) "Remember, O Lord, your great mercy and love, for they are from old...according to your love remember me, for you are good, O Lord."

Challenge for today: Extend grace to others, even as you have received His grace.

One day I looked out our back door and right in front of me was a big turtle uprooting our landscaping to lay her eggs. She had gone through the fabric and dug a deep hole, spreading dirt everywhere. I tried to scare her off but she was not to be deterred. We live on a high hill from the lake and yet she decided to lay her eggs right outside our door. It made me think of how sometimes, through no fault of ours, someone comes along and makes a "mess" for us. We may question why but in the end we have to deal with it and clean it up. If we do it with the right attitude there can be blessings and fruit as a result in our lives. (For example- many little turtles!) I was reading in <u>The Message</u> from Matt. 5 where Jesus speaks a lot about such situations. "If someone takes unfair advantage of you, use the occasion to practice the servant life. No more tit-for-tat stuff Live generously...I'm telling you to love your enemies. Let them bring out the best in you, not the worst. When someone gives you a hard time, respond with the energies of prayer, for then you are working out of your true selves, our God-created selves....Live generously and graciously towards others, the way God lives toward you." I think that says it all!

Challenge for today: Ask the Lord to show you a way to express love for an "enemy" and follow up by doing it.

I am still left with a sense of awe as I picture in my mind the group gathered last night to welcome the Holy Spirit. Over 60 gathered at the Life in the Spirit seminar that desired to let the Spirit have more room in their lives. I was impressed with the Father who shared with the group about the importance of being open to all that God has for us. He told how the Holy Spirit gave him different messages at 3 services, one right after the other, with things he had not planned to say. He had so much knowledge of the Word but was humble and so open to let the Spirit flow through him. We all can have lots of Bible knowledge and get puffed up rather than letting His love flow through us. This Father was so full of God's love that he could have given the message without words! Paul says in I Cor. 8:1b (The Message) "We sometimes tend to think we know all we need to know to answer these kinds of questions—but sometimes our humble hearts can help us more than our proud minds. We never really know enough until we recognize that God alone knows it all." When he finished speaking all of those gathered sat quietly praying with a background of someone playing the guitar and singing softly. God touched each one in His own unique way and we went home blessed and with full hearts.

Challenge for today: Humbly and wholeheartedly ask God to help you to be open to all that He has for you and allow His love to flow through you.

When Al and I go on long trips he likes to do most of the driving and often arrives at our destination rather tired. On the other hand, I sleep a lot in the car, read books, play games on my I-Pad, or write letters. If we drive late into the night, Al may want me to give him relief for a couple hours. I thought of the Body of Christ and how this would not be good thing. Is it right for some to do all the work and others just to "play" and not responsible for any of the work? I recently read from II Thess.3 how Paul warns against the idle in the church, who end up being busybodies. In our new church there is plenty of work for all ...not just physically but also teaching, serving, praying, visiting the sick etc. God has gifted each one of us as part of the Body and as Paul says in Eph. 4: 15 & 16 (Phillips) "But we are meant to speak the truth in love, and to grow up in every way to Christ, the head. For it is from the head that the whole body, as a harmonious structure knit together by the joints with which it is provided, grows by the proper functioning of individual parts, and so builds itself up in love." We need to do what God has gifted us to do; and grow to full maturity so the Body may work properly and build itself up in love.

Challenge for today: When prompted by the Spirit, joyously say "yes" to something you have been reluctant to do.

Have you ever had a dream where you were floating through the air or water, completely relaxed or free? One day I went to the Point (a piece of land and dock across the lake that belongs to our whole family) and the day was so beautiful. I floated on an air mattress and noticed the blue sky overhead, felt a refreshing breeze, and soaked up the sunrays. It was a little bit of heaven! When we allow the Spirit to have complete control of our lives, it seems just like floating, for our cares are given over to Him who is able to handle all of them. It may be surprising where He leads us, just as I floated near the lily pads, on the other side of the dock and into deep water etc. When I just relaxed and shut my eyes, I really didn't care where I went. Sometimes when I opened my eyes, there was an eagle overhead, or loons nearby. I wanted to enjoy the moment and just savor it all. When the Lord has permission to direct our lives, it is like He leads us to the place where we know we belong...we feel one with Him and we are truly "home". Let us give up directing our own lives and float in freedom. Paul says in II Cor. 3:17 (Amplified) "Now the Lord Is the Spirit, and where the Spirit of the Lord is, here is liberty (emancipation from bondage, freedom)." We will have deep joy and His peace when we let Him lead us wherever He wills.

Challenge for today: Walk in the Spirit, willing to go wherever He takes you. (Even if it begins as small steps it is blessed!)

Perhaps we have all said at one time or another, "I will never make that mistake again!" I thought that just today as I was making rhubarb/cherry jam. I said to myself," I will never forget all the ingredients again!" One time I forgot to add the 2 boxes of gelatin just before they go into the jars and today I remembered with the first batch. But making the second batch I was not paying as much attention (I was reading while stirring) and started putting the jam in the first jar before I remembered. My immediate thought was, we really don't know ourselves and how frail we are. We can say "I would never do that!" but we are on slippery ground when we make such statements. We are most vulnerable when we are so self-assured and think we wouldn't do something or *ever* make a mistake! We are to be on guard that we don't become presumptuous and overly confident. When we assume and think we know, we don't go to the Lord as we should but depend on ourselves. In I Cor. 10:12 (Amplified) Paul says, "Therefore let anyone who thinks he stands (who feels sure that he has a steadfast mind and is standing firm), take heed lest he fall (into sin). " Let us be humble before Him and rest confidently in Him and not ourselves.

Challenge for today: Begin telling the Lord how dependent you are on Him as you make decisions and plans, relying on Him more and more.

Sometimes we may feel like we are not making a lot of progress in our Christian walk and wonder if we are growing at all. We want to hurry to become spiritual giants overnight but need patient endurance as we are in the transformation process. When we were in our parish in Brunswick the 75 year old church was moved off its present foundation to a new foundation in a field about 2 blocks away. Now this was not a speedy process. In fact, when they put the church on wheels and began moving it, we had a hard time knowing if it was moving at all. But in reality it was moved one inch at a time. If you watched the wheels you could then see it was actually moving but much of time was spent waiting and watching. When it got to the intended place and was set down; the Fellowship Hall was then built on to it. We had a model of what the church would look like when it was completed with the addition. We had to hang on to that while we waited expectantly! Our lives may look rather messy and we may feel we are making little or no progress; but God has us on track and moving us closer and closer to Him. We need patience and hope that we are being changed into His image more and more. David says in Ps. 27:13 & 14 (Amplified), "(What, what would have become of me) had I not believed to see the Lord's goodness in the land of the living! Wait *and* hope for *and* expect the Lord; be brave and of good courage and let your heart be stout *and* enduring. Yes, wait for *and* hope for *and* expect the Lord." We may be surprised some day at the finished project which is temporarily under construction!

Challenge for today: Be patient and trust God, keeping your focus on Him and not on your progress.

When I was young we went to up north to spend our summers by the lake. Now that was okay for a short time but I never wanted to live there and I welcomed even the smell of the city when we returned. But God can change the desires of our hearts to be one with His will and purpose. One time when Al and I went to Michigan in February we did some snow-shoeing out in the woods. We came to a clearing and I was overwhelmed by the beauty and God touched my heart and I knew it was Him. I told Al, "I could live up north! I would like to live up north!" It wasn't too long later that we began our move from Iowa north and later all the way up to Hackensack, MN. This was the very place He had in mind for our Retreat House and there is no place I would rather live. I love every season here and I love the quiet beauty that is before me each day. David says in Ps. 37:4 (Amplified) "Delight yourself also in the Lord and He will give you the desire and the secret petitions of your heart." I am so thankful that God will actually change our desires and when we are in His will, we find our hearts are saying, "Yes, this is it! Perfect! Thank you Lord!"

Challenge for today: Commit your way to the Lord and trust that His way is perfect!

Sometimes we think we know just what someone else needs. Maybe we have been through a similar situation and know what helped us, and certainly that would help them, wouldn't it? Not necessarily, for we are all unique and there is no one else anywhere who is quite like us. One day a friend was outside studying and happened to see a woman in a wheelchair near the lake. She decided how nice it would be to pick some lilacs and give to her. But when she approached the woman put her hands up and said, "No, no! I am allergic to them!" Those flowers would not have been welcomed and would have caused her discomfort. We all have needs and the bottom line is that our real help is from the Lord. The Holy Spirit directs how our needs are met in each circumstance and He is our peace in the midst of whatever we go through. Sometimes we may be given flowers, a card, a visit, and other times someone may just sit and listen to us and pray for us. Paul said in II Thess. 3:16 (Amplified) "Now may the Lord of peace Himself grant you His peace (the peace of His kingdom) at all times and in all ways (under all circumstances and conditions, whatever comes). The Lord (be) with you all." Our pain and problems are only meant to draw us closer to Him and He fills our needy empty places with Himself.

Challenge for today: Be open to whatever way the Holy Spirit would use you to help someone else who is hurting.

Sometimes we are overly focused on outward things and may neglect our inward lives. I remember when we were going to be interviewed in a church up north. I took pains to pick out the clothes I thought would create a fine first impression and helped Al do the same. But when we arrived the heat was off in the church and we never took off our coats the whole time. No one saw what was underneath. What is going on inside us if far more important than what is happening outwardly. We need to focus on the Lord and feast on His presence, and the less important outward things will diminish. I just came home from a party and am so full that I have no desire for anything more. When we practice His presence and experience His love on a deeper level, we feel filled and satisfied as if we have just experienced a feast. He wants us to seek Him first that His life may be poured into us and our hearts would pant after Him. It says in Ps. 42:1 (Amplified) "As the hart pants *and* longs for the water brooks, so I pant *and* long for You, O God." May our hearts long to be filled with His loving presence and all the while letting go of the lesser things.

Challenge for today: Ask the Lord to expand your heart that you may come to know more of His love.

As I recently preached on the story of Lazarus as he emerged from the tomb at the sound of Jesus voice speaking to him. Jesus told him to come forth and He also invites us to leave behind our grave clothes and come forth and become our true selves in Him. We can recognize His voice as it is the voice of love and He wants to speak into our everyday lives. It may not be as dramatic as it was to Lazarus to come forth or to Moses when He spoke to him from the burning bush; yet we heard it and received Jesus to be our Lord and Savior! But if we slow down we may notice His voice speaking to us in our physical and relational surroundings and see things we haven't seen before. Just this morning I happened to look out our bedroom window and there was a bear in our front yard. What a surprise and he meandered off down the hill to our cabin. God can use creation to speak to us, or He can use other people to speak life giving words into our lives to call us out of our tombs. His Word is the most powerful way He uses as everything *must* agree with it! As we learn to recognize Jesus' voice in ordinary ways, it will help us get unwrapped from those things that have us bound. May we hear Him as He knocks at our heart's door for it says in Rev. 3:20 (Amplified) "Behold I stand at the door and knock; if anyone hears *and* listens to *and* heeds My voice and opens the door, I will come in to him and will eat with him, and He (shall eat) with Me."

Challenge for today: Open wide your heart's door and listen for His voice of love.

When we travel in the summer we often hear zap, zap, zap as the bugs hit our windshield. Soon it gets covered over with them so our vision is not good. We can choose to keep going with the dirty windshield or we can get it cleaned. It is a reminder of how our spiritual vision can get clouded by unforgiveness in our lives. We all have hurts and forgiveness doesn't mean forgetting or minimizing the offense done to us. The offender is still answerable to God and He will deal with that person. Our part is to forgive and give up our right to pay back or get even with the person who hurt us. One time we stopped for gas and the manager came out quickly and washed every window on our SUV free! It was his habit to do it one day of the week for his customers and we came just at the right time! It was so great to see clearly when they were all washed. Jesus washes the windows of our hearts and only needs our permission and then does it all. Paul says in Eph. 4:32 (NIV) "Be kind and compassionate to one another, forgiving each other, just as Christ God forgave you." When we forgive we find freedom!

Challenge for today: Think of someone who has hurt you and choose to forgive, remembering how much the Lord has forgiven you.

A missionary friend in the Philippines e-mailed that she was asked by one of the orphaned boys where her dad lived. She told him he had died and he proceeded to ask where her mom lived. When she told him she also died he said, "You mean you are an orphan too?!" Later that day we got a call from a former parishioner (only child) that her father had just died. Now she was also an "orphan" for her mother had also died recently. But when we are in the family of God, we are never left orphaned as Jesus promised us the Holy Spirit will be with us always. Jesus said in John 14: 16 & 18 (Amplified) "And I will ask the Father and He will give you another Comforter (Counselor, Helper, Intercessor, Advocate, Strengthener, and Stand-by), that He may remain with you forever.....I will not leave you as orphans (comfortless, desolate, bereaved, forlorn, helpless); I will come back to you." We are given the Holy Spirit, the Spirit of Truth, who teaches us, comforts us, and strengthens us. He wants to work in us and be our helper and our part is to welcome Him and give Him freedom to work within and through us. We are never alone for we belong to the family of God with a loving Father and so many brothers and sisters!

Challenge for today: Ask the Holy Spirit to open your heart more and more to the Father's love and to share that love with your brothers and sisters in Christ.

The Lord is our refuge and a safe place. David said in Ps. 31:1, 14 & 15a (The Message) "I run to you, God; I run for dear life. Don't let me down! Take me seriously this time! Desperate, I throw myself on you: *You* are my God! Hour by hour I place my days in your hand." This was especially true as we felt His protecting presence when we drove back home from the cities in a storm. I had been at the dermatologist and it took a long time to get into see my doctor. He was teaching a resident and stitching me up seemed to take forever. We got on the road much later than usual but found out that the delay was good. If we had gone sooner we would have been in the midst of a bad storm that hit shortly before we arrived. The county road to our house was blocked by downed trees and electrical lines so we had to wait and hour in our car. An ambulance finally got through to take a person to the hospital that had been struck by a tree. We did eventually get home and were so thankful. I thought of how impatient in my emotions I had been with the long wait for the doctor; but it was actually a good thing. The delay had prevented us from being caught in the brunt of the storm. Sometimes what we think may be delays are truly God's way of protecting us. Over and over again we read in scripture how Jesus was always on His Father's time schedule. Let us also be in His time for He knows best!

Challenge for today: Be sensitive to what God has for you today; and don't rush where He is not leading.

When I went for a walk the other day, I saw a huge tree that was broken off about 1/3 of the way up. I was quite surprised to see green leafy branches growing out of the stump and looked almost like a bush that was 15 feet off the ground. It struck me that sometimes in our lives our hearts may get broken like the top of that tree that came crashing down...maybe a great loss, an accident, rejection, cancer, loneliness etc. We think our life can't go on. Each day may be so painful that we wonder if we will ever heal. It's true, life won't go on as before; and somehow we wish we could get better faster. We can no longer cling to what was, as everything is changed! But as we reach out to God in faith with our hearts, and trust that He will take care of us, He will provide what we need to go on. As time passes we are surprised that hope starts rising in us. We can live again and it seems like a miracle, which in many ways it is. Just like the green growth on the top of the big tree stump, we have something to give again and to bear fruit. Perhaps because of our brokenness, others receive from us in a greater way for we have lived what we speak. David said in Ps. 31:24 (Amplified) "Be strong and let your heart take courage, all you who wait for *and* hope for *and* expect the Lord!"

Challenge for today: Trust that God will bring hope in what you have considered a hopeless situation.

When we planted our shrubs one of them looked like it was not going to make it. The other 4 were already showing green leaves and blossoms and this one had none. We thought we would give it one more week and much to our surprise it came to life and is now full of blossoms. Sometimes I am overwhelmed with awe as I see God's work in someone's life that has so radically changed. It is like a miracle unfolding and you know it is only the power and love of God! Recently I sat next to a young father who prayed for the group we were in, shared from his heart, and was concerned that his daughter would grow to love the Lord. It wasn't so long ago that he was drinking and on drugs and an undependable father. His mother had talked to me and we prayed for him, never realizing how God would answer in such a dramatic way. It is true that we never know how He will answer! Paul says in Eph. 3: 20-21 (Amplified) "Now to Him Who, by (in consequence of) the (action of His) power that is at work within us, is able to [carry out His purpose and] do super-abundantly, far over and above all that we [dare] ask or think (infinitely beyond our highest prayers, desires, thoughts, hopes or dreams) --To Him be glory in the church and in Christ Jesus throughout all generations for ever and ever. Amen—so be it." When we are filled with His Spirit, we have no idea how He will work and change us from the inside out. We only need to yield our will over to His and let Him go to work within us...and we may even be surprised at the deep changes that take place in us!

Challenge for today: Surrender to the Lord an area you have been holding out on and give it to Him.

Yesterday Al and I gave some of our shrubs a "haircut"! Some really needed it as they had branches growing rather wild and sticking up to be noticed rather than symmetrical. Others had dead branches that also had to be cut out. As I was clipping away, I thought of how necessary it is for the Lord to also prune us and cut off those things in our lives that are out of balance with the whole. It seems cruel at first to cut away but as it says in John 15:2 (NIV) "Any branch in Me that does not bear fruit (that stops bearing) He cuts away (trims off, takes away); and He cleanses and repeatedly prunes every branch that continues to bear fruit, to make it bear more and richer and more excellent fruit." When we allow Him to trim us and shape us, we will be more fruitful and become whole and complete as he planned. When we do our own thing or stand out from the center, we ruin the shape. He should be central in our lives and we are meant to bring glory to Him and not cause the focus to be on ourselves. He wants to bring us back when we insist on our own way and wander off on our "wild" course. How important it is to draw our nourishment from Him so we do not dry up and wither away. He is so willing to trim off what is old and dead and no longer fruitful, even though it may have been fruitful at one time. Remember, we are part of a huge garden He is planting for eternity! Let us allow the Master Gardener to clip and shape us into something beautiful that will bring much glory to Him.

Challenge for today: Ask the Lord to make you fruitful and welcome and grateful for His pruning shears!

When I asked the Wildmen (the name of various groups of men who gather together, study the Word, and are accountable to the each other and the Lord) about a time they felt especially close to the Lord, for most of them it was a time of pain or difficulty. We have a choice in such times if we want to seek God in our pain or if we want to try to exert more control and avoid intimacy with Him. Pain makes us aware of attachments and the things we cling to that are not of God. Letting go may be painful but actually there is more pain as we try to hang on or grab onto something or someone else rather than by the Lord. We may have to face the feeling of emptiness for a time after letting go, and it is very tempting to try to fill it with something else right away. But if we quiet ourselves before Him, we will find that God is holding us in our pain until our brokenness is healed by His love. He is with us in our pain and will strengthen us. Peter says in I Peter 5:10-11 (Amplified) "And after you have suffered a little while, the God of all grace—Who imparts all blessings and favor—Who has called you to His [own] eternal glory in Christ *Jesus*, will Himself complete *and* make you what you ought to be, establish *and* ground you securely, *and* strengthen (and settle you) to Him be the dominion—power, authority, rule—forever and ever. Amen—so be it."

Challenge for today: Seek Him in your pain and open yourself to the healing power of His love.

We say we want change but change is not always fun! I recently got a new refrigerator and when I started putting the food from my old fridge into it, some of it wouldn't fit. The filter pitcher and the juice bottle were too tall etc. and the crisper pans too small and I told Al, "I want my old frig back!" But after making some adjustments with the shelves and moving food around, I discovered I may come to like this one even better, although I'm not quite there yet. It may be the same with the Lord. We need to be always open to the new things He brings into our lives. Just like the old fridge was not dependable and varied in temperature all the time, what was once good for us in our spiritual lives may need to be released? Often we find as we grow and mature, we need to go on to deeper things and relinquish the former things. Sometimes it is hard to let go of the familiar but when we do, we may find the new has greater possibilities. Life also gets more exciting as we don't know what is ahead. When we welcome the new it brings spontaneous joy and unlimited good things. He has designed us to feel the peace and fulfillment of obedience! Let us not settle for the familiar and the predictable but let ourselves be stretched with the new. John says in Rev. 21:5a (Amplified) "And He Who is seated on the throne said, See! I make all things new."

Challenge for today: View your life like constantly changing adventures and welcome the new!

When we are at the Point (property belonging to my siblings and myself) we have to get water from the well as there is no plumbing in the cabin. It is a very old well and I remember as a child priming the pump and waiting for the water to flow out. Sometimes in a spiritual sense we may feel thirsty and wonder if the well has gone dry. Those times are best met with priming the pump with thanksgiving and focusing on the goodness of the Lord. It may take faith as we may not "feel" like doing that but when our minds are off ourselves and on Him, the channel is cleared. Gratefulness helps us to receive the blessings He wants to pour out on us and live from our true center. Jesus invites us to come to Him for that living water. John 37-38 (The Message) says "On the final and climactic day of the Feast, Jesus took His stand. He cried out, 'If anyone thirsts, let him come to me and drink. Rivers of living water will brim and spill out of the depths of anyone who believes in me this way, just as the Scripture says.'" The Holy Spirit is the living water that flows within us but also should flow out of us to others. When times come that we feel the flow has been blocked, let us prime the pump with praise and thanksgiving.

Challenge for today: Ask the Lord to fill you to overflowing with His Spirit and to reveal any way that you block the flow.

Does your mind wander, like mine, at the most unexpected moments? Maybe we are listening to a sermon and all of a sudden our mind might be on the fishing we are going to do in the afternoon, or the meal we are going to prepare when we get home. Surprisingly, we realize we have missed the third point in the sermon. Our soul (mind, will, & emotions) wants to run our lives and grab our attention just when we are going to hear something that the Lord is trying to get through to us. Or, we may be listening to a friend share what is on his heart and find our mind has wandered and we missed seeing the whole picture. We need to discipline our drifting minds and focus on what is at hand or we feel aimless. It takes practice to take our minds captive to Christ. When our minds are on the future while we are living in the present, we can get stressed and miss the joy of the present moment. But as we have our minds set on the Lord and what is happening in the present; we experience His peace and rest. In Isaiah 26:3 (Amplified) it says, "You will guard him *and* keep him in perfect *and* constant peace whose mind (both its inclination and its character) is stayed on You, because he commits himself to You, and leans on You, and hopes confidently in You."

Challenge for today: Ask the Lord to help you discipline your mind to be stayed on Him!

I think we all say we know how important prayer is and can quote scriptures about prayer and read books on prayer; but how much do we practice it? While at our church in Brunswick we had Bible study groups where prayer was an important part of it, and we studied about prayer. But more than that, we had people who were serious about prayer. Al and I have always had our devotional time early in the morning and some of our congregation must have known. Two men asked if they could come to church each morning and join us in prayer. Now Al and I had only to walk from the parsonage, through our back yard and a short distance to the church; but they had to get in their cars and drive several miles... that included cold winter dark mornings! They were so faithful and came each morning for 3 years at 6:30 a. m. (until we moved)! We sat in a dimly lit church and prayed together and had periods of silence as we waited on the Lord. If one morning we didn't "feel" like going, we knew they were there waiting and that encouraged us to press on. The early church met together daily also and Paul said in Heb. 10: 23-25 (NIV) "Let us hold unswervingly to the hope we profess, for He who promised is faithful. And let us consider how we may spur one another on toward love and good deeds. Let us not give up meeting together, as some are in the habit of doing, but let us encourage one another—and all the more as you see the Day approaching."

Challenge for today: Encourage someone else and take time to meet together as the Spirit directs.

Every now and then we meet a person who is so full of love that we feel like we are in the presence of the Lord. We may sense we are on holy ground and our hearts are touched in new ways and blessed. So much in our culture is all about "me" and what I will get out of it. But a truly self-giving person is focused on others and not on self. Rather than waking up in the morning and thinking of how this day will go for ME, we can ask the Lord how we can bless someone else. Love is expressed in giving and like I Cor. 13 says it is not self- seeking. We can do many good things for others but if we don't have love we gain nothing and are just a noisy gong. God is love and He wants to pour His love into our hearts. But if we are full of self, there is no room. We need to become empty of self so He can fill us and cause that love to over-flow on others. We will find His joy bubbling up within us as we desire to do His will in His way in His timing with His love. Paul says in II Cor. 5:15 (Amplified) "And He died for all, so that all those who live might live no longer and for themselves, but to and for Him Who died and was raised again for their sake." Let us be vessels full of His love, spilling out all over!

Challenge for today: Ask the Lord to use you to bless some unsuspecting person today!

One day I walked to the Point where we swim, and there on sun deck were large branches and sticks. Recently we had been swimming there with lots of relatives and now a beaver was trying to take it over and make a home. I told Al and he dismantled it but we have to be vigilant as he may not give up so easily. Spiritually speaking, it seems like enemy also comes when we are least suspecting and tries to move in to areas we are especially weak. He tempts us and wants to take over in any way he can. Sometimes we need to give up certain activities that seem to give him an inroad into our lives. We can't avoid all evil, but we can cut off those things that strengthen temptations. Our need is to turn to the Lord whenever temptation comes and ask Him to make an escape for us. It says in I Cor. 10:13 (The Message) "No test or temptation that comes your way is beyond your course of what others have had to face. All you need to remember is that God will never let you down; He'll never let you be pushed past your limit; He'll always be there to help you come through it." We must not think in our pride, that we can handle it on our own but instead seek His help. He has promised to be faithful and to give us the strength of resistance and power to bear up under it.

Challenge for today: Seek God's help in an area the enemy has been trying to gain entrance into your life.

When we take trips I like hotels with a pool so I can enjoy a relaxing swim while Al goes for a walk. One such time there was no one else at the pool site and I just prayed as I swam and enjoyed the freedom. I thought I was alone but I looked up and there was a security camera! I thought of the verse in Luke 8:17 (Amplified) "For there is nothing hidden that shall not be disclosed, nor anything secret that shall not be known and come out into the open." Little did I know that I was not alone and someone was indeed watching me. I thought of times when we feel like we are going through hard times alone and wonder where God is in all of this. But, He is there all the time and if His eye is on even a sparrow then certainly His eye is not too busy to watch over us. He sees it all and waits for us to call out to Him for help. It says in I Peter 3:12 (Amplified) "For the eyes of the Lord are upon the righteous (those who are upright and in right standing with God), and His ears are attentive to their prayer." We are not meant to be self-sufficient but to be totally dependent on Him who is always there. It is our decision!

Challenge for today: Visualize the Lord right by your side all day and see what a difference it makes.

When our grandsons were with us on vacation I decided to surprise them with waffles one morning. Since they have to be gluten-free I had to use special flours that require more mixing. As a result the waffles turned out rather hard and I called them "awful waffles"! It didn't stop the grandkids from eating every one of them but was humbling for me. I read the same day from Eph. 4:1-2 (Phillips) "As the Lord's prisoner, then, I beg you to live lives worthy of your high calling. Accept life with humility and patience, generously making allowances for each other because you love each other." We are to be humble and meek, in other words, live in lowliness of mind so our behavior is a credit to the Lord. A spiritual writer said he prays for one good humiliation a day! I'm sure most of us find that we have many humbling experiences each day and at the end of the day find ourselves asking for forgiveness and a fresh start. When we have humiliations it cuts through our pride and shows us how dependent we are on the Lord and His righteousness.

Challenge for today: Ask the Lord to make you aware of any behavior and attitude that is prideful and to form in you a humble spirit.

Today we had a visit from Scott and Kathy as we processed the news of his latest MRI. His brain tumor has activity in 3 spots so the prognosis is maybe 6 months left at best. What impressed our hearts as Scott struggled to communicate is that Christ is most important in his life and then Kathy and his 3 girls. He can't remember other details but he has his priorities in order and faces the future secure in the Lord. Kathy shared how their daughter Ellie is soon coming to spend time with Scott and the others are here at the lake now. On the day of Scott's last MRI Ellie was in the chapel of Northwestern University Hospital in Chicago praying. A worker on her way to lunch felt God telling her that someone in the chapel needed prayer. When she got there, 2 gals were praying but the other one got up and left. So she knew it was Ellie and asked if she could pray for her and what her concern was. Wow! The Lord is so faithful to send His ministering angels to those in need and at just the right time. We need to be always ready in case He should call on us to be such a loving representative of Him for a person in need! We can trust Him and as it says in Ps 62: 6 & 8 (NIV) "Find rest, O my soul, in God alone; my hope comes from Him…. Trust in Him at all times, O people; pour out your hearts to Him, for God is our refuge."

Challenge for today: Give God your greatest concern and thank Him that He is big enough to handle it.

I make several trips to town a week and love singing and praying in the car. One day I was asking God to speak to me, and as I drove along I noticed the T.V. transmitting tower with its high antennae. I had just asked God to give me His signal, so to speak, that I could hear Him. I became aware of how important it is to have my spiritual antennae up too. How often do we ask the Lord to speak to us but make no effort to be in a place that we would hear Him when He did? It helps to be quiet before Him so we are in a listening mode. We can welcome the Holy Spirit and ask that He make us sensitive to His signals. There are times we may not know what to do in a situation or need a word of wisdom, and after inviting the Holy Spirit to speak, things become clear. Only moments before we may have had no idea! Words of scripture stored in our hearts can also be used by the Spirit to direct us. I believe the Lord is pleased when we tell Him we want to hear His voice to our hearts. It says is Heb. 3:7-8 (NIV) "So, as the Holy Spirit says: 'Today, if you hear His voice, do not harden your hearts as you did in the rebellion, during the time of testing in the desert,'" Moses had to remind the children of Israel often to listen and respond with humility and willingness to follow. Let us do the same.

Challenge for today: Put your spiritual antenna up so you can hear Him speak to your heart.

One day a friend was sharing about an employee that was a vegetarian and quick to tell everyone around her how they should eat...why this was good and why that was bad etc. But one day she had to be taken to the hospital only to be told by the doctor that she was malnourished and dehydrated herself. Sometimes we are quick to tell others what is good for them, but don't discern for ourselves. We may even put the problems we refuse to face in our own lives and transfer them on to others. God deals with us individually and He knows exactly what spiritual food we must eat and what we should not eat! He may use various means and sources to do this as He wants us spiritually healthy and well balanced. That's why He doesn't always feed us only the things we want to hear or constant correction. But what He feeds us will give us a sense of being filled to overflowing ready to be poured out as He wills! The Psalmist says in Ps. 81:16 (The Message) "You'll feast on my fresh-baked bread spread with butter and rock-pure honey." Let us trust that the Lord will feed us what is exactly right for us!

Challenge for today: Welcome what the Lord feeds you and give Him thanks.

Welcome to the family of God! Those are words we love to hear but sometimes it is not all it is cracked up to be. When we come to Christ we also come into a family of Christian brothers and sisters. The family is not to be a clique or membership based on social or economic status, but on the presence of God in our lives. Christian community should give us a sense of belonging but many have found it sadly to be a place of hurt and pain. We must remember that we are together because we have the same Father and we all want to listen to His voice that calls each of us His beloved. Community is created through prayer as we recognize God' presence in our midst and our focus is on Him. Without community our individual prayers can get very self-centered. It is so wonderful when we find a community that is warm, gracious, vibrant and full of love. Too often the community may be cold, condemning and critical. When people who are suffering come into the Family, it should draw us closer together as we join in prayer for His healing Presence. Paul says it well in Eph. 5:1-2 (Phillips) "So then you should try to become like God, for you are His children and He loves you. Live your lives in love-the same sort of love which Christ gave us and which He perfectly expressed when He gave Himself up for us as an offering and a sacrifice well-pleasing to God." What a wonderful example to follow!

Challenge for today: Go out of your way to welcome new people into the community of Christ.

I'm sure we all have regrets for things we have done or said that are unloving and sinful. I was reading from II Cor. 7:1 (Phillips) where Paul says "With these promises ringing in our ears, dear friends, let us cleanse ourselves from anything that pollutes body or soul. Let us prove our reverence for God by consecrating ourselves to Him completely." Isn't it a wonderful miracle how when we commit ourselves to the Lord and ask Him to cleanse us that He gives us His righteousness? We get a clean heart and His righteousness in exchange for our sinful thoughts and ways. On our trip to the mountains we went past the dome of the sports arena of the University of S.D. in Vermillion. Many years ago when Kurt, our son, played football for Augustana, we were at a game there. We sat in the bleachers and the player's bench was almost beneath us. It was quite shocking to hear their foul language. But recently Kurt called home and told us he was sending a video of one of these same players to watch. We listened to his excellent preaching and his passion for God was so evident. He is now a pastor of a thriving church. Wow! Was this really the same guy? What a difference the Lord makes! It is a beautiful thing to see the change the Lord makes when we give our lives to Him. We truly become a new creation.

Challenge for today: Thank the Lord for His robe of righteousness and give Him anything that is polluting your life.

Have you ever felt like everything is the same and you are "stuck" and not moving forward? Sometimes the Lord closes a door and we are actually pushed out of the comfortable place we have known, and have no choice but to move on. The Lord may give us some time to mourn those familiar things now gone but then encourages us to reach forward to the new things waiting. I have been reading about Joshua and wondering how he must have felt when Moses died and he was now given the enormous task of leading the children of Israel into the Promised Land. He and all the people were given 30 days to mourn Moses' death but then they had to move on. Joshua's life would never be the same and he must have clung to the promise that he was given in Joshua 1:9 (Amplified) "Have not I commanded you? Be strong, vigorous, and very courageous. Be not afraid, neither be dismayed, for the Lord your God is with you wherever you go." What a change for him and he had to rely on the strength of the Lord to accomplish this huge undertaking. When God closes a door to us, let us not be afraid to go on to the next thing He has in store. Life is never boring when we are willing to let Him free us up from what is now over and move on.

Challenge for today: Thank God for how He has led you in the past and tell Him you are willing to take hold of the new things He has planned for you.

Canaan's Rest is a place of quiet and we especially try to keep it that way when retreatants come. The most important thing is for them to listen to the Lord and hear what He is saying to their hearts, and not our words. Jesus said in John 10:27 (Amplified) "The sheep that are My own hear *and* are listening to My voice, and I know them, and they follow me." How good are we at listening to Him? How about following His instructions? I read how after Jesus used Simon's boat to preach from, He told him to go out into the deep water and let down his nets. Even though he hadn't caught one small fish during the whole night he listened to Jesus and obeyed. The result was astonishing and not only was his boat filled with fish but his partner's boat as well. Sometimes as our hearts are listening to Him, we are asked to say something or do something that may not even make sense to us. But if we obey, our "nets" may be filled and others are blessed. Just a couple days ago, I was praying over the phone with a friend. A strange picture and word came to my mind so I added it to my prayer. It didn't make sense to me; but it made a lot of sense to her as it was something she was in the midst of dealing with. The Lord used that to bring encouragement to me as well. God wants to speak to us and as we obey we will see His hand on all that touches our lives.

Challenge for today: Seek a quiet place and spend some time just listening to Him with the intent to obey.

Grace is such a wonderful gift and when we make mistakes we come to realize it in a deeper way. I was made aware of that on Friday when I should have put our large red plastic garbage bag out for pick up. We had retreatants and I totally forgot until Al reminded me at breakfast. It was too late for the garbage pick-up truck had already come and gone. But all of a sudden we heard the commercial garbage truck that you have to sign up for, come down our road. His habit is to turn around in our driveway each week, so I ran outside and asked him if he would take our garbage. He doesn't have to as we do not have a contract with him. But he showed grace and took it away willingly and I thanked him and hugged him. It was a reminder to me of how the Holy Spirit ministers God's grace to us. We don't deserve it and we can't earn it but only have to open ourselves up to receive His over-flowing grace. No matter what we have done, no matter how we mess up, His grace is there for us if we come to Him and receive. It says in Eph. 2:8-9 (Phillips) "For it is by grace you have been saved, through faith. This does not depend on anything you have achieved. It is the free gift of God: and because it is not earned no man can boast about it." He does it all from start to finish and we simply trust and receive. His grace is sufficient to cover all we have done and all we ever will do so let us praise Him from the depths of our hearts.

Challenge for today: Spend time reflecting on the gift of His grace and notice during you day how many times grace is extended to you.

Timing is everything and we are especially reminded of that when we are too late for something or a day early for an event etc. Well, this morning my new stacked washer and dryer were to be delivered; and the big question was would they fit into the main floor closet that the old ones were in. My uncle is a very competent handyman so we asked him to be on call if needed. It wasn't long before the delivery guys determined the washer/dryer weren't going to fit and Stanton came immediately and saved the day! He cut a large hole in the sheet rock and cut the piping to fit and it was solved! We were so grateful as otherwise it would have meant the delivery men would have left them unconnected and not come back until we found someone to enlarge the closet. If Stanton had not been home and decided to go fishing we would have been without washing facilities with the kids and grandkids coming for 11 days. In the spiritual realm timing is important and Jesus speaks often of obedience. We need to be aware of what He is asking of us but also not to delay for if the timing is off, everything is off. We are to be watchful to obey Him as it says in Deut. 5:32 (Amplified) "Therefore you people shall be watchful to do as he Lord your God has commanded you: you shall not turn aside to the right hand or to the left." Let us walk in His ways and in His timing.

Challenge for today: Be aware of what the Lord is asking of you and do it on His time schedule, not yours.

Our son, Mark, had to get progressive tri-focal glasses so now he can read menus and maps etc. I have reading glasses as I have to admit I am "blind" when it comes to reading a map, or my Bible, even though I don't need glasses for driving or watching T.V. etc. We all have some spiritual blindness at times. Often we are not aware of how spiritual blind we are! It is much easier to see farther away at the sin in someone else rather than close up of our own sin! Jesus said in Matt. 7:3-5 (Phillips) "Why do you look at the speck of sawdust in your brother's eye and fail to notice the plank in your own? How can you say to your brother, 'Let me get the speck out of your eye', when there is a plank in your own? You hypocrite! Take the plank out of your own eye first, and then you can see clearly enough to remove your brother's speck of dust." We need to allow the Spirit to reveal areas we need to change and humbly accept however God reveals it to us. Yes, it is much easier when God shows us through scripture or a loving brother or sister that something needs to change. But sometimes He uses even our enemies to challenge us to change. But however He does it, it is out of His heart of love and He desires that we become like Him.

Challenge for today: Ask God to reveal a specific area you need to change and humbly accept help in whatever form He sends.

When Al was in seminary it was inferred that you don't make good friends within the congregation and maybe that has changed now. But the Lord has always given me the gift of a "soul friend" in each church in which He has called us. We all need "soul friends" on the journey and spiritual friendship is clearly God's idea and desire for us. Soul friends are people with whom we can be open and honest with our souls. It is very important that God chooses who these "soul friends" are. In return, they reflect God's love for us in their words, their attitudes, and their actions. These are the ones that exemplify God to us so we come to really know His love. Our soul is our inner essence, our spirit, the core of our will and our desires...it's who we really are. Our soul is rooted in our unconscious, and we don't always pay attention to, or even know, what it needs. We can get so preoccupied that we ignore our soul and that is not good. Soul friends listen to our souls and look at us with spiritual eyes, helping us respond to our own souls. But sometimes we don't want to know what is in our soul because of fear, or maybe not wanting to deal with the issues we are facing. But soul friendship is a place where we can experience the companionship of God and hear the whispers of the Spirit. Prov. 19:20 (Amplified) tells us "Hear counsel, receive instruction, *and* accept correction, that you may be wise in the time to come." Let us desire to know what is under the surface of our lives and be led into greater freedom.

Challenge for today: Tell the Lord you are willing to let Him show you more of what is in your heart through whatever means He chooses.

Often unexpected things happen and we have to switch gears in our thinking and planning. We were looking forward to our son's family from Kansas and our daughter's family from Texas coming for a visit and fun times with extended family as well. Our daughter arrived quite sick and because our granddaughter was also sick, their family did not make it here at all! Not the plans we had in mind! But God's goal for us is to live in constant communion with Him and that means accepting what happens as it comes. The Lord desires to carry us through all that touches our lives. Our only responsibility is to let go and allow His protection! The Holy Spirit desires to help us to cooperate with Him and rest within His strength and enjoy His plan. Then we can relax and be at peace and not be moved by the circumstances around us. We did that last night as we joined with extended family and lifted up our sick loved ones in prayer. Paul says in I Cor. 15:58a (NIV) "Therefore, dear brothers, stand firm. Let nothing move you." No matter what is happening, we need to humble ourselves and give to Him every situation of our lives and just trust. We are told in I Peter 5:7 (Phillips) "You can throw the whole weight of your anxieties upon Him, for you are His personal concern."

Challenge for today: Bundle up all your concerns and hand them over to the Lord in trust!

My heart felt sad for our daughter as we segregated her from our family gathering one night because she had a virus with a fever, achiness etc. The rest of us sat at the table eating and catching up with one another but Ann reclined on the sofa and had her dinner on a TV tray. Now we tried to include her but she still was not where the main action was and missed out. I wonder if we ever feel like that in the Body of Christ or in our gatherings with friends and family. Do we feel left out? Do we miss the closeness of fellowship with the Lord? It says in Song of Songs 2:4 (NIV) "He has taken me to the banquet hall, and His banner over me is love." He invites us to come to His table of delights and abandon ourselves to Him, without holding back. Too often there is distance between us and the Lord as we are caught up in busyness and things of the world. He tries to woo us and it is up to us to respond and let Him draw us in. As we do this we will find that His love flowing into us bridges the gap and there is no longer distance between us and others. Let us not hold back but quickly respond to His overtures of love.

Challenge for today: Abandon yourself to the Lord and respond to the ways He pursues you.

One of my friends was running the 4th of July one mile race with her 7 year old grandson. She had only run on flat roads and was panting hard at the first steep hill in the woods. She told her grandson to go ahead and she would catch up when she caught her breath! She was sure she would be the last one into the finish and was feeling a bit old and discouraged. After resting she ran about 1/4 mile and came to a fork in the trail and the "guide" standing between the two trails said to turn left. But the man with his two children that were running almost alongside of her but a bit behind said, "No, I have run this race for many years. We must go right!" The guide, who obviously was new, panicked because he had just sent about 25 runners the wrong way–the 10K route!!! My friend jogged the other 1/2 mile through the woods to the finish line all the way praying for those who had gone the wrong way and for the guide who made the mistake. Her feelings of discouragement turned to joy. She let the father who knew the way and his two children win first and she won as the first woman! She will never forget her first trail race! Doesn't that make You think of the scripture in Matt. 19:30 (NIV) "But many who are first will be last, and many who are last will be first." I think heaven will be full of surprises. Those that left houses and lands and families for His sake may come in first. Jesus looks at things from a higher perspective and also knows what is in our hearts. May we run the appointed race set before us with patience endurance!

Challenge for today: Stay focused on the Lord and the particular path He has set for you, throwing off anything unnecessary that would weigh you down.

Isn't it wonderful that God has made each of us unique and one of a kind? He has a plan for each of our lives and it is good! We do not fit into anyone else's mold! This became more evident when a friend sewed a couple dresses for my daughter Ann. She was given an old dress of Ann's and created a pattern with a couple minor alterations. She had never seen Ann and when Ann tried on the dress, it didn't fit right at all! When she actually pins it on her, I'm sure the fit will be perfect in the future. God's plan for us is perfect too; and we are not a carbon copy of anyone else so their plan will not fit us. We are told in Eph. 2:10 (The Message) "He creates each of us by Christ Jesus to join Him in the work He does, the good work He has gotten ready for us to do, work we had better be doing." He has plans for our lives and they are for our welfare and peace. Our joy comes as we fit into those plans and do the good works He preplanned for us. Of course we don't obey perfectly so we may find when we get off course we need to repent and get back into His plan. Let us not go our own way and create our own plan for it is not anything compared with what He has for us.

Challenge for today: Thank God for His workmanship in your life and ask for His grace to do the works He has created you to accomplish and prepared for you.

When we had a houseful of *loved ones* for 11 days, I missed Bible Study for 2 weeks in a row. That is my favorite time of the week so when I return it will be even more meaningful to me! Sometimes the Lord will withhold things for a time that we have come to depend on and may even get *ho hum* about. But He may use that time in our lives to create in us a greater desire for Him and to wake us up from taking things for granted. Often we do not appreciate what we have until it is taken from us, even for a season. He wants us to live in moment by moment communion with Him and trust Him with every detail of our lives. I was reading today from Eph. 4:23-24 (Amplified) "And be constantly renewed in the spirit of your mind (having a fresh mental and spiritual attitude), and put on the new nature (the regenerate self) created in God's image (Godlike) in true righteousness and holiness." Let us not ignore the Lord or be distant from Him but have an open and receptive heart.

Challenge for today: Ask the Lord to renew your mind with a fresh spiritual and mental attitude.

When our children and grandchildren are coming to visit we like to have all the housework done and lots of food in the freezer. Nevertheless, when they come we still have to put some things on hold as we just want to enjoy them! One such matter was the yard work and I was shocked at how many weeds grew up in the 11 days they were here. I surveyed the situation and thought it will take me forever to weed the yard and flower beds. It was discouraging but I thought I could do a little at a time so got started. I was reminded of how the children of Israel conquered their enemies and took the land a little at a time and not overnight. It says in Ex. 23:30 (NIV) "Little by little I will drive them out before you, until you have increased enough to take possession of the land." The Israelites could have been overwhelmed if they looked at the vastness of the land and the enemies they needed to conquer but the Lord fought for them so they could possess the land. We may look at some areas in our lives that need changing and feel defeated but we have to remember Who it is that fights for us. We are told to cling to the Lord and He will thrust out the enemy. (Joshua 23) I was pleasantly surprised at the progress made on the yard and was thankful I didn't put it off any longer.

Challenge for today: Ask the Lord to show you any "weeds" in your life and for His help to root them out.

I was getting dressed for church and noticed my new long skirt was shedding sequins everywhere. I quickly found where the thread was loose and had to mend and secure it. Had I gone to church without doing that I would have left a path wherever I walked. Now isn't that just like anger when we spew it out quickly and it lands all over others? We leave a path of hurt feelings and even the atmosphere is charged with emotion. Paul tells us in Eph. 4:26-27 (Amplified) "When angry, do not sin; do not ever let your wrath (your exasperation, your fury or indignation) last until the sun goes down. Leave no (such) room or foothold for the devil (give no opportunity to him)." Now even if we are not the kind to spew all over others, we can store up anger and get ticked off inside. That is not any better and either way we are not to let the sun go down while we are still angry or it gives the devil and inroad into our lives. Instead we need to let go of our expectations of others and how we may feel they failed us and replace the anger with a passion for God. May we allow the Lord to make us so secure in Him, that what happens around us is only a minor thing.

Challenge for today: Ask the Lord to increase you passion for Him and let go of the periphery things in your life.

I think we have all met people that share their positions on issues and impress us with their knowledge but really don't know what is going on in their heart. I am a *feeler* but raised by parents that were both *thinkers*. When I married Al who is also a feeler, he helped me to become more aware of what is going on in my heart and how to express my feelings. Jesus was a great teacher but His stories and sermons were not to impress people with His knowledge but to help others become transformed within. He used symbols and metaphors to explain spiritual things to help us grasp what is actually important. It is not about getting more knowledge (or even knowledge about Him) but all about helping us connect with Him. He wants an intimate relationship with us. It says in Jer. 9:23-24 (The Message) "Don't let the wise brag of their wisdom. Don't let heroes brag of their exploits. Don't let the rich brag of their riches. If you brag, brag of this and this only: That you understand and know me. I'm God, and I act in loyal love. I do what's right and set things right and fair, and delight in those who do the same things. These are my trademarks." Let us be about what is really important in life and let Him transform our hearts.

Challenge for today: Spend time enjoying the Lord and letting Him soften your heart.

It is not a pleasant experience to realize someone really doesn't like you. When we were at the nursing home visiting Al's mom, there was a resident with Alzheimer's there who I must have reminded of someone she detested. She took one look at me and started screaming at me and shaking her fist. I did not know her at all but we had to go behind closed doors to have a visit with Al's mom. I didn't try to defend myself as I'm sure that it would have done no good at all. The apostle Paul was not liked by many, especially the religious leaders, but that didn't stop Him from preaching and carrying on the ministry he was given. He tells the Philippians in chapter 1 to stand firm and not (for a moment) be frightened or intimidated in anything by their opponents and adversaries. We don't need to be concerned about what other people think of us and when attacked it is usually best to remain silent instead of explaining. We can't control other people's opinions of us but God can use such things in our lives to help us to die to self. We are to remain confident in the Lord and stand firm. We have a perfect example in Jesus who emptied himself and embraced the cross for us as the greatest act of self-giving love.

Challenge for today: Ask the Lord to help you not to be self-absorbed but self-giving!

Have you ever noticed when the Lord puts something before you two or three times, that He is speaking to your heart and wants you to get it. Lately the word has come to me to just enjoy God. Enjoy life with Him. A man in our small group said it at the close of our gathering and today I read it again while having devotions. Too often we get caught up in trying to do the right thing and keeping the rules, and miss the point of just enjoying the Lord. Paul did keep the rules before he had the encounter on the Damascus road but he needed his eyes opened by the Holy Spirit. He says in Phil 3:10a (Amplified) "(For my determined purpose is) that I may know Him ((that I may progressively become more deeply and intimately acquainted with Him, perceiving and recognizing and understanding the wonders of His Person more strongly and more clearly)"... Enjoying the Lord and knowing Him more intimately doesn't come by rule keeping or we would think we earned His favor. It comes more by recognizing our weaknesses and knowing how much we need Him. We aren't perfect and neither are the people around us but we can relax in His grace. Our dependency is on Him and may we just enjoy this relationship of love for He delights in us.

Challenge for today: Talk to the Lord and focus on His love … not if you are doing everything right.

Have you ever wanted to pull up stakes and quit? Maybe it is a job that is frustrating or a relationship that is difficult. Today when I was picking raspberries I really wanted to quit many times. The mosquitoes were fierce and also the deer flies. They were attacking my eyes and ears and any place on my body that was not covered. I had on mosquito spray but didn't seem to make a difference. The other day there was a breeze and no mosquitoes and I sang and prayed as I picked. But today was different and so hard to keep on with my task. But when I got home, even though I didn't pick as long, I had about the same amount of berries. If *invited* into all of our circumstances the Lord will get us through the difficult times and bring songs of gratitude in the good and bad times of our life. It takes faith to praise God in all circumstances but when we do, He is free to work it for our good. Paul surely practiced this and told us to press on and keep our eye on the goal. He didn't let his circumstance make his faith waver. His words in Phil. 4:13 (The Message) "Whatever I have, wherever I am, I can make it through anything in the One who makes me who I am."

Challenge for today: Trust God with each circumstance in your life and sing praises to Him in the difficult times.

Quite a few years ago we bought 2 blueberry bushes that were *supposedly* going to grow and produce lots of berries. But each year it seemed like they didn't get much bigger and only one produced a few berries. But one day I noticed that particular bush was just loaded with plump blueberries! When I walk by, I can't resist popping a few into my mouth. The other one hasn't produced yet, but maybe one day it will surprise us too. When the Lord looks at us, does He see lots of luscious fruit or are we like the bush that is barren? On our own we can produce no good thing for none of us are righteous in ourselves, but only through Christ are we made clean. Our lives are dramatically changed as He pours His love into our hearts and the Holy Spirit gives us the desire to live for Him. Then our lives begin making a difference in those around us also. Paul's prayer for the Colossians is one for us too: Col. 1:10 (Phillips) "We also pray that your outward lives, which men see, may bring credit to your master's name, and that you may bring joy to His heart by bearing genuine Christian fruit in all that you do, and that your knowledge of God may grow yet deeper."

Challenge for today: Do something for someone else that tangibly expresses God's love.

Have you ever been surprised at the people God chooses to use that result in His glory being manifested in a big way? I have been reading about Gideon and he was not a likely candidate to be used by God to deliver the Israelites from their enemy. He didn't hesitate to tell God that and asked for signs (fleeces) to be reassured that God was with Him. It seems he didn't have a great self-image but he came to know that it was God's power and not his ability that won the victory. I think the Lord wants to get us to the place where our confidence rests in Him and we are totally dependent on Him. That is the best place to live and a place of constant peace. When we are self-sufficient we do not see our need for God and depend on our own strength. But, when we are humble and trust Him, we can praise Him even before we see the victory, as Gideon did. Let us not be moved by any circumstance in our lives but totally dependent on His power. Paul reminded the Colossians in 3:17 (Amplified) "And whatever you do (no matter what it is) in word or deed, do everything in the name of the Lord Jesus *and* in (dependence upon) His person, giving praise to God the Father through Him." Let us not be surprised if God shines more through our weaknesses than our strengths!

Challenge for today: Trust God in a weak area of your life to display His power and glory.

Lately I have been picking berries on my cousin's property since her life has been too busy to harvest the raspberries. Usually it is very quiet as I pick, except for the sounds of the wind and birds overhead. It is a perfect time to just commune with the Lord and I love to sing and pray and just listen for anything He has to say to me. But one day it was entirely different as they were hosting an Art and Craft festival. People were coming and going, eating and buying, and listening to the band playing and songs from the singers. It was anything but quiet and I found it difficult to focus on the Lord. In fact, since I was dressed in ragtag berry-picking clothes, I did my best to not let anyone see me. I picked more from the low bushes than the tall ones that were in view of the crowd. I found scriptures coming to my mind about the world creeping in and squeezing us into its mold as more and more people arrived. Rom. 12: 2 (The Message) says, "Don't become so well-adjusted to your culture that you fit into it without even thinking. Instead, fix your attention on God. You'll be changed from the inside out." The Art and Craft Fair was fun and a good thing that I enjoyed too, but we need to be aware of anything that begins to take our attention away from the Lord and our ability to hear Him. When that happens we need to reassess our lives and hide ourselves in Him.

Challenge for today: Seek the Lord to show you if there are things in your life that are robbing you of hearing and enjoying Him.

One sunny warm day I walked over to the Point (lakeshore property belonging to my siblings and me) and was surrounded by dragonflies the whole way. I felt like "Pigpen" in the Peanuts column that had a film of dirt around him. But dragonflies are not bad as they eat the unwanted mosquitoes that we do our best to avoid. Happily I didn't have one bite the whole time I was at the Point. Instead of visualizing them as unwanted intrusions, I saw them as an army going before me and freeing the way. Sometimes there are upsetting circumstances in our lives and we immediately try to get out of them as quickly as possible. But if we look deeper, maybe they are the very things that God is using to do a work in our lives; or is protecting us from something more harmful. He has a plan and purpose for each of us and uses many ways to direct us where we need to be. David says in Ps. 138:8 (NIV) "The Lord will fulfill His purpose for me; your love, O Lord, endures forever—do not abandon the works of your hands." May the Lord fulfill His purpose in our lives for His thoughts and plans are for our welfare and peace and to give us hope.

Challenge for today: Thank the Lord next time there is an unwanted intrusion in your life, even before you know how it can work for your good.

Here at Canaan's Rest we live in such peaceful sur-roundings. Today I woke up to the sunrise over the quiet lake and it was like a mirror or a sea of glass. Other days it seems less tranquil with huge whitecaps on the lake. But even if we may be in a quiet secluded place we can be stirred up inside and lack a sense of peace and calmness. Peace is a gift that is offered to us and it is not dependent on wonderful circumstances or even peaceful surrounding but rather Whom we put our trust in. Anxious thoughts can quickly fill our minds and we can forget that He is here with us all the time. He is our peace! Some days when there are whitecaps on the lake I think of Jesus word on the stormy night to the waves of the sea, "Peace be still. " We can ask Him to calm the sea of our hearts and hush the turbulent waves. The Psalmist said in Ps. 85:8 (Amplified) "I will listen (with expectancy) to what God the Lord will say, for He will speak peace to His people, to His saints (those who are in right standing with Him)—but let them not turn again to (self-confi-dent) folly. "

Challenge for today: Give Jesus (The Prince of Peace) your anxious thoughts and listen for His word of peace.

This week we had friends come to visit that we haven't seen for over 30 years and it was an extraordinary time of wonderful fellowship and prayer together. The house echoed with much laughter as we reminisced about nursing school days and times together as couples. Way back then, we all knew the Lord but didn't know what plans He had for each of our individual lives. The sharing of how He has led us caused us to see more deeply His faithfulness to us. The Spirit bridged the gap of all the years and it was if we had just talked with them the day before. I was made more aware of how God uses others in the Body to bring encouragement and strength as I was reading in I Thess.3:2 (Amplified) what Paul says, "And we sent Timothy, our brother and God's servant in (spreading) the good news (the Gospel) of Christ, to strengthen *and* establish *and* to exhort and comfort and encourage you in your faith." When Timothy came back again after his visit, Paul was also encouraged with the news of their steadfastness, faith, and affection. God uses others in the Body to strengthen us and let us know we are not alone on the journey. He has given us others to stand with us and help us remain firm and strong in Him. Let us receive the ones He sends to help us along the way!

Challenge for today: Thank a person in the Body of Christ that has brought you encouragement.

One day I looked down at my watch and realized the battery was dead as it was much later than the time displayed. It was nearly a week before I could get to the mall for a new battery but in the meantime it caused me to contemplate the vital work of the Holy Spirit in our lives. Without His input in our lives we are like a useless watch. We need to guard against quenching the gentle Spirit and what He wants to do. We can so easily do our own thing and ignore His promptings. Paul warns of suppressing the Spirit and tells us just beforehand to do good to one another, to be happy in our faith and to pray unceasingly. Another key way is in I Thess.5:18 (Amplified) "Thank (God) in everything—no matter what the circumstances may be, be thankful and give thanks; for this is the will of God for you (who are) in Christ Jesus [the Revealer and Mediator of that will]." If we have a grateful attitude and accept the way the Spirit is leading us, even when we may not understand, we will be less likely to suppress His actions in our lives. When the Spirit is quenched, just like my watch, it may look nice but we have lost God's perfect timing. Just recently we had a couple from Mexico speak at our church and their simple sharing flowed in the Spirit and caused our hearts to be blessed. Let us give the Spirit free course in our lives and we will be surprised at what He will do.

Challenge for today: When you sense the Spirit directing you, say "yes" and immediate respond to His prompting.

Last night we got home from Scott's beautiful *home-coming* celebration. My cousin was rather quiet and reserved as I remember him in my growing up years. But things changed dramatically around the time he was diagnosed with brain cancer 3 ½ years ago. Scott began opening his heart as he faced the unknown future. He wanted God's help and began to share his spiritual journey with my husband and allowed Al to become his spiritual guide. We were awed as we saw how his trust in the Lord grew and together they kept the focus on Jesus. Al often said, "Scott it is not you, but Jesus living in you." Knowing his days were numbered Scott's concern was not for himself but for his lovely wife and 3 daughters and dad. He wanted to prepare them for life without him. He gave himself away as he let go of life in freedom to be given to others as a source of hope in Christ. A favorite verse of Scott's was in II Cor. 4:16 (NIV) "So we fix our eyes not on what is seen, but on what is not seen. For what is seen is temporary, but what is unseen is eternal." His life was a testimony of grace of how to live; but also to die wrapped in God's peace and constant love. He told us several times that either way he wins…to be healed and live or to die and be with the Lord. He is now in the presence of the Lord for all eternity and our lives will never be the same because of him and his living testimony!

Challenge for today: Live your life in such a way that when you die, your unwavering faith is a blessing to others.

Lately, Al and I have been talking about how we hope when we step into eternity our family will have great joy and encouragement through memories of our lives. They will understand more fully the faith and grace it took to run each one of our separate races to the finish. Our last and greatest gift to our loved ones can be the importance to live our lives well day by day. Seeing how my cousin Scott prepared his family for his death made a deep impression on us. His *homecoming* was truly a celebration of a life that left behind the fragrance of Christ and an anticipation of glory. The priest who conducted the service made us feel like we were almost at heaven's door peering in to heaven's glory. It is important that we live in forgiveness and love so that we give our lives away as Jesus did. Then what we leave behind will be nurturing by the fruit that remains forever in their memories. Paul shows his concern for the Thessalonians as he says in II Thess.1:11-12 (The Message) "Because we know that this extraordinary day is just ahead, we pray for you all the time-pray that our God will make you fit for what He's called you to be, pray that He'll fill your good ideas and acts of faith with His own energy so that it all amounts to something. If your life honors the name of Jesus, He will honor you. Grace is behind and through all of this, our God giving Himself freely, the Master, Jesus Christ, giving Himself freely." May our lives be honoring to Him and that those we leave behind may feel His presence and receive His love.

Challenge for today: Live this day as if it was your last day on earth, honoring the Lord in all things.

The longer I walk with the Lord, the more I see my sinfulness and need of His mercy and grace. When I was a new Christian I was aware that I needed forgiveness and cleansing but seems like the closer I am drawn to Him, the more I see how very sinful I am. One day when we came from swimming I mentioned that our 6 year old grandson, Grant, may not need a bath that night as he had spent the afternoon in the lake. But by the time we had our campfire and he had played in the sand and done charades, there was no question that he needed a bath! His face had soot marks, he smelled of smoke and his feet were so dirty that it left a ring around the bath tub. I wonder if that is a picture of us also. Just being out in the world we get *dirty* and influenced by sinful behavior around us. But also, as the Lord shines more of His light upon us, we see our own sinful hearts in need of forgiveness. Paul realized this and says in I Tim. 1:15 (Amplified) "The saying is sure and true and worthy of full and universal acceptance, that Christ Jesus (the Messiah) came into the world to save sinners, of whom I am foremost." Paul acted in ignorance when he persecuted the Christians and we also may sin unintentionally. But whether it is in our actions, our thoughts, our disobedience, or our unintentional acts, we need His grace all the time!

Challenge for today: Ask the Lord to show you areas of your life that need to come to the foot of the cross.

Each day that is before us we may be given opportunities to share the Lord with others. We are to be lights in the world and to let them shine so others will be drawn closer to Him. Do we take advantage of those openings or do we pass them by and remain silent? During vacation time when our relatives are together we observe the older ones challenging the younger to live out their faith. It is often during these casual times of fishing and swimming together questions are often asked about how God is leading in their lives and prayer requests given. Even the little ones love to play Bible charades and they seem to get refreshed on what they have learned in Sunday school. Families are drawn closer together when they focus on the Lord and bring encouragement to one another. David said in Ps. 22:30-31 (Amplified) "Posterity shall serve Him: they shall tell of the Lord to the next generation. They shall come and shall declare His righteousness to a people yet to be born-that He has done it (that it is finished)." Let us not be silent but use every opportunity to pass on to others what the Lord has done and will do!

Challenge for today: If you sense the Lord giving you an opportunity to share the Good News, don't pass it up.

It seems like the youth of today have a harder time to remain true to the Lord in the culture that is turning more and more from God. We need to use every opportunity to encourage young people and pray for them as the Lord puts specific ones in our path. Our niece's son is a junior in high school and although he is young, he has felt for some time that God is calling him to be a pastor. He admires his younger sister for her boldness in witnessing and desires to be a strong witness too. He recently went on a mission's trip to Nicaragua and was blessed to work and share the Lord there. We pray for our niece's son daily, as I am sure others do, and look forward to the day we can hear him preach and teach. The apostle Paul took young Timothy under his wing and treated him like a son in the faith. He said in I Tim. 4:12-14 (The Message), "And don't let anyone put you down because you're young. Teach believers with your life by word, by demeanor, by love, by faith, by integrity. Stay at your post reading Scripture, giving counsel, teaching. And that special gift of ministry you were given when the leaders of the church laid hands on you and prayed—keep that dusted off and in use." May we be inspired by the examples of the young people who live a life of faith and cheer them on to remain strong.

Challenge for today: Watch and pray for the youth that God puts on your heart.

Have you noticed how God's ways are so oppo-site of the world's way that continually strives for power, prestige, and wealth? Jesus said if we want true greatness we are to be a servant. If we want to be rich we should give more away etc. Lately I have seen how His ways can be almost contagious as we practice His prin-ciples. My neighbor gave me 4 ripe peaches since she knows I like peach pie. I made an almond crusted peach pie topped with heaps of whipped cream and brought 2 pieces back for her and her hubby. Then I picked rasp-berries and brought them to a farewell dinner, and the hostess turned around and sent me home with 2 pack-ages of blueberries she had picked! It seems like every time you give away it just comes back in another way with even more. The secret is to be content with the pro-vision God has for us but also to share with others as the Spirit directs. Paul sends a message to Timothy in I Tim. 6:18-19 (The Message) to tell those who are obsessed with riches: "Tell them to go after God, who piles on all the riches we could ever manage-to do good, to be rich in helping others, to be extravagantly generous. If they do that, they'll build a treasure that will last, gaining life that is truly life." Let us give up worldly ways and live in contentment that comes from knowing Him who gives life abundant.

Challenge for today: Give something away that you know would bless someone else.

Isn't it easy to slide into people pleasing and miss the *best* that the Lord has for us? When the Lord is not number one in our lives we end up trying to please others which is doomed for failure. I think we have all discovered we can't please everyone all the time, whether it is our boss, our parents, our friends etc. The Lord wants to be our focus, and we may need to just call out to Him many times during the day to refocus on Him when our attention is on pleasing others. David cried out to the Lord and in Ps. 27:7-9 (The Message) he says, "Listen, God, I'm calling at the top of my lungs, 'Be good to me! Answer me!' When my heart whispered, 'Seek God,' my whole being replied, 'I'm seeking him!' Don't hide from me now!" David had a lot of enemies but he came to seek the Lord first and to rest in Him. He was called a man after God's own heart. May our primary desire be to seek the Lord with our hearts open wide to His love and approval and not waste our energy trying to win the esteem of others. It's God's opinion that counts! May our desire be to please Him and seek His face always.

Challenge for today: Delight to please the Lord first and disregard what others may think.

Our family came for a week's visit. I didn't get to the berry patch and was excited to get out there again. But when I did I was surprised at the many berries that were overripe and fell off the bush before I could get them in my pail. I had been too busy to pick and realized I missed the opportune time for the big luscious berries. I wonder how frequent our timing is off when the Spirit prompts us to do something but we wait and don't act. Perhaps the person in need gets the gift we were to give them; but it can no longer be used for the specific purpose since the time is past. Or maybe we were to help someone and now they had to change courses since the need wasn't met. It's important that we listen to the Spirit and there is deep joy when we follow in obedience. Just yesterday I sensed the Lord telling me to make a phone call and I prayed before making it. The person needed encouragement and said it was just what she needed before going to bed. My heart was also made lighter and I went to bed with a sweet peace. Wouldn't it be wonderful if we always listened to the Lord and promptly obeyed? I'm sure we have all blown it. The Psalmist says in Ps. 119:35 (NIV) "Direct me in the path of your commands, for there I find delight." Let us hear what the Lord is asking of us and joyfully obey.

Challenge for today: When prompted by the Spirit, obey without delay.

One day when I was out in nature, I asked the Lord to speak to me and a simple phrase came to mind, "Lead by example." What does that really mean for us? Talk is easy but what about walking it out in our lives? Isn't it easy to share scriptures about being His servant and loving others, forgiving others, turning the other cheek etc. But when it comes down to living it out, we need lots of help....His help! Our natural inclination is not always the same as what Jesus would tell us to do. It can be difficult to forgive someone who has hurt us or to serve someone who is ungrateful etc. But the Lord gives us grace, and as we seek His help, can use us as an example to others. One night I was in a group and a lady blurted out how some of our friends who came to visit had been too boisterous and taken over the church party with their loud laugher etc. She was very offended. I apologized for them and told her our friends would feel terrible if they knew and would certainly want to apologize themselves. Later another woman in the group told me that God used my response to the incensed woman to speak to her heart as she would have responded in anger. Who knows what God will use? Sometimes even our mistakes or failures. Paul tells Timothy in II Tim 2:22 (The Message) "Run away from infantile indulgence. Run after mature righteousness—faith, love, peace—joining-those who are in honest and serious prayer before God." Let us leave behind childish behavior behind and go on to maturity as examples to others.

Challenge for today: Ask the Lord to help you be an example of His grace that brings glory to Him.

Each Wednesday I work in town at Share and Care, a shop for slightly used items. It is a large building with 3 floors and I work on the lower floor sorting through the clothes and other items that are donated. There are rare times that we get all caught up but the last time I worked there was an avalanche of bags everywhere! One huge pile was almost to the ceiling, other bags filled the sides of each aisle, and even the toy room was completely filled so one couldn't move. Surveying the situation, it looked rather impossible that we could ever get through all those bags but one by one we started. It made me think of mountains in our own lives that seem impossible and the temptation may be to give up. But God makes all the difference and specializes in things we think are impossible. We have only to look at scripture to read one example after another of His power at work. I just read of Samuel who was a miracle baby in answer to Hannah's prayers. The crossing of the Red Sea on dry land was not exactly common place either! Our part is to trust Him whatever comes our way; for He is sovereign. Paul said he held on to the faith and had fought the good fight through all the trials he suffered and told Timothy in II Tim. 4:5a (Amplified) "As for you, be calm and cool and steady, accept and suffer unflinchingly every hardship.." Whether God removes our mountains or helps us over them, let us accept His ways and not give up.

Challenge for today: Walk in faith, accepting and trusting Him in each circumstance.

Last night our Small Group met outside on the deck as it was a lovely warm evening. Our leader had us spend a half hour alone in silence and to ask the Lord what He wanted to do for us. We could sit or walk but were to remain quiet before Him. When we regrouped it was inspiring to hear how individually God had spoken to us. Each of us had heard in our own *language*! We can never fully comprehend His mysterious ways but only seek to let His Spirit lead us along the path that is for us. I found the Lord asking me to adjust my sails to the wind of His Spirit, which means being flexible for all the changes coming. We never know when He may change directions but He is in control and I need to do the flexing. Another person felt God was speaking about the desire for her and her family to stand together solidly on the rock. It says in I Sam. 2:2 (Amplified) "There is none holy like the Lord, there is none beside You; there is no Rock like our God." Someone else shared he felt God was saying He was going to do some work in his basement, perhaps getting to some early foundational issues. Isn't it amazing how God loves us so much and knows what each of us need, as He seeks to draw us closer to Himself? May we respond to His quiet whispers and be aware of His loving presence.

Challenge for today: Spend a few minutes listening in quiet for His voice to your heart.

Perhaps all of us have felt at one time or another that we are in a desert time and our life seems barren and dry. If we want to know the Lord in a deeper way, chances are we will be called into the desert place and we will come face to face with our false self and see our great need. It is a time of testing and we can learn more of who we really are; rather than who we believed ourselves to be. We may find we aren't as loving as we thought. We may have anger issues that we aren't aware of. Or, maybe we continually rehearse our hurts and harbor bitterness. The desert may actually be a place of blessing in disguise as we depend on Him to cleanse and transform us. We may have to give up our false identities; but will then find who we truly are in Him. It is a humbling time and a time of death to what is not of Him....our insecurities, fears, idolatries etc. When we give these things over to Him our hearts are purified and healed and enlarged to contain more of His love, resulting in peace and contentment in Him alone. In Titus 2:14 (Phillips) Paul says, "For He gave Himself for us, that He might set us free from all our evil ways and make for Himself a people of His own, clean and pure, with our hearts set upon living a life that it good." Let us welcome the desert times so we can be set free and walk in His love.

Challenge for today: Ask the Lord to show you any blind spots and illusions you have about yourself and bring His cleansing and healing.

When we were going through a *challenging* time in one of our churches, I memorized blocks of scriptures and one of them was Ps. 34. I found myself reciting it and others while I working around the house or swimming laps at the fitness center. Today as I was making the bed the word, "Hang on tighter!" flashed before me and I have been pondering that ever since. We are all going to be assailed by darts that the enemy sends to knock us off our feet. But in Ps. 34:1 & 6 (NIV) David says, "I will extol the Lord at *all* times; His praise will *always* be in my lips...This poor man called, and the Lord heard him; He saved him out of *all* his troubles." First of all it is hard to praise the Lord when we encounter problems in a time of warfare, but that should be our first line of defense. We are in essence saying to the Lord that our focus is on Him and we are giving the problem to Him. He is so capable and will help us to walk it out together. We may be amazed as we see the enemy's power broken and our hearts get flooded with peace. David said that even the angels encamp around those that fear Him. No matter what is happening to us, we can cry out to the Lord and know we are heard and begin to praise Him for how He is going to work it all out. It is an opportunity to hang on tighter to Him and draw closer.

Challenge for today: Give the Lord something that you have been holding on to and begin to praise Him as you watch Him handle it.

After we have had guests for a period of time, the food in the freezer gets depleted and must be replenished. This week I served 5 or 6 different kinds of baked goods for the coffee time at church, our Bible study, and the kid's group after having company too! So the sweet section of my freezer is nearly non- existent and I started baking again. I wonder if we also feel rather depleted when we have been busy serving the Lord and putting out lots of energy for an extended time. We may not realize we are tired and on empty as there are more things to demand our attention but we find we have no reserve. Instead of keeping on, we may need to go apart and get refueled and allow the Spirit to fill our tank again. We can't give to others what we don't have and spending time getting refueled is just what is needed. Sometimes the most spiritual thing is to take a nap and get rest and renewed that we can again get poured out as the Lord directs. God promised Moses rest even as he had the enormous task to lead the children of Israel through the wilderness. He said in Exodus 33:14 (Amplified) "And the Lord said, My presence shall go with you, and I will give you rest." The most restful place to be is in His presence and in His will and timing.

Challenge for today: Set time apart to just sit quietly with the Lord and let the Spirit fill you.

A friend was scheduled to come this weekend for a quiet time of retreat. She is a busy mom with 8 kids and quite weak being a cancer survivor. I have food in the freezer and her room prepared but plans may suddenly change as she may not be able to come. We have to be flexible and adapt to change as the Lord is in charge and sees the big picture. Sometimes the timing is wrong and there is better time in the future and it is worth waiting for. Or if our plan is not good in the beginning, submitting to God's plan will bring far greater blessing than our own. I often wondered as I read about the children of Israel if they always wanted to get up and go when the cloud moved or if they would have rather stayed put another day or week. Or maybe they thought they had been in one place entirely too long and wanted to move on. God is in charge and it is important that we are flexible and change with His plans. We need to just trust and know that He is with us and His Spirit will guide us. Moses asked the Lord in Exodus 33:13a (Amplified) "Now therefore, I pray You, if I have found favor in Your sight, show me now Your way that I may know You." His way is best of all and will draw us closer to Him!

Challenge for today: Seek to be flexible and flow with the plan that He has for you.

I think we have all known people that have been hurt by someone or been in difficult circumstances and gotten very bitter. They have an edge about them and a negative spirit that is projected on others around them. Bitterness is like a poison and when it takes root can take over our lives if we don't deal with the hurts. Many people have not gone to church for years as they were wronged by someone in the Body and unwilling to forgive them. Spouses ask for a divorce when grievances pile up and are not dealt with or forgiven. None of us are perfect and we all are in need of forgiveness as well as extending forgiveness to others. We all have weeds growing in our gardens and if we don't take care of then, they will take over... just as hurts not dealt with and forgiven often result in bitterness. Sometimes when we come home after being gone a few days we find the garden is so full of weeds it is hard to know where to begin. Also, when we hang on to the weeds in the garden of our hearts we end up bitter and only hurt ourselves. Paul says in Heb. 12:15 (Phillips) "Be careful, too, that none of you fails to respond to the grace of God, for if he does there can spring up a bitter spirit which can poison the lives of others." Let us give to Him all our resentments and bitter attitudes and receive His grace and forgiveness.

Challenge for today: Ask the Lord to help you to forgive all those who have hurt you

It seems like in our present day, taking a stand for the Lord brings on a negative reaction from the world. Why are we surprised? Scripture says the wicked will plot against the righteous and shoot arrows at them. Sometimes it appears that those who do wrong are getting by and yet the Lord sees it all and says that one day they will be cut off. He tells us not to fret and get all upset in the meantime. Instead, as it says in Ps. 37:3-4 (Amplified) we are to "Trust (lean on, rely on, and be confident) in the Lord and do good; so shall you dwell in the land and feed surely on His faithfulness and truly you shall be fed. Delight yourself in the Lord, and He will give you the desires *and* secret petitions of your heart." We are to commit our lives to Him and confidently rest in Him and not be stressed by those that do evil. This is evident when we see someone who is surrounded by evil and yet at peace and flowing with love. Their trust is in the Lord! Let us keep our focus on Him and as David says in verses 39-40 (Phillips) "The spacious, free life is from God, it's also protected and safe. God-strengthened, we're delivered from evil- when we run to Him He saves us."

Challenge for today: When you get negative reactions for your faith, rest confidently in Him

I wonder how many of us have been in the presence of angels and yet been unaware. We know from scripture that God sends angels to protect and help us. I was just reading from Heb. 1:14 (Amplified) "Are not the angels all ministering spirits (servants) sent out in the service (of God for the assistances) of those who are to inherit salvation?" It is comforting to know that angels are all around us to protect us from harm. I remember my dad telling us of a near death experience for him. He needed to go to the post office and had to park on a busy icy street. Just after he got out of his car, a vehicle came from the opposite direction and skidded right into him. His body was hit and flew over the roof of the car and landed in the snow. My mom who was in the passenger seat, thought she would find him dead when she quickly got out to check. But there he was getting himself up and had only a small scratch. They were both mystified and felt there must have been an angel that cushioned his hit and spared his life. They were so filled with gratitude. People in the Bible entertained angels and saw them at different times and welcomed them. Next time you are afraid, ask that His angels encamp around you as David said in. Ps. 34:7.

Challenge for today: Be open to all the supernatural ways God comes to you.

L ife can be so exciting when we live in the flow of the Spirit and respond to His prompting. But of course, it can also be unpredictable. We may have our own plans as we face each new morning, but we need to hold them loosely and be open to the Spirit's guidance. Our obedience is important for we either hear and obey or we hear and harden our hearts. Those times I have not responded to the Spirit, I find my heart is grieved afterwards. We are warned in Heb. 4:7b (Amplified) "Today if you would hear His voice *and* when you hear it, do not harden your hearts." This morning as I was in prayer, it came to mind to send gifts to a couple missionaries. My heart was full of joy as I sent them cards and wrote out checks. Another day I planned to go home from working at Share and Care but felt led to take a friend out for a birthday lunch, as no one had remembered her special day. Joy followed! I'm sure we all have also been recipients of the Spirit prompting others to show kindness and love to us in a variety of ways as they were led by the Lord and obeyed. Just yesterday a friend stopped over with a gift that was something I desired. When we act in obedience, who knows who has more joy ... the one giving or the one receiving!

Challenge for today: Listen closely to the Spirit and obey promptly as He directs.

Our lives are sacred as they are meant to be lived for God. He wants us to live in close communion with Him and desires that we spend time listening to Him and not just calling on Him when we are in a tight spot. He tells us we can approach Him with confidence and boldness as it says in Heb. 4:16 (Phillips) "Let us therefore approach the throne of grace with the fullest confidence, that we may receive mercy for our failures and grace to help in the hour of need." We don't have to fear but come to Him confidently and recognize our need for His grace and mercy. I find the best time for me is early in the morning when the day is fresh and my special place is our bedroom where it is quiet. Even though He is always speaking to us it may help to have a special time and place to listen and just enjoy the closeness of His presence. Some people have a special chair that is their *holy place* and one gal said she goes into her closet. Or you may want to sit on your deck or by a lake. It is a time to 'unclutter' our minds and listen to the One who loves us most and to put our cares into His hands. Then we can enjoy our day and cherish each moment for He is with us, giving us grace for all that touches our lives.

Challenge for today: Spend quiet moments with Him and listen to His words to your heart.

I'm sure we have all met people that seek attention and seem to revel when the eyes of all are on them. We are more likely though to find saints in a hidden place as they don't need the approval of others since they are secure in knowing God loves them. Many people don't believe they really matter unless they are noticed by others. But if we live in fear what others think, we can hinder love from taking root in our hearts. We actually spend our lives being manipulated by the approval of others rather than living in the fullness of real love. The important thing is that we know that God loves us, He sees us, and we matter to Him. When the angel came to Hagar after she ran away from her mistress Sarai, the message from the Lord told her what to name her child, "You are the God who sees me!" (Gen. 16:13) God sees us and we matter so much that He was willing to die for us so that we may live for Him. One of the scripture songs we taught our children when they were growing up comes from Zeph. 3:17 (NIV) and says it all. "The Lord your God is with you, He is mighty to save. He will take great delight in you, He will quiet you with His love, He will rejoice over you with singing." Let us remember His eye is on us always and we matter to Him.

Challenge for today: Find a scripture that speaks of God's love for you and carry it always in your heart.

I'm sure we have all wondered at various times in our lives, what is the value of suffering? What do we learn through suffering that we don't quite learn through other means? When I was younger, I had occasional migraine headaches that made me feel incapacitated. When one hit, I just wanted to lie very quietly in a dark room and have no one jiggle the bed in any way. I would ask Al to pray for me as I felt so terrible and helpless. But after my head was fine again, the feeling I had was almost euphoric. I felt so alive, so appreciative of good health, and had much more empathy for those who were sick and hurting. It was like I was living from a deeper place and felt closer to the Lord. When sickness strikes we know we are not in control and so dependent on Him and that is the best place to be. Isn't life all about giving up the controls and dying to ourselves so that we might live for Him and for others? Paul says in II Cor. 5:15 (NIV) "And He died for all, that those who live should no longer live for themselves but for Him who died for them and was raised from the dead." When we go through suffering, we hopefully can emerge from a deeper place in Him with healing water flowing out of us to bring to the world that is hurting.

Challenge for today: Give up the controls and ask the Lord to use all your sufferings to bring you to a deeper place and healing to others.

I usually wake up happy and have a steady disposition without high highs and low lows. But after I had surgery I was given a medication for pain that had adverse effects. It caused me to feel down and depressed and like the walls were coming in on me. This seemed worse than the surgery and I shared how I felt with a friend who was visiting me at the time who was a nurse. She quickly ascertained that it was my medication and I refused it after that and was fine. But in that time span, I felt what it was like for many of you who may struggle with depression on a daily basis. Today I was reading from Psalm 42 and the sons of Korah were depressed. They questioned their hearts asking themselves why they were depressed. They felt forgotten and longed for God's presence as they were far from the sanctuary where they corporately worshipped. But they go on to tell their souls in verse 5b (Amplified) "Hope in God *and* wait expectantly for Him, for I shall yet praise Him, my Help and my God." Their course of action was to change their thinking and put their focus on God. They remembered where to put their hope and waited for the Lord who would bring them victory. When we feel down and like God is far from us, may we put our eyes upward and hope in Him and as it says in verse 8, "Yet the Lord will command His loving-kindness in the daytime, and in the night His song shall be with me, a prayer to the God of my life."

Challenge for today: Turn your thoughts on the Lord and praise Him when you feel forgotten or down.

Everyone wants to be loved and to know they are valued. We are told so many times in scripture to love our neighbors, to do good to them, to be a servant, to share with them, to show hospitality etc. But fleshing this out will bring us to the point when we know we are not able to do it in our own selves for our love runs out quickly. It is easier to have power over people than to love them for it means death to our selfish selves. I remember when we were newly married, a gal I sewed for came over regularly for fittings. I found it hard to love her and would listen to her talk about how great she was etc. I prayed before she came each time and would have to admit after she left that I still *didn't* love her. Finally one day I confessed to the Lord that I didn't have it in me to love her. I couldn't. I needed His love! That is when he poured His love into my heart for her and I didn't struggle to love her after that. Sometimes the Lord puts people in our lives that are hard for us to love so that we know that we are dependent on Him. His love is unfailing and like David said in Ps. 51:1a (NIV) "Have mercy on me, O God, according to your unfailing love;" We don't have to do extraordinary things to show others love but we need to see them as valuable human beings who are precious in God's sight.

Challenge for today: Ask God for His love to flow through you to someone you find difficult.

hange is good! Sometimes we have a choice about change but other times circumstances are out of our control and change happens. But with it brings a new perspective and fresh outlook...and of course some adjusting. When we were at our son Kurt's, I noticed the creative things our daughter-in-law had done in their house. Brenda showed me a pile of things she no longer wanted to use to decorate her house, and it resulted that we had more things going home that altered the look of our house. It felt good to have a cushy carpet runner in the kitchen, more light in two of our bedrooms with taller lamps, brighter pillows on the sofa, and oriental rugs in the great room. Why do we often want to keep everything comfortably the same? The Lord has so many new things for us and we must let go of the old. He may show us a new way of looking at something, a broader perspective than our narrow view, a verse that is waiting for our obedience, or a change of direction. But one thing we know, if the Lord initiates the change we can trust Him that it is for our good. We may find ourselves singing a new song as it says in Ps. 40:3 (Amplified) "And He has put a new song in my mouth, a song of praise to our God. Many shall see and fear (revere and worship) and put their trust and confident reliance in the Lord." May we open our hearts to the One who makes everything new!

Challenge for today: Let go of the old and welcome change in some new way.

My second cousin Linnea is becoming famous for her scrumptious Artisan bread that is baked in her outdoor brick oven. Her name has been in the paper and people come to see her oven and taste her home made pizza and many different kinds of bread. She didn't become well known overnight and it took lots of hard work and perseverance. Al and I and a couple others helped a few times in the building of the brick oven; but she and her husband shouldered the work often into dusk and even in the rain and sleet. They quickly realized this project was going to be a lesson in patience and going to take a lot longer than anticipated. It had to be done exactly right. If you are off in laying a brick in one layer the next layer above will be off too. The leveler was being used constantly with the laying of each brick. It is also that way in our lives when the foundational things are being laid. If something is off, we may see life from a perspective that is rather *crooked.* Often we need to go back to those places and let the Lord heal us and put our *brick* in properly. When things are in the right placement, life will take on a new and right perspective. We read in II Tim 2:19a (NIV) "Nevertheless, God's solid foundation stands firm, sealed with this inscription: 'The Lord knows those who are His,'" Let us allow Him to go to those places and do the necessary changes so that His glory will shine forth unhindered in our lives.

Challenge for today: Ask the Lord to show you where your foundation may be crooked and ask Him to correct and bring healing.

We had a blind couple in one of our churches that Al had the privilege of marrying. They seemed to be able to do most everything that seeing people can do and often to the amazement of us all. After knowing them for several years, Terry expressed a desire to know what I looked like and I told him he could touch me and I could fill in the blanks with color of my hair eyes etc. He started laughing in this process; for he pictured me as hearty and very plump and found out I was more on the thin side etc. I thought of how much we base our impressions of people from what we see on the outside and the Lord by-passes all that. The Lord said to Samuel in I Sam. 16:7b (Amplified) when he was to choose a king to replace Saul, "Look not on his appearance of at the height of his stature, for I have rejected him. For the Lord sees not as man sees, for man looks on the outward appearance but the Lord looks on the heart." When we are willing to look past the exterior of a person and see more of their heart, we may also be pleasantly surprised and find a *jewel*. God is most interested in what is inside and so should we; or we will miss out on many gifts of friendship and love He desires to give us. Let us also be aware of our own hearts that we allow Him to change our bad attitudes and thoughts and motives and to give us more of His pure heart.

Challenge for today: Ask the Holy Spirit to give you a heart like His and to see others through His eyes.

Have you ever stopped to think of what you want to leave behind and pass on to your children and others? David gave his son Solomon instructions of how to build the temple and was so specific about each room, the weight of gold for each article, the division of labor etc. But the important charge he gave him in I Chron. 28:8b (NIV) "Be careful to follow all the commands of the Lord your God, that you may possess this good land and pass it on as an inheritance to your descendants forever." Here at Canaan we had fathers come with their sons for a weekend retreat and there was great freedom and respect between them. Many boys would not want to retreat with their parents but these boys seemed very comfortable around their dads. Each one of them wanted to follow the Lord so the sharing had to do with how best we can do that. Their fun was not limited as they had a sauna and jumped in the lake, had target practice, etc. But beneath it all, they had a desire to seek the Lord and draw closer to Him. David goes on to tell Solomon to serve God whole heartedly with a willing mind and to be strong and courageous. Don't we also want that for ourselves and for our children and for them to pass it on to theirs? There is no greater joy!

Challenge for today: Seek ways to encourage your children or a younger person to be courageous and strong in the Lord.

During the winter months we take about 3 weeks and travel south to see our children and grandchildren. The deeper into the south we go, we notice that nearly everyone has a front porch. I have never seen so many and most of them were furnished with rocking chairs. One such house had at least 8 rockers but the strange thing is we never once saw anyone sitting on their front porch! I remember Al's mom and how she loved to sit with her coffee on her front porch that faced the traffic from their corner lot. She wanted to know what was going on and did not want to miss anything. What use are porches and decks if we never go outside to enjoy them? I wonder how many gifts the Lord gives to us that go unused. Many of us just stay inside and don't venture out into the new things He has for us. The Lord is always up to new surprises, new ways of relating to us, new ways of blessing us. Let us go outside our routine busy days and sit in our contemplative rockers and let the blessings fall. God says in Ezek. 34:26b (NIV) "I will send down showers in season, there will be showers of blessings."

Challenge for today: Take time to enter into *His rest* and receive the blessings the Lord desires to rain down upon you.

Our Small Group is studying a book on healing and this week we are to note how words spoken to us when we were young have impacted our lives. We may have been hurt by careless words, or overreacted to something that was not intended in the way we received it. But their words may still have left us feeling wounded. One day I walked to a friend's house and she welcomed me with a steaming cup of hot chocolate topped with whipped cream. When it touched my hand, I quickly said to her, "Don't let go of the cup!" I had burned my fingers a few days before on our wood stove and when the hot cup touched my hand it was just like a fresh burn! Ordinarily, I could have handled it, but not that day! We need to cut people slack when we unintentionally hit an area of hurt in them, and remember that we also have those areas where we are wounded. The Lord is compassionate and wants to bring freedom and healing to every area of our lives. Our healing won't be complete until glory but He has given us Himself and each other to help in the healing process. James 5:16 (The Message) says "Make this your common practice. Confess your sins to each other and pray for each other so that you can live together whole and healed. The prayer of a person living right with God is something powerful to be reckoned with." We may find that confessing our sin to a friend often breaks the power of it and healing results. Let us receive healing and be bearers of His healing power to others.

Challenge for today: Be intentional to listen to a friend and pray for healing if the Holy Spirit leads.

Sometimes we want to be so helpful that are actually in the way if we are not led by the Spirit. We are told to "keep in step with the Spirit" but do we practice that? We need to pay careful attention to how He leads us and follow that lead. One Monday we were quilting at the church and a visitor stopped by from another town. She went over to where one woman was sewing and told her she could fix the brushes on the sewing machine. The gal answered her politely but told her the machine was working just fine and didn't need fixing. But this *helpful* gal persisted that she could fix it and wanted to know when she could come back. Eventually she got the message, that her help wasn't needed. That same day another woman in our group saw another gal and I measuring off and cutting quilt-size pieces of batting. She was free then and volunteered to help out of the goodness of her heart. But it actually took longer with her *help*. I wonder how many times the Lord has to tell us to get our hands off of something and let Him do it. We are in the way when we are doing what He has not called us to do. David says in Ps. 37:23 (Amplified) "The steps of a (good) man are directed *and* established by the Lord when He delights in his way [and He busies Himself with his every step]." May we do only what He asks us of us!

Challenge for today: When asked to fill a role or do a task, pray before answering and see if it is something He is asking you to do.

Our hearts are so full of gratitude to the Lord as we got the wonderful surprising news last night that we are going to have a new grandchild. Little John Mark, who will be 5 very soon, is going to get a new brother, also from Korea. They have already picked out the name Anders Joel (A.J.) and he should arrive when he is about 3 years old. The government has opened a window of opportunity for a brief time for parents who are older than the specified age to be able to adopt. That in itself is an answer to prayer. John Mark and his mom and dad are preparing to welcome the new member of their family with much anticipation. The verse that came to mind when we got off the phone from hearing the news was James 1:17 (Amplified) "Every good gift and every perfect (free, large, full) gift is from above; it comes down from the Father of all (that gives) light, in (the shining of) Whom there can be no variation (rising or setting) or shadow cast by His turning [as in an eclipse]." What a wonderful gift they are receiving from heaven and our hearts are full of praise.

Challenge for today: Thank the Lord for a gift you have received from the Lord and share the news with someone else today.

Each day we pray for our family and ask the Lord to outfit them with spiritual armor, for one never knows what will come against us. When our son Kurt was in grade school he came with me to the mall and for the first time I let him shop on his own for an hour. When I went back to pick him up I was met at the store entrance by a security officer and he asked if I was Kurt's mom. I wondered what he had done but he quickly reassured me that Kurt was fine and had done nothing wrong. But he told me that 3 teenagers had pulled a knife on him while he was shopping and demanded his billfold. An employee just happened to be looking out of a small security window that overlooked the shoppers and saw what happened. He rushed to Kurt's aid and caught two of the boys but one got away. We were so thankful that God protected him and used this man to keep him from getting stabbed. It is good to make a practice of praying protection over our families each day. Besides praying the Armor of God in Ephesians 6; also pray a prayer based on the Jabez prayer found in I Chron. 4:10 (Amplified) but put in these words, "Oh Lord, bless our family and enlarge our territory. May your hand be upon us and may your keep us from all evil." Let us use the protective means God has given us and be prepared.

Challenge for today: Read Eph. 6:13-18 and pray for God's protective armor on your loved ones.

While out celebrating the August birthdays a friend shared how her birthday is Dec. 30th. She always felt deprived since it is so close to Christmas and the New Year. When she was quite young she asked for a soft blue angora scarf and matching gloves and was appalled that her cousin received them for her Christmas gift rather than her. She was sorely disappointed and cried and carried on for some time. Finally her mom had had enough, and went to the closet and grabbed her intended birthday present and said, "Here!" She opened it up several days early to find she did get the scarf and gloves she wanted but now was embarrassed for her behavior. What about us? Do we complain and carry on that the Lord is not being fair? After all we are busy serving Him and He gives what we want to someone else who *we judge* is not nearly as *worthy*! We may feel God is holding out on us or taking way too long to give us what we *want!* How quickly we can forget that we are the apple of His eye and He gives us what is good for us, all in His perfect timing. If it is all in His hands, never mind what someone else receives. It says in Ps. 84:11-12a (The Message) "All sunshine and sovereign is God, generous in gifts and glory. He doesn't scrimp with His traveling companions." So let us remember God doesn't hold out on us but the greater of His gifts is living in His presence.

Challenge for today: Ask forgiveness when you complain to God for not being *fair* and trust what He gives you comes from His perfect plan for you.

What a difference the Lord makes! When I was a young nurse, there was a patient whose call light seemed to be on all the time. When he was my patient for the day I often took my charting into his room just to keep him company as he seemed afraid. He did not know the Lord at the time but God used the sharing of us Christian nurses to help him come to accept the Lord into his life. After that things changed and with his fear gone, his call light was rarely on. He seemed to know that he was dying but had a desire to give one last Christmas present to his wife. I offered to go downtown and bought a gift and wrapped it for him. He gave her the necklace on Christmas Eve when she came to visit him and he died on Christmas day. I will never forget him as I saw what a difference Christ made in his life. He went from a man filled with fear to one of peace, knowing he was now in Jesus' hands. It says in Heb. 13:5b-6 (The Message) "Since God assured us, 'I'll never let you down, never walk off and leave you,' we can boldly quote, God is there, ready to help; I'm fearless no matter what. Who or what can get to me?" There may be times we feel totally helpless and forsaken but we have a safe place to go and a Helper who won't let us down.

Challenge for today: Pray for an opportunity to share with someone else, the difference the Lord has made in your life.

God prepares us for things ahead even when we are not aware. When we lived in Brunswick my worst nightmare happened on Sunday morning when Al woke up and said he was too sick to preach. I tried to tell him he was not too sick and he would be fine; but to no avail. I called the men who offered to preach for Al at other times and no one was available. I had to go and preach 2 services and also teach adult Sunday School. But that was not all. We had the Alpha course in the evening and I had to lead that. But when we went to our Small Groups, someone came to the church and asked for the pastor. When I told her he was at home sick she grabbed my hand and told me to come with her as her mother was dying. I went to the house and prayed over her and she died shortly afterwards. Relatives came and I prayed with them and went to church and got all the left-over food to feed them. When I got home, I thought of how the Lord had prepared me for I had just spoken at a retreat a couple weeks before and used that message for the sermon. I felt the Spirit instructing me all along the way and as it says in Ps. 32:8 (NIV) "I will instruct you and teach you in the way you should go; I will counsel you and watch over you." When I went to bed that night my heart was full of gratitude for I felt the Spirit had directed me through each circumstance. If anyone knows me well, they know I could not do this on my own; as I don't like to be *up front* in public at all! But God is faithful and prepares us for what is ahead.

Challenge for today: Thank God for what He is doing in your life; and ask Him to use you in whatever way He chooses.

One day I was taking my supplement pills and swallowed the big ones like glucosamine but couldn't get the little Vitamin D pill to go down. I had to take more and more water before I could finally swallow it. I thought of how often we can sail through major hard times and yet seem to fall apart when something ever so much minor occurs. Could it be that we know we need to trust Him for those big things and put ourselves under His control but then try to handle the smaller things ourselves? We need Him to be in charge of *everything* that touches our lives for He knows what is best for us since He sees from a higher perspective. Life is exciting when we commit everything to Him and *allow* Him to work everything out. We are in for surprises, and as we look back, we are full of amazement for how He did it. Today I read from Ps. 25:4-5 (Amplified) "Show me Your ways, O Lord, teach me Your paths. Guide me in Your truth *and* faithfulness and teach me, for You are the God of my salvation; for You [You only and altogether] do I wait (expectantly) all the day long." May we commit our whole life into His hands, the big things and the small things.

Challenge for today: Begin trusting God with *everything* that concerns you.

I am preparing to lead our Small Group, and gave them for homework the writing down of names or words that were spoken of them as a child. Now these may be positive things on the surface but what about when we internalize them. Perhaps we have all come away with many diseased or distorted images of ourselves that need healing. I was told how responsible I was and how helpful and always happy. Now those are good qualities but it also left me feeling guilty if others served me rather than me serving them; or doing the responsible expected thing rather than something spontaneous and fun; or listening to other people's hurts rather than sharing some not so happy things in my own life. The Lord wants to heal us and help us discover our real identity and live as His beloved child. That involves renouncing our unreal self and letting that false-self die. Then we can embrace our true self in Christ and we will discover who we really are. In fact, God will give us a new name as He says in Rev. 2:17b (Amplified) "To him that overcomes (conquers), I will give to eat of the manna that is hidden, and I will give him a white stone with a new name engraved on the stone, which no one knows or understands except he who receives it." Let us become authentic and real and truly who God has lovingly designed us to be.

Challenge for today: Be quiet before the Lord and ask the Lord what name He has for you.

H ave you ever felt like you *jumped the gun*? I certainly have and blew it when we showed up for our former church's rummage sale a week early! I didn't listen carefully and had it marked down in my date book for the wrong weekend. Now it can be good to think ahead and plan but if we go ahead of what God has planned for us, we are not in His will. Sometimes it is hard to be patient as it seems so long when we are waiting for answers for something we have prayed and prayed! In fact, we can think we need to *help* God to get it done but we only get in the way. Just like Al and me when we got to the church and saw there were only 3 cars in the parking lot. We *then* knew our timing was wrong. We expended our time and energy for nothing as they weren't ready for the sale and very busy marking things. We can make plans and spin our wheels but it says in Prov. 16:1 (The Message) "Mortals make elaborate plans, but God has the last word. " Let us desire His timing, His way, and His will and *then* He will establish our steps! It says in Verse 9 "We plan the way we want to live, but only God makes us able to live it."

Challenge for today: Exchange your plans for the day for His plans.

I think we may have all been to a party or some kind of a gathering where someone does all the talking and doesn't allow others to get a word in edgewise! Maybe we have something special to say but there isn't an opening to speak. We can end up going away without sharing what is on our hearts or hearing what another person has to say. Perhaps when that happens to us we may see more clearly the need expressed in James 1:19 (NIV) "My dear brothers, take note of this: Everyone should be quick to listen, slow to speak, and slow to anger." If we get frustrated when not given a chance to say anything, I wonder how the Lord feels when it is only a one way conversation and we do all the talking? We need to listen and be quiet enough to hear what He has to say. He already knows whatever is happening in our lives but we need to hear what is on His heart for us. When Samuel was a child and realized it was the Lord calling out to him, he responded with, "Speak Lord, for your servant is listening." I Sam. 3:10b (NIV). Let us listen intently for His voice and respond as His voice is one of love and unfailing wisdom.

Challenge for today: May we slow down our lives and spend more time just listening to the Lord and enjoying His presence.

A friend was preparing to have a rummage sale with her son's family and had a huge amount of fabric she wished to sell. She measured over 500 yards and marked each remnant piece. But all the while she doing this, her family told her it would never sell. Who would want to buy it?! She was almost discouraged from even putting the material out on the large table but did any way. Much to everyone's surprise one of the first customers bought a large amount for their church quilters and more people came and continued to buy. What about us? Have we been told messages that have caused us to doubt or become discouraged? Messages like "You will never amount to anything!" Or "What makes you think you could ever accomplish that?" God may ask us to do things that might seem unlikely to the world's way of seeing. It may even seem impossible in our eyes, but if He asks it of us He will equip us as well. I'm sure Noah didn't get encouragement when he was building the ark in obedience to God's instruction! Neither did David give up and go home when his brothers ridiculed him for coming to the battle. Instead, God caused his little slingshot to do what the whole army could not do. Let us not think or say, "I can't do that" and give up and quit! Instead, let us listen to the Lord and follow whatever He tells us to do, remembering who is on our side. May we, like David, say in Ps. 41:11 (NIV), "I know you are pleased with me, for my enemy does not triumph over me."

Challenge for today: Give any negative messages over to the Lord and act on what He tells you.

There is a small sunflower shaped vase in my kitchen that was given me by a special friend and holds an actual sunflower. It sits by my sink and is a constant reminder of my friend, causing me to smile and prompting me to pray for her. She is a woman of faith and I know she also prays for me. Just as with the vase, the Lord fills our surroundings with reminders of Him but we so often miss them. We are so busy with our mundane lives and these special evidences escape our notice. There may be times we wonder where God is in our situations. But He is always there as He has promised and encircles us with manifestations of His presence. Sometimes we just need to be quiet and still and slow down to receive what He is sending our way. He may put before us a beautiful sunset that takes our breath away. Or He may have someone give us a gift that comes just at the very time it is most needed. Or maybe a word comes through a friend that we needed to hear. That is God! Let us be alert and open to all the reminders He sends to let us know He is right here with us every moment. David says in Ps. 9:10 (NIV) "Those who know your name will trust in you, for you, Lord, have never forsaken those who seek you."

Challenge for today: Be aware of the many ways the Lord comes to you and thank Him.

Ps. 127:1 (Amplified) says, "Except the Lord builds the house, they labor in vain who build it; except the Lord keeps the city, the watchman wakes but in vain." One thing we noticed when we traveled on our trip out west is the variety of homes and their locations. We saw some lovely mansions built on high bluffs without a single tree near. Being from Minnesota we can hardly imagine doing that as we love being surrounded by a forest of trees. In fact we like that our house cannot be seen by people from the lake. But the people whose houses stand on the cliffs for all to see would probably feel *suffocated* if they live where we do! There was a time in ministry when my husband and I were more up front and seen, but now the Lord has us more hidden and it feels so right. Al calls us a monk and a nun in the woods. People who come to Canaan's Rest are often those whom God is bringing into a more quiet contemplative time alone with Him. We're not all alike or serve in the same way but we need to pay attention to where the Lord would have us dwell in each season of our lives. But most importantly may each of our dwelling places be filled with the fragrance of Christ just as Mary poured perfume on Jesus feet and the house was filled with the fragrance.

Challenge for today: Ask the Lord to make your house a place where people feel His presence.

Two of our children were born in southern California while Al was going to seminary. After he did his internship in a church there, the congregation gave us a send-off with gifts and prayers for our journey back to Minnesota. We were poor at the time and hoped our car and the U-Haul trailer could make the long trip back. We were going through the hot desert of Nevada in the middle of the night when all of a sudden the car quit as the gas tank showed empty. The baby was sleeping and Mark was a toddler and what would we do with 2 kids in the middle of the hot desert at night? We prayed and waited and God sent along two Air Force men that stopped to see if they could help. We were able to pull out a hose from our overflowing U-Haul and they generously siphoned gas from their tank into ours. We were so grateful and felt like they were angels sent from above. Now, it was our fault we ran out of gas as we should have been more watchful but the Lord had mercy on us and sent what was needed. We felt His protecting hand over us. It reminds me of verses 3 & 4 from Ps. 91 (The Message) "That's right-He rescues you from hidden traps, shields you from deadly hazards. His huge outstretched arms protect you—under them you're perfectly safe; His arms fend off all harm." May we walk this day knowing His protecting arms are always all around us.

Challenge for today: When difficulties come, first call upon the Lord and then wait for His answer and thank Him.

Today I struggled with finding a pair of comfortable shoes to wear for work and had to end up with sandals. Yesterday I noticed there was blood on the basement floor and I wondered where it was coming from. I had been downstairs earlier in my bare feet and didn't give it a thought that I had nicked the top of my little toe on the hearth of the wood stove earlier. I had blood all over my slipper etc. and I never knew I was hurt. I wonder how many hurts we have that we are unaware of but affect how we approach our daily lives. We need to be quiet before the Lord and let Him minister to the needs of our hearts. We don't know the depth of our hurts and may be surprised at times when tears come to our eyes or we have feelings of abandonment or loss etc. We may think what happened long ago in our past is over, but maybe it's not! It can still be like my sore toe that is not yet healed. Even the healing process can't be hurried or forced to happen. We can only give ourselves to Him who understands fully and is our Healer. It is much like opening the door and inviting Him into our inner sanctuary and giving Him permission to pour out His healing love on us, for however long it takes. It says in Jer. 30:17a (NIV) "'But I will restore you to health and heal your wounds,' declares the Lord." I haven't been able to walk on these cold days as my boots hurt my toe too much; but in time I will be on my prayer walks again!

Challenge for today: Lay your hurts before the Lord and receive His healing love.

While on my prayer walk today I was singing a song based on Ps. 42:1-2 (Amplified) "As the hart pants *and* longs for the water brooks, so I pant *and* long for You, O God. My inner self thirsts for God, for the living God. When shall I come and behold the face of God?" Our longing should be for God and He wants to be our source, our strength, our nourishment. Too often we look to others or to things to fill the void in our souls. But the Lord wants to be number one and anything or anyone else becomes an idol. Maybe we missed being nurtured and we try to find it in many unhealthy ways. But all along He is waiting for us to come to Him for He has promised to quench the spiritual thirst of our souls. His nourishment and His alone, gives us a feeling of being fully satisfied and content. But if we are putting anyone or anything else before Him we need to renounce that and ask His forgiveness. Then He can take His place on the thrown of our hearts and fill it with His presence. He will give us the strength to choose Him over all the false idols we encounter every day. The absence of peace in our hearts is a sure tipoff that we are not filled to the fullness He longs to give us!

Challenge for today: If God reveals anything that comes before Him in your life, repent and seek forgiveness.

We are often surprised how God chooses to answer our prayers and we need to wait in anticipation and faith. When I was in the hospital recovering from my hysterectomy, the doctor seemed concerned about my blood work. He said things were not normal and he may have to do a spinal tap on me the next day. A friend from church was there at the time and said, "Judy, I'm supposed to pray for you right now!" She laid hands on me and prayed fervently and before doing the procedure the next day the doctor had more lab work done again. He couldn't believe it but things were perfectly normal. When I went in for my post op check-up, he did more blood work as he was still in disbelief. But I shared with him that God had healed me through prayer and I was so very thankful. Now why did God heal me in that instance; but not my endometriosis so I needed surgery? Only He knows but He is sovereign and has a plan for all of our lives. Our part is to pray and put our confidence in Him as it says in Ps. 57:7 (Amplified) "My heart is fixed, O God; my heart is steadfast and confident! I will sing and make melody." We remain in *His rest* when we trust our lives into His hands with confidence and faith that He does all things well!

Challenge for today: Place in His hands a concern you have and wait in faith for His answer.

We have many scriptures about being obedient and as His children we need to practice obedience to the Lord. It always brings rewards! One night I was soundly sleeping when Al shook me and said; "Hon, I don't want you to ask any questions. I just want you to get up and go out of the room and shut the door." I could not think why he would make such a request but I obeyed quickly. After I had done this, he told me the news that there was a bat in the bedroom! He said he would get rid of it and then let me know when it was safe. I do not like bats and I was so glad I obeyed and slept like a baby after the bat was taken care of. Sometimes God asks us to do things that may not make sense at the time and we don't understand the *whys*, but we are to obey. In fact we are to be like the sheep that follow our shepherd. He wants to lead us for He knows the dangers, the pitfalls, and the enemy's tactics. Jesus said in John 10:27 (NIV) "My sheep listen to my voice, I know them, and they follow me." Let us not be sheep that go their own way but ones who are quick to hear and obey from our hearts.

Challenge for today: Ask for discernment to recognize His voice and to follow quickly in obedience.

When we were at our son Kurt's home I had my devotions early in the morning in his office. I noticed on his desk was his computer, his Bible and a figure of a muscle man bench-pressing with heavy weights. It made me think of how our lives have many facets but need balance. Any one of those things that is out of order can cause trouble. If Kurt only read his Bible and neglected his work or taking care of his body he would run into problems. Or if he just focused on work he may soon burn out without the spiritual dimension. Or if he gave all his time to just working out at the fitness center he could look good on the outside but be deficient on the inside. We need all 3 dimensions and in their proper balance. I think the monks have a good rhythm and we try to do that here at Canaan's Rest too...our day starts with devotional time and study, then work, and later time to exercise and play. We can't separate them all as they blend together but hopefully we strive for balance. Just as Kurt works out daily, may we care for our bodies, recognizing they are temples of the Holy Spirit. But let us also not forget Jesus words in Matt.22:37 (The Message) "Love the Lord your God with all your passion and prayer and intelligence. "

Challenge for today: Seek the Lord as you spend time in the Word, working, and exercising.

While driving to the cities we saw a gorgeous flaming red tree in the midst of other trees that had barely started to turn their autumn colors. It stood out above all the rest in its brilliance and was like a sign post to me. It seemed to say that even as we are aging, we can still be a light and flame to others that can cause them to seek the Lord. It won't be long until all the leaves will drop and the trees will become bare as winter sets in…but even in this barren time we can still shine and bring Him glory. We may all be in different seasons of life; some barely beginning like our 5 year old grandson and others in their 90's with only a few short years left to live. But one thing is sure, winter will come to us all and we will die. The Psalmist said in Ps. 71:18 (The Message) "God, don't walk off and leave me until I get out the news of your strong right arm to this world yet to come." No matter where we are in our journey may our hearts be raised upward to bring Him praise all of our days…and even after we have *shed our leaves* that our memory will live on. May our last days be our best days!

Challenge for today: Allow His spirit to shine through you and proclaim His power to those around you.

God is concerned about every detail of our lives; and waits to be invited to meet each need in our day. When Al was in college he took care of a country church in Wisconsin and drove there each Sunday to preach. I was in nurses training at the time and accompanied him when I could. One winter Sunday I was driving so Al could put the finishing touches on his sermon when all of a sudden we hit a patch of ice. The car went into a tailspin and we landed in the median between the freeways. Now if we were on a pleasure trip, it wouldn't have been so important but there was a congregation waiting for their pastor to come and give the sermon! We sat there for a few moments and prayed, realizing that time was so crucial. Very soon two guys knocked on our window and said they thought they could push us back on the freeway again. It wasn't long before we were on our way, thanking and praising the Lord for sending His messengers to help us. We have a promise from the Lord in Isaiah 65:24 (NIV) "Before they call I will answer; while they are still speaking I will hear." Let us be so mindful of where to go for help and then give Him praise as we see His hand move in our behalf.

Challenge for today: Bring every concern to Him and be amazed at how He works in your behalf.

We have so much to learn from children if our hearts are open. It says in Prov. 20:11 (Amplified) "Even a child is known by his acts, whether (or not) what he does is pure and right." I love observing our young grandkids, as what they think or feel seems to come out so plainly in their words and actions. My heart was touched by Sam, a 7 year old boy, who was helping at his family's garage sale. When I was browsing he came over and showed me his toys and how they worked, as I was on a mission to buy for our grandsons. Later a 13 year old African American boy came with his grandma and looked at Sam's superhero action figures. He went up to the check-out table and asked the price for 7 of them that he was holding. He was short even though his grandma offered him $1 more. Sam's mom said she would accept what he had but thought Sam might feel bad that he was not getting enough for them. That night as she tucked him in bed, he asked her what she thought the boy was going to do with them...just collect them and look at them or to play with them? Then he said, "Mom, I was going to give them to him for free!" His mom's eyes filled with tears as she saw the generosity of his heart. She had thought he might be upset that he was short changed but instead he showed compassion. May we become child-like and do what is pure and right.

Challenge for today: Be abandoned as a child and put your faith into action.

When we are at our son Kurt's house, I often sit at the kitchen table in the morning and have my quiet time before everyone comes downstairs. His I-phone lies on the counter and it keeps buzzing every few minutes with another message for him. When he awakens he will find message after message which may help determine how his day will be spent. Wouldn't it be great if we could pick up our phone and hear God's audible voice giving us clear instructions for the day? We do have so many ways that He speaks and the Holy Spirit faithfully unfolds Father's plans for each day before us. But we need to be quiet and receptive with openness to receive what He has to say. Isn't it easy to respond with, "No way! I don't have that in mind for my day!" or "I have something more important in my schedule and don't have time for that!" But there is joy and peace when we lay down our own agendas and embrace what the Lord has rather than clinging to our own plans. May we be as David in Ps. 143:8 & 10 (The Message) "If you wake me each morning with the sounds of your loving voice, I'll go to sleep each night trusting in you. Point out the road I must travel; I'm all ears, all eyes before you...Teach me how to live to please you, because you're my God."

Challenge for today: Ask for His plan for your day and follow in obedience.

Watching the news and reading the paper of the wars and conflicts in the world can cause us to become fearful. Even sending our children to school may bring anxiety because of all the shootings, bullying etc. Anxious thoughts can begin to dominate our thinking. Peter addresses fear as he talks about the last days and the coming destruction of the earth, and tells us to be people of peace and integrity. In II Pet. 3:14 (Amplified) he says "So beloved, since you are expecting these things, be eager to be found by Him (at His coming) without spot or blemish and at peace (in serene confidence, free from fears and agitating passions and moral conflicts)." Our peace is found in Him and He is our safe place. Since He lives in us we are His dwelling place. We can't control what goes on around us but we can lively deeply in Him and trust His love. He is our confidence! When anxious thoughts come to us, we need to cast them all on Him and let Him calm our fears. Let us trust Him completely that we may walk with Him faithfully into the future.

Challenge for today: Tell the Lord all your anxious thoughts and present them all to Him without taking them back.

Who says God's children can't have fun?! I think because we know the Lord and find our love and security in Him; we should have more fun than those in the world! It is evident in the Bible Study I attend each week. We share the Word together but also exhibit joy and deep laughter. We go home feeling refreshed and renewed. Just as we love to see our children having fun and enjoying life, I think the Lord is pleased when He sees us entering in fully. My uncle who is 81 ½ years *young* stopped by on his new Spyder motorcycle that he just bought. It's a flashy red color and even has room for his favorite friend to ride on the back. We are applauding him as it was something he desired and didn't stop to say, "I'm too old for this!" or "What will people think?" Never mind! Let us not be held back by the opinion of others but be free in the Lord. Jesus said in John 10:10 (The Message) "I came so that they can have real and eternal life, more and better life than they ever dreamed of." May we enjoy our Heavenly Father and enjoy His children and enjoy His gifts!

Challenge for today: Do something that you have not had the courage to do before.

The father-in-law of one of our sons had quadruple bypass surgery as his 5 heart arteries were blocked. When I was on my prayer walk and praying for him, I thought of our spiritual hearts and how they can get blocked up too. For the most part, we come into the world with open healthy hearts, but along in life we too can shut down our hearts. So many things can cause blockages like when we refuse to forgive; or anger when problems occur; or wounds from words spoken against us; or grief over the loss of a loved one etc. When an artery shuts down, other vessels try to take over. Likewise when we shut down in one area, we may try to make up for it in other ways. We may go on spending sprees or be constantly busy and overextended. Perhaps we shut down from others and isolate ourselves. It isn't long before we need the Great Physician to operate on us and open up those clogged places. It may be painful as in surgery, but if we want to live fully, let us be willing to allow Him to do His necessary work. He has promised to give us a new heart as He says in Ezek.11:19 (The Message) "I'll give you a new heart. I'll put a new spirit in you. I'll cut out your stone heart and replace it with a red-blooded, firm-muscled heart."

Challenge for today: Ask the Lord to reveal blockages you may have and give Him permission to open them up.

L iving in truth and speaking the truth is God's way and it results in peace from a clear conscience. But it is so easy to be deceived by our own sinful hearts and as we listen to the culture that strays from the truth. We may know what we are doing is not right but because others do it, we are influenced by them, rather than the truth of the Word of God. It can be big things like David who had Uriah killed after committing adultery and covering his sin for almost a year. Or it can be small things like the boy who was tempted to eat an extra marshmallow at the church campfire last night when his grandma said only 2. But who would know? God knows and sees. The Psalmist said in Ps. 66:18-19 (NIV) "If I cherished sin in my heart, the Lord would not have listened, but God has surely listened and heard my voice in prayer." It is a gift when we can repent and have a tender conscience rather than making excuses. After Nathan exposed David's sin, he finally came to the place where he could say he had sinned against the Lord. We need to be quick to confess our sin when we know we have done wrong. We have the wonderful promise in I John 1:9 (Phillips) "But if we freely admit that we have sinned, we find him reliable and just—He forgives our sins and makes us thoroughly clean from all that is evil." Let us walk in the light and freedom of a clear conscience.

Challenge for today: Ask the Holy Spirit to reveal anything in your life that is not in conformity to His will.

When my husband was in his last year of seminary we had dreams of working with the poor in the inner city. But he was referred by a pastor to go to his friend's church who needed a youth director. It turned out to be in the most affluent suburb, directly opposite of what we had in mind. Al being from a very small town in upper Michigan and I being an introvert, wondered what we had to offer kids that had everything. We started the youth group with 3 girls who came to our house to pray together for God's plan. We felt led to call it Pit Stop, and we found ways to decorate our lower level to resemble one. God answered our prayers and gradually more teens started coming. Before long we often had 100 high school kids crowded together praising the Lord and being challenged to grow in their faith. We had a large group of junior high and college kids as well. They witnessed to their friends and many came off drugs and carried their Bibles to school. Some of those turned out to become pastors. What was the secret? Truly a sovereign work of God! It says in Eph. 3:20-21 (The Message) "God can do anything, you know—far more than you could ever imagine or guess or request in your wildest dreams! He does it not by pushing us around but by working within us, His Spirit deeply and gently within us." Later a friend shared how he had wanted to be pastor at our affluent church and Al told him how he had wanted to go to his inner city church.... put I suspect God put us in just the right place!

Challenge for today: Pray for God to work in sovereign ways and yield to His Spirit.

A crew of us lefse makers got to church before 9 a.m.; full of energy and eager to get started. We looked energetic and fresh and ready to meet the challenge. But 6 hours later this same crew was dragging as we tried to clean up the floury mess in the kitchen and fellowship hall, after making 70 dozen lefse. You might say we looked rather haggard...like coming through a war. I think sometimes in the Body of Christ there are those that are presently going through a spiritual war and are worn down. It's so easy to give them a quick word to "Hang in there!" Or "Things will get better!! Or "Rejoice in the Lord always!" We do not understand where they are coming from as we may be fresh on the scene just like the fresh lefse makers. But when we have come through a war ourselves, we can relate and be there for them. We know what it is like to feel war torn and attacked so can give words that will bring them comfort, strength, and courage. Like it says in Prov. 25:11 (Amplified) "A word fitly spoken and in due season is like apples of gold in settings of silver."

Challenge for today: Pray for His words to give to others before you speak your own.

I just came from a prayer walk to my cousin's house with a quart jar full of Kefir (a health drink I make daily) in each arm. It is almost a mile there and I held them quite close to me so that I wouldn't let them drop out of my arms. I couldn't walk my usual fast gait as I was heavy laden. But once I deposited them on her porch, I could walk swiftly and even jogged part of the way home. I kept thinking of our earthly burdens and how we so often insist on carrying them ourselves and they weigh us down. David said in Ps. 55:22 (The Message) "Pile your troubles on God's shoulders—He'll carry your load, He'll help you out. He'll never let good people topple into ruin." Each day we have a choice of what we will do with the day's problems. Will we worry and hold on to them or will we cast them onto the Lord? When we give everything up to Him, we will find He is all the while holding our hand and keeping us from falling and keeping us in His peace. Let us rest everything upon Him, thanking Him even *before* we know how He will work everything out.

Challenge for today: Put all your concerns into His hands and then trust Him completely.

We've all heard that laughter is good for the soul and haven't you felt *lighter* after you have had a good laugh? The Bible refers to a joyful heart like good medicine for our souls. Potential laughter is everywhere to find and to share. It is a universal language. Recently we had a longtime friend here at Canaan that causes laughter to just roll from our very bellies. Al's sister was also visiting at the time; and she and I dressed up as senoritas and did a *hot tamale dance*. Laughter filled our house the rest of the day and we felt refreshed as we went to bed that night. Eccl. 3:1 & 4 (NIV) says, "There is a time for everything and a season for every activity under heaven: a time to weep and a time to laugh, a time to mourn and a time to dance," While living in Des Moines we met to pray for a friend who was in ministry. We gathered in the prayer chapel and the Lord just filled us all with *holy laughter.* It was a surprise to all of us, but we went home feeling so much lighter and full of joy. It's not that we don't take life seriously enough but rather we know into Whose hands we have placed our lives.

Challenge for today: Purpose to see the light side of life today and let laughter roll!

Al took me for a boat ride around our lake and when we got near the Point the depth finder read it was 6' deep. Just a short distance from there it went down to 91' deep. Hard to believe! It made me think of the deep things of the Lord and how careful we need to be to listen to His Word for our lives. Sometimes we are going along in our ordinary lives and reading the Word or listening to someone speak when suddenly we know we have just received a deep piece of His truth! It could have come through a new Christian or a seasoned preacher but it doesn't matter as it hits us deeply in our soul. We feel we want to hang on to it, savor it, and reflect upon what the Lord is saying to us. How we hear and the attention we give is important as the Lord wants to impart His words to our hearts. I read from Mark 4:24-25 (NIV) where Jesus said, "Consider carefully what you hear," he continued. "With the measure you use, it will be measured to you-and even more. Whoever has will be given more, whoever does not have, even what he has will be taken from him." Let us not miss the deep things He sends our way but pay closer attention to what we hear lest we drift away.

Challenge for today: Rehearse throughout the day what you feel the Lord has personally said to you with the intent for you to apply it to your life.

There is nothing better and richer than to know our children and grandchildren are following the Lord. David says in Ps. 103:17 (NIV) "But from everlasting to everlasting the Lord's love is with those who fear Him, and his righteousness with their children's children." What a blessing it is for Al and I to hear about the Bible Study group that our son Kurt leads as it continues to grow. Also to see our grandkids do skits about the Bible stories that have heard in Sunday School and ask questions about heaven etc. They even set up a *pulpit* to do church and preached to us. While at our daughter's church it was a special joy to be able to be present for Joe and Paul's confirmation as they confirmed their faith. When we were at Mark's I read Bible stories to John Mark who was only 2 at the time, and he already knew what would happen. In III John 4 (NIV) Paul said, "I have no greater joy than to hear that my children are walking in the truth." We pray for our family daily and also know we are experiencing the answered prayers of our own parents and grandparents who also prayed for us so long ago. Let us not grow weary in prayer but pray for our loved ones daily.

Challenge for today: Ask your children and grandchildren for prayer requests they may have and be faithful to pray for them daily. Also, share your prayer needs with them!

Just recently we were invited to the home of a couple who is also interested in running a retreat house. Now there set up is so different from ours and has such amenities as a swimming pool, a tennis court, sauna, jet ski etc. Ours is a much smaller contemplative place of quiet where people come to pray and seek God. This couple is asking the Lord what He has in mind for their spacious home and is it to be a place of rest and restoration? When we have questions and desiring to know God's will for our lives, advice from others is good and to be considered, but most of all we need to seek God's face. "What is it You have for my life?" The children of Israel looked around them at the nations that had kings and insisted that God give them one too. But He wanted to be their king, and even though he gave them what they wanted it was not His best plan for them. Do we settle for Plan B or Plan C in our lives, because we do not go to God first and find out His Plan A? Do we want most of all to be in His will? Let us not insist on something the Lord does not have for us or get ahead of Him in His timing. We had the desire for a prayer house almost 20 years before it actually came to fruition. But when it did, we could see God's plan unfold; and His time of preparation needed for us. Instead of settling for a prayer house in a busy city, we have one by the lake and 40 acres of land to walk and talk and listen to the Lord. Job said in Job 42:2 (Amplified) "I know that You can do all things, and that no thought or purpose of Yours can be restrained or thwarted."

Challenge for today: Before making your own plans, ask the Lord for His Plan A.

I went to the garden just before lunch and came home with tomatoes and peppers to put on top of our hamburgers. There was lettuce for our salad, and green beans for our vegetable; all fresh from our garden and right to our table. I didn't have to go to the store to get veggies that had been picked, sent by truck to be put on shelves and then sat there for some time. I thought of how wonderful it is in the spiritual sense to get fresh *manna* every day as the children of Israel did. It says in Ex. 16:11-12 (NIV) "The Lord said to Moses, I have heard the grumbling of the Israelites. Tell them, 'At twilight you will eat meat, and in the morning you will be filled with bread. Then you will know that I am the Lord your God.'". Every day we can go to the Word ourselves and get our bread for the day, digest it, and let it nourish us. Yes, it is good to hear the Word preached, read spiritual books, listen to Christian CD's etc., but we can also receive it *first-hand*. The Holy Spirit wants to teach us as we feed on the Word, nourish us, and help us apply it to our lives. Have you noticed how often He takes a verse or two and it seems to speak precisely to our particular situation that very day? Let us not just receive day old bread but fresh from our Father's heart.

Challenge for today: Spend time in the Word, and ask the Holy Spirit to speak to your heart.

When we had a church in Des Moines the Women's Group was quite large. After teaching for several years, I felt led to have gals volunteer to take turns teaching, although no one was forced to do that. One gal that came from another church was in class almost 2 years and listened but never talked and added to the discussion. I was surprised when she volunteered to teach and prayed for her throughout the week before it was her turn. The day came and she did a fine job of leading the study and then did something that shocked us all. She said the Lord had given her a song and she went to the piano and played it for us and sang. We all knew how hard that must have been for her introverted nature but we also knew it could only be the Lord. What a testimony of His grace and strength. The Psalmist said in Ps. 73: 26 & 28 (Amplified) "My flesh and my heart may fail, but God is the Rock and firm Strength of my heart and my Portion forever....But it is good for me to draw near to God; I have put my trust in the Lord God and made Him my refuge, that I may tell of all Your works." We all were so aware of the strength of the Lord demonstrated in her life and she would be first to give Him praise.

Challenge for today: Share with someone else how you see the Lord manifested in their life.

Children have a hard time hiding how they feel and often their motives are quite obvious. How about us? Do we hide our true feelings from others and also from God? We tell God we are willing to do His will and yet are we really willing? I have been tested on this lately as we take turns leading a study in our Small Group which meets twice a month. When it was our turn I told Al he should lead it as he is more qualified and not something I like to do. But I told the group I would pray about it and asked the Lord to make me willing so I would do whatever He said. I proceeded to study the chapter and all kinds of things came to mind to share and even a homework assignment. It went well and I thought that my turn was over but they all wanted me to do the whole book. I agreed to pray about the next chapter and certainly God wouldn't ask me again. But sure enough it happened again and then again and each time He gave me what to teach. But in my heart there was joy for I felt He blessed my obedience. Too often I have obeyed out of great reluctance and not from my heart! I am not a person who likes to be leading and visible; and often am put in the position. Let us be like David who prayed in Ps. 143:10 (NIV) "Teach me to do your will, for you are my God; may your good Spirit lead me on level ground."

Challenge for today: Dare to pray His will and then *will to obey.*

One Sunday our pastor shared an example in his preaching that has stayed with me. What if a friend knew I was in need and gave me 10 one dollar bills? But as I leave, I turn around and give him one dollar back as my tithe, shouldn't he be real thankful? Hummm! Maybe that is how we often view our giving to church or even going to church...like God should be so pleased with our giving to Him or taking the time out of our busy schedules to go to church...like we are doing Him a favor. But just like this friend, He gave it all to us in the first place and we should give back with delight and hearts of deep gratitude. Worship is really a celebration of what He has done for us. When we sing and give Him praise it is because we can't hold it inside. It says in Isa. 66:1-2 (NIV) "This is what the Lord says: 'Heaven is my throne, and earth is my footstool. Where is the house you will build for me? Where will my resting place be? Has not my hand made all these things, and so they came into being?' declares the Lord, 'This is the one I esteem; he who is humble and contrite in spirit, and trembles at my word.'" Let us give him the worship due His name.

Challenge for today: Give Him worship freely and deeply from your heart and also joyfully give to others.

One day when Al was pasturing a church I got a call at the parsonage inviting me to coffee at a parishioner's home nearby. I said no at first as I just had a perm and hadn't had a chance to calm my hair down. But he kept insisting as there were several women there along with his wife. So I went and we were laughing and having a good time around the table when all of a sudden he slumped over. We knew something was terribly wrong and lowered him to the floor. As a trained nurse; I quickly gave instructions for helping, as we needed to get his heart going. One gal waited out by the road to guide the paramedics, another called 911, and I began trying to resuscitate him. Nothing seemed to work at first and finally I just stopped and asked that we all join in prayer. Then I tried some chest compressions once more and he gasped and started breathing again. The paramedics came and rushed him to the hospital where his heart stopped again but they were able to shock it into rhythm. He lived for several more months and had time with his family and friends, celebrating each day as a gift. We don't all get such a dramatic wake-up call to live each day to the fullest, but we need reminders. Before we even get out of bed, we can greet the Lord with the words in Ps. 118:24 (NIV) "This is the day the Lord has made; let us rejoice and be glad in it." We don't know what each day may hold but we can welcome it with joy for He has promised to be with us every moment.

Challenge for today: Give your day to the Lord and enjoy His presence with you and in you.

Our 3 grandsons and I were invited over to a friend's house to make tie-dye shirts with her 2 granddaughters. We put rubber bands in many places throughout the shirts and then sprinkled on several colors of dye. They sat overnight before washing them and the next day we saw the beautiful and unique results. I thought of how much it is like our lives when circumstances come that may cause us restriction and pain...situations of hard learning etc. It is not pleasant and yet necessary for our growth. Then grace (dye) is poured out upon us and we wait while God does His work in our hearts as we remain still. It says in Isa. 30:18 (NIV) "Yet the Lord longs to be gracious to you; He rises to show you compassion. For the Lord is a God of justice. Blessed are all who wait for Him!" The glorious thing is that after waiting for a time and the rubber bands are removed we can see the beautiful patterns of what He was doing all along in our lives. He knows what it takes for each of us and sees the end result. Our part is not to resist His hand upon us but cooperate and trust that He knows what He is doing.

Challenge for today: Thank God for a hard time in your life and ask Him to show you the good that resulted.

Our granddaughter, Lily, has a soccer ball that appears to be squashed into her bedroom wall with fake cracks all around it. When you press it, it lights up as a nightlight and is perfect for the décor of her room since she is a good soccer player. But we heard the story of how she happened to get it as a Christmas gift from her sister who made the sacrifice. Paige was shopping with her mom and had two pictures she wanted in her cart when suddenly saw the soccer light that she knew Lily would like. Her mom said they had spent enough, so Paige offered to put her 2 pictures back to get this gift for Lily. Now every time Lily sees it, she not only appreciates the light but remembers her sister's sacrifice of love for her. Isn't that the way it is when we see the cross? It was a cruel instrument of torture but because Christ died for us, it is a symbol of love and victory. Heb. 9:28 (NIV) says, "...so Christ was sacrificed once to take away the sins of many people; and He will appear a second time, not to bear sin, but to bring salvation to those who are waiting for Him." May the cross be for each of us the greatest symbol of His love...and let us also sacrifice for others when the Spirit prompts us, as it may be the very thing He uses to lead others to Him.

Challenge for today: Make a sacrifice for someone else today, even if it is as simple as making them a cup of coffee.

During our Bible Study a gal shared how she had gone to church at the usual time and was surprised at how many people were already there. She heard a missionary speak for a short time but no sermon from pastor and no offering. Unusual!! She had coffee following the service and went home and didn't realize until the next week, that the time for the service had changed. In fact, there were now 2 services instead of one due to increased attendance. She had missed out on half of the service and didn't even know it. Are we like that too? God has so much for us and we receive only a portion of what He is desirous to give us. Maybe we aren't open to changes He wants to make in our lives; or maybe we are lagging behind in the new things He has for us. It could be that we *really* don't' want His will in an area that we find it hard to face. David prayed in Ps. 25:4-5 (NIV) "Show me your ways, O Lord, teach me your paths; guide me in your truth and teach me, for you are God my Savior, and my hope is in you all day long." Let us be open and receptive to the Lord and not miss all the rich things He has for us.

Challenge for today: Ask the Lord for a teachable heart that seeks Him.

We woke up early this morning to prepare for the Wildman gathering at our house. Al remarked that he wondered if he should keep having the group as he got very few responses when he e-mailed them of this date. We discussed how even a small group is important to the Lord and not to get discouraged. I was hopeful and planned for a big group and even set the table for the maximum. Well, the men started coming and they dribbled in for an hour and a half so that the table was not only going to be full, it was going to be overflowing. It is so easy for all of us to go by outward signs and think *small*? I am quite sure the servants at the wedding in Cana did not expect the water in six large stone jars to turn into the best wine; or the invalid for 38 years at the pool of Bethesda to walk again; or the 5,000 hungry people to be fed with 5 loaves and 2 fish! Sometimes we miss what the Lord has for us as we are going by what our eyes see. Maybe we can't see where the funds will come from, or where the time will open up. But if the Lord tells us to do something, He will provide in every way. Let us keep our focus upward on Him as He can turn the darkest circumstances into light. David knew that well and says in Ps. 18:28 (NIV) "You, O Lord, keep my lamp burning; my God turns my darkness into light."

Challenge for today: Believe God for what you feel He has spoken to your heart, and thank Him before you see it come to pass.

When I went for my prayer walk I was aware of how autumn leaves just let the wind blow them freely about until they make a landing on the ground. Some try to hang on and make it through part of the winter but maybe they miss the joy of the *free fall*. I wonder how many times we are like those tenacious leaves that hang on and want to be in control. But are we ever really in control? When we hang on so tightly and don't release ourselves to Him, we miss the wonderful freedom God has for us. Paul says in II Cor. 3:17 (NIV) "Now the Lord is the Spirit, and where the Spirit of the Lord is there is freedom." But when we let the Spirit blow us where He wills, it takes trust on our part as we don't know where He will take us. When our son Mark's family was praying for the job the Lord had for him, they didn't know what part of the country that would take them. They left it up to Him and they were blown all the way to North Carolina from their home in Colorado. May each of us release ourselves daily so the Spirit can move us as He wills.

Challenge for today: Let go of anything you are holding onto tightly and catch the wind of the Spirit.

Before our last retreatants came I thought I would spruce up the bathroom and also give it a fragrance of lavender. I used a little atomizer and attempted to spray, but didn't think anything was coming out. So I sprayed more and more. All of a sudden I did get a whiff and it was overpowering. The whole bathroom was not pleasant but rather *nauseating* to my sense of smell. We tried to air it out but it was still much too much. There are things that are pleasant in their proper proportions but too much of a good thing can be rather *nauseating*. Sometimes we want God to give us all sunshine, no rain, all easy joyous experiences and no difficulties. But how would we grow without those *rainy* experiences in our lives? We are most likely to see His power manifested in our weakest times. It may be that others are also drawn to the Lord when they see us trusting God in the midst of our difficult experiences. Paul reminds us in II Cor. 12:9b-10 (NIV) "Therefore I will boast all the more gladly about my weaknesses, so that Christ's power may rest on me. That is why, for Christ's sake, I delight in weaknesses, in insults, in hardships, in persecutions, in difficulties. For when I am weak, then I am strong."

Challenge for today: Ask the Lord for strength to face the challenging times in your life and thank Him for His presence and strength to overcome.

Have you ever gotten your own way and then wished you hadn't? When our children were young we decided to take them to Mackinaw Island while we were visiting grandma and grandpa in Michigan. Al wanted to take the first boat that would ferry us to the island and was more costly than the one I wanted to take. I persuaded him to go with the more economical choice but was soon very sorry I did. It was a windy day and the waves were crashing against the boat and spraying water all over us. Plus I have motion sickness and our boat was going up and down like a bobber. In the distance we saw the larger boat we would have taken and it was like the Lord said to me: "Look what happens when you insist on your own way!" The Israelites also had a problem and it says in Ps. 81:11-14 (NIV) "But My people would not harken to My voice, and Israel would have none of me. So I gave them up to their own hearts' lust and let them go after their own stubborn will, that they might follow their own counsels. Oh that my people would listen to Me, that Israel would walk in My ways! Speedily then I would subdue their enemies and turn My hand against their adversaries." How sad when we go our own way and miss God's protecting hand that saves us from our own selves.

Challenge for today: Ask the Lord for grace to seek His will above your own.

Have you noticed how there is an *in language* for various groups? When I was in nurses training we had secret pals and would do funny prankster things for them often using our medical lingo that not everyone else would understand. Lawyers have their legal language and the clergy have their theological terms etc. One pastor was saying how we need to learn the language of another when we want to share the Lord with them. Sometimes the words we use may scare people and push them away; even other Christians. I think in a sense, everyone has their own individual language. It takes some time to learn their language and to see where they are coming from before we can speak into their lives. It says in James 3:17 & 18 (NIV) "But the wisdom that comes from heaven is first of all pure; then peace loving, considerate, submissive, full of mercy and good fruit, impartial and sincere. Peacemakers who sow in peace raise a harvest of righteousness." We must be patient as we listen to another and *learn their language*, waiting for an opportunity to share the Lord with them. Let us not short circuit the process and rush in and turn people off. Love is willing to be patient.

Challenge for today: Listen to others and wait for the right time and right words to speak into their lives.

Yesterday I walked about a mile to the garden and joined a friend to pick the produce and pull up all the plants and vines so the rototiller can be used on the soil. I didn't realize it would be so hot and had not carried any water. It took some time even though we worked quickly, and all the while both of us were getting thirsty. Walking home again with veggies in hand, I could only think of a cool drink of water. I didn't need coffee or something to eat but water to quench my thirst. My mind was flooded with scriptures about water and our spiritual need for Jesus. Nothing and no one else will satisfy us! Jesus gives the invitation in John 7:37-38 (NIV) "On the last and greatest day of the feast, Jesus stood and said in a loud voice, 'If anyone is thirsty, let him come to me and drink. Whoever believes in me, as the Scripture has said, streams of living water will flow from within him.'" When our hearts are filled with Him our thirst is truly quenched! His love springs forth within us and we are totally satisfied. He said the water He gives will become a spring in us and joy will bubble up. Our need is to drink deeply of Him. Also, let us remember there are so many others around us that are thirsty and need to know where to find the living water.

Challenge for today: Share with someone else today how Jesus satisfied your thirst.

Many things in life are not *either-or* but rather *both-and*. Those that know me well are aware that I don't' like to stand out publicly and try to avoid being upfront as much as possible. But sometimes it is good to stand out and the other day was one of them. I went for my prayer walk and put on a neon pink jacket that made me stand out as I was walked on the road. I didn't get very far down the gravel road before I heard the sound of gun shots that interrupted my silence. I immediately thought that whoever it was would have no trouble seeing me! We are told we also need to stand out from the worldly crowd and be different because of *Whose* we are. In scripture it says we are to stand out as stars, or like the sun. Matt. 13:43a (NIV) says "Then the righteous will shine like the sun in the kingdom of their Father." We are also told in Matt. 5:16 (NIV) "In the same way, let your light shine before men, that they may see your good deeds and praise your Father in heaven." The color neon is bold, bright, dazzling, lively, radiant, positive and cheerful. Just think of the light that would be shed on others if we displayed those neon colors? Take care for what you wear for sometimes it is good to *stand out* that others may be drawn to Him.

Challenge for today: Wear the garment of praise today that others may see Christ in you.

Isn't it wonderful when we get a welcoming reception and we know we are well received? When our children were young we went to Upper Michigan and arrived at Al's folks late at night. After knocking on the door for some time, Al's mom finally appeared. She almost didn't let us in as she had the date mixed up and thought we weren't coming until the next night. Other times we were so heartily welcomed like the times when we moved to a new church. We found many of the congregation waiting for hours at the parsonage to help us unload the van and even set up our appliances. We felt so welcomed and cared for. I wonder how each of us views our Heavenly Father? Is He seen as one who is not that aware of us and hesitant to receive us; or is He like the one who is eagerly awaiting our arrival and receiving us with outstretched arms? Our picture of Him is often like the lenses through which we see our earthly father. But we need to go to scripture and believe what is written so we might say as is spoken of David in Ps. 89:26 (NIV) "He will call out to me, 'You are my Father, my God, the Rock, my Savior.'" Even if you feel rejected by your earthly father remember the promise in Ps. 27:10 (NIV) "Though my father and mother forsake me, the Lord will receive me."

Challenge for today: Find a scripture on the love of your Heavenly Father and carry with you for several days.

We had 3 generations under the roof while at our son's home and had much laughter and fun. We shared stories of times past and saw how the Lord has blessed us and our children and children's children. We see evidences that they are following the Lord and that brings us great joy. When I was dusting I noticed by each bed is a Bible and a devotional book. But even more is the love we see between them as they interact throughout the day. I read from Ps. 90:1 & 16 (NIV) "Lord, you have been our dwelling place throughout all generations. May your deeds be shown to your servants, your splendor to their children." Our prayer is that they may continue to grow in the ways of the Lord and see His hand in their lives and pass it on to the next generation even beyond them. I am reminded so often of the heritage left to me by my parents; of their example as they put the Lord first. They especially believed in giving Him the first fruits of their labors and I see that carried out in the generations since. May we leave godly footprints for the next generation to follow.

Challenge for today: Live today as if it was the last opportunity to be an example for others to follow.

Each day we are given the choice to live close to our Father and to commune with Him throughout the day. It is easy to get busy with our own things and not include Him or even ask Him for His plan. Even though we may accomplish a lot something will be lacking when He is left out. But if we begin the day seeking Him and His will first, we will find that we carry His peace in our hearts, even if fearful things happen. Everything during the day is an occasion for prayer and He is so faithful to show us how to handle difficult situations. We were not meant to walk alone but walk in step with our Heavenly Father. I find that with my long legs I often walk faster than Al and am several steps ahead of him. I need reminders to walk beside him and with him and enjoy our time together. Do we need that reminder also, to slow down and seek to walk closely with the Lord and enjoy His presence with us? He will turn our darkness and confusion into light. He says in John 8:12 (NIV) "When Jesus spoke again to the people, He said, 'I am the light of the world. Whoever follows me will never walk in darkness, but have the light of life.'" Let us joyfully walk step in step in the light of His presence.

Challenge for today: Start the day by spending time in His presence and asking for His plan.

Our family has been avid Viking fans as long as I can remember. Later in life my folks did not like to accept any dinner invitations on Sunday as they wanted to hurry back to their apartment to watch the Vikings play. I like football also, although not quite as enthusiastic as the men in our family. But passion is good and how wonderful it is when we are passionate for the Lord. Do we get excited when we read a verse of scripture that speaks specifically to our hearts and recognize it is Him? Do we desire His gifts so we can share with others to encourage them and build them up? Do we delight to just sit in His presence and hear His whispers? We are given the warning that He gave to the church of Laodicea in Rev. 3:16 (NIV) "So, because you are lukewarm- neither cold nor hot- I am about to spit you out of my mouth." God does not want us to be apathetic and indifferent; but passionate about Him. He must be delighted when we ask Him to reveal more of Himself to us and when our hearts overflow in worship of Him. He has promised in Heb. 11:6 (NIV) "And without faith it is impossible to please God, because anyone who comes to Him must believe that He exists and that He rewards those who earnestly seek Him." Let us be passionate and diligently seek Him!

Challenge for today: Be earnest in your desire for the Lord and spend some time just worshipping Him.

When we were on our way home we caught sight of an eagle flapping his wings in flight. Later, when I went for a prayer walk I saw another one soaring and it was such a beautiful sight. Eagles have enormous wing spans and use lots of energy when flapping their wings. But if they choose to glide and use the air currents and updrafts to aid their flights, they use only 1/20th of the energy as when flapping! It made me think of how often we get to *flapping our wings* spiritually and may think God loves us more when we are performing and working hard for Him. When we blow it we may feel even more unworthy and try to do more and more for Him. But all the time He tries to reassure us of His unconditional love and wants us to lay back in that love and *soar*! When we quiet ourselves in His presence and soak in His love, we feel like we are soaring...loved just for who we are. Zeph. 3:17 (Amplified) tells what He thinks of us. "The Lord your God is in the midst of you, a Mighty One, a Savior (Who saves)! He will rejoice over you with joy; He will rest (in silent satisfaction) and in His love He will be silent and make no mention (of past sins, or even recall them); He will exult over you with singing." Let us not be *flappers* but *soar-ers*, resting in His love for us.

Challenge for today: Spend some time just absorbing the thought of Him singing over you.

Do we live on the surface or do we experience the abundant life that Jesus promised us in John 10:10b (Amplified) "I came that they may have and enjoy life, and have it in abundance—to the full, till it over-flows." We have a choice to live superficially or deeply and abundantly. When we had a farewell coffee time for our interim pastor, our council president knitted him a beautiful prayer shawl. We could have thought it was just an ordinary shawl at first glance but looking closer revealed it had special significance. Marlys had done it in several patterns of 3 stitches signifying the Trinity. It was bordered by 6 stitches called a seed stitch, which was significant of all the seeds pastor had sown in our midst. She also used a diamond pattern that reminded us that God sees us as His most valuable creation, a jewel. The center and the largest panel was a cross which helped us remember what God has done for us through Jesus' sacrifice on the cross. Sometimes used is a cable pattern that looks like 2 vines twisted together. This can remind us that Jesus is the vine and we are the branches. I put the prayer shawl on pastor's shoulders as Marlys read about the patterns in it. But we all took a closer look after these things were pointed out. Do we take time to look deeper into what is happening around us; to see what God is up to; to listen more intently to a friend's story; to live below the surface? Let us not be surface dwellers but ones that dwell deeply in Him!

Challenge for today: Live in the present moment and be a careful observer of what God is up to.

While at our grandsons I played several different wii games with them. They were very accomplished but grandma has a long ways to go. I did the best in bowling and often beat everyone else, but in some of the other games I was pathetic! I found that the games that were hard for me were so easy for them. Isn't that the way it is in life? Sometimes what is a *baby step* for someone else can be a *giant step* for us and vise-versa. God knows the difficulty or ease of what we go through each day and we shouldn't fear what others think. Nor should we judge others for the things that seem to be easy for us. We need to focus on the path the Lord has for each of us and know that we can trust Him even when we are being led to take a giant step of faith. It says in Rom. 8:31 (Amplified) "What then shall we say to (all) this? If God is for us, who (can be) against us: (Who can be our foe, if God is on our side?)". God accepts us even when we fail and is for us. He is right there cheering us on so let us not let the fear of what man thinks keep us from entering into all that He has for us.

Challenge for today: Step out in faith to do whatever it is that God is prompting you to do and be at peace.

When we went to our Canaan's Rest board meeting, one of the members was rejoicing that he found out he had diabetes. Now you may think that is strange but he was happy to know there was a reason for how awful he felt; his total lack of energy, his thirst and many other symptoms. It was a big relief that he knew what was wrong and could do something about it. He is careful of his diet now and eats 6 meals a day, and no more diet cokes or things that are not good for him etc. When he shared with us, I thought of the condition we were in before we came to the Lord. We were feeling bad and knew something was wrong as we lacked inner peace. But the good news is that we are guilty and can go to the Great Physician for the remedy. He already paid the price for our salvation and wholeness and wants us to agree with Him that we are sinful and in need of His grace and forgiveness. It says in Rom. 3:23 (Amplified) "Since all have sinned and are falling short of the honor and glory which God bestows and receives." We need to receive His diagnosis and accept His treatment for He paid for it on the cross. Then we are on the road to health and healing for our bodies and souls. So it is good news and it is the news we need to share with others for He came for all.

Challenge for today: Thank Him for the gift of forgiveness and look for an opportunity to share the Good News with someone else.

When we moved to Des Moines I started a *Clothes Closet*, which was a place for needy people to come to get free clothes and blankets. It was housed in a room at the church but also spilled out into the hallway. Clothes were donated and often I would get a truck load to sort through and organize. It was evident that some who came to get warm clothes were living out of their cars and very needy. Our congregational members were also free to use the closet as there were treasures to be found. One day I came across a pair of pink ballet shoes and wondered if they would fit a young girl in our church. Unbeknown to me, she was to be in a ballet recital in a couple days and had only one pair of black ballet shoes. She needed pink ones in order to dance with the other gals and her mom suggested they pray about it since she couldn't afford to buy them. The next day I casually asked her if Alyssa could use some pink ballet shoes and she looked like she was in shock. God answered their prayers so quickly and what encouragement it brought to her daughter! The Lord loves to give gifts to His children and has told us to come to Him and ask. I love the verse in Is. 65:24 (NIV) "Before they call I will answer; while they are still speaking I will hear." Let us go to the giver of all good gifts and ask not only for material things but for eternal blessings.

Challenge for today: Before purchasing something you need, ask the Lord to provide in His way.

When we were on our way home we decided to stop at Culvers and get something eat. A family came in after us with 4 adorable little children (probably around 2, 4, and 6 years old plus a baby), and we never heard one word from their booth. The parents were deaf and the children were using sign language. They were so well behaved and helped one another as their actions spoke louder than any words. The love between them all was so evident. Al gave them the *high sign* when we left to show them how impressed we were with their family. What about us? What kind of a witness would we be if we couldn't speak? Would our actions be enough to cause others to see Christ? Would they see us acting out of a grateful heart and showing the compassion of Jesus? James 1:19 (The Message) says, "Post this at all the intersections, dear friends: Lead with your ears, follow up with your tongue, and let anger straggle along in the rear." James is saying we are to listen to others and wait to speak and not take offense. If we did this, I'm quite sure others would be drawn to the Lord.

Challenge for today: Ask the Lord to make you to be a loving witness to all you meet today.

While working in the kitchen at our son's home I spilled and got a stain on the shirt that I happen to like a lot. When I washed it, I noticed the stain was just as prominent as before. Since it had gone in the dryer too, I felt it was futile to wash it again and it would probably have to be thrown away. But when I got home, I sprayed it and then washed it a second time. Much to my surprise, the stain was completely removed and I could wear the shirt again. Have you ever wondered if you could ever get over something traumatic in your life….something you did or was done to you? Perhaps a big stain that you still *wear* every day of your life! It may seem impossible but not with the Lord. He is able to wash us and make us 100% clean and white and whole. We may try other ways to get over it, but when we give it to the Lord, He is able to remove it completely. After David had committed adultery with Bathsheba and Nathan revealed his sin, he cried out to the Lord in Ps. 51:7, 10&12 (NIV) "Purify me with hyssop, and I shall be clean; wash me, and I will be whiter than snow. …Create in me a pure heart, O God, and renew a steadfast Spirit within me. ..Restore to me the joy of Your salvation and grant me a willing spirit to sustain me." Let us go to the One who can cleanse us and heal us and make us new.

Challenge for today: Give to the Lord a wound that still festers and ask for His forgiving, healing balm.

Today I read the book of Esther and for a while it looked like wicked Haman would win and Mordecai and all the Jews would die. A very tight situation! Applying that to us, does it also seem at times that we are losing and the enemy is winning as we go through adversity? A friend sent me these verses from Ps. 13:1, 2b-4 (NIV) this morning: "How long, O Lord? Will you forget me forever? How long will you hide your face from me?. ..How long will my enemy triumph over me? Look on me and answer, O Lord my God. Give light to my eyes, or I will sleep in death; my enemy will say, 'I have overcome him, and my foes will rejoice when I fall.'" I think we can all identify with David when things are out of our control and we seem to be losing the war. It is a time when we sense our inadequacy but that is the best place to encounter the Lord. He wants to fight for us, and we need to call out to Him and ask Him to work in our behalf. The Lord did fight for Esther and Mordecai and the situation was totally reversed; Haman was hung on the gallows he intended for Mordecai and the Jews were saved. Even before we know how God will rescue us, let us be like David in the last 2 verses of this Psalm when he exclaims, "But I trust in your unfailing love, my heart rejoices in your salvation. I will sing to the Lord, for He has been good to me."

Challenge for today: Give the Lord the battle you are in and praise Him for how He will work it out.

One day my brother and sister-in-law went out to eat and after ordering Alison talked with a young guy who had on a t-shirt with the letters DGA. She asked him what it meant and was it "Do Good Always!"? She was so impressed that a young man would display that kind of a message on his shirt that she secretly paid for his meal which came to about $14. Later when she and Paul went to pay out, the waiter said that their meal of $28 was already paid for by someone else! Shock! They had no idea who would do that. The young man that they had bought the meal for previously was really quite wealthy and seldom did anyone offer to give to someone like him; instead people were usually looking to get something from him. He was so touched that he turned around and not only paid for their meal but left a generous tip. When he went home he shared with his mom, who was Alison's beautician, about his experience and the word got back to Alison. Isn't it true we can never out-give God? How important it is to be sensitive to the Spirit and as it says in Matt. 10:8b (The Message) "You have been treated generously, so live generously."

Challenge for today: Give to an unsuspecting person as the Spirit directs you.

Hang loose! Make room! Give space! Today I got up early and took out of the freezer twice baked potatoes, ribs, and peanut cake, but a call from my uncle changed everything. He sounded terrible and is sick so was canceling the dinner at our house. There are reminders every day that we need to be flexible as one call can change everything. Instead of a big meal, I got baking done and took out the winter clothes. Just yesterday we had a nice surprise as my sister unexpectedly stopped in, giving us time to catch up as we had coffee on the deck. But what if we are so *locked in* that we miss what is happening right before us? The Lord wants to call the shots and direct every part of our day. But we need to be listening and open, and have space for the Holy Spirit to move in our lives. If we are receptive we will hear as it says in Isa. 30:21 (NIV) "Whether you turn to the right or to the left, your ears will hear a voice behind you saying, 'This is the way; walk in it.'" May we let the Holy Spirit be in charge of every detail of our lives and stay on the perfect path He has for each of us. Who knows what is in store for us today?!!

Challenge for today: Tell the Lord the day is His and to instruct where you should go.

Have you ever started a project and found it led to another and to another? I have an idea it is like that with our heart *make-overs*! A friend wrote that they were going to redo their kitchen completely but when they tore out everything to the studs, they found that their balcony overhang needed attention, and their bedroom and the hallway. It seems similar with our hearts. The Lord works in one area and we think well that is taken care of and then there is another big area that needs attention. I suspect He will always be working on some area in our lives for the completion; but it won't happen until Glory. But we can rejoice that our Father loves us enough not to leave us as we are; but wants to transform us to be more like Him. It says in II Cor. 3:18 (The Message) "And so we are transfigured much like the Messiah, our lives gradually becoming brighter and more beautiful as God enters our lives and we become like Him." Wouldn't it be nice if someone hasn't seen us for some time and would say, "My but you have changed and I see more of the Lord in you!" May we allow His work to continue in our lives until we see Him face to face.

Challenge for today: Give the Lord permission to work in any room of your heart for He knows what needs to be done and what order it is to happen.

Perhaps we all have handicaps and limitations; some very obvious and others hidden and may be yet unknown to us. Paul spoke of his *thorn in the flesh* as a gift to keep him humble. He begged God 3 times to take it away but instead he received God's strength and power in his weakness. He was told in II Cor. 12:9 (The Message) "My grace is enough; it's all you need. My strength comes into its own in your weakness." Ever since I can remember I have been directionally handicapped. I have absolutely no sense of what direction is north, east, south, or west and could get lost at a moment's notice. There have always been places I didn't go and things I never tried because of my weakness. (That is before the days of the GPS) While on a mission in Mexico I dressed as a clown and had a large group of children following me. Fortunately I ran into our youth director who directed me back to the church. I had no idea how to get back there and we were soon to have a program for them. I was so grateful for his help! Whatever our limitations are, God wants to use them to keep us dependent on Him and to experience His strength in our weak areas. Then one day we can actually celebrate them as Paul did. He said in II Cor. 12:10 (The Message) "I quit focusing on the handicap and began appreciating the gift. It was a case of God's strength moving in on my weakness. Now I take limitations in stride, and with good cheer, those limitations that cut me down to size- abuse, accidents, opposition, bad breaks. I just let Christ take over! And so the weaker I get, the stronger I become."

Challenge for today: Celebrate a handicap you have and thank the Lord for the evidence of His grace and power.

None of us have it all together but together we have it all! We need one another! I grew up in the city and had no experience on the farm. But when Al received a call to Brunswick, Minnesota, the congregation not only had the parsonage sparkling clean but had planted and cared for a large garden behind the parsonage just for us. I had lots to learn and many people to teach me. In fact, the following spring we had a garden party for the seniors and they all came with hoes and seeds and helped plant the whole garden. We had lots of laughter and fun planting and then in the fall we had a harvest party. We made various dishes from the garden produce and had games with a garden theme. It was a group effort and later we continued to have the harvest parties even though I was now caring for the garden myself. God did not mean for us to be *lone rangers* but to help one another and stand alongside one another. Sometimes it is just for a time and then we can launch out on our own. But other times it is more for the long haul. When we see sisters and brothers in the Body struggling; we can ask to give them a hand, or a listening ear, or prayer support and word of encouragement. Other times we may be the recipient and know how good it feels to know we are not alone. Let us be there for one another as it says in Col 3: 15 (The Message) "Let the peace of Christ keep you in tune with each other, in step with each other. None of this going off and doing your own thing. And cultivate thankfulness."

Challenge for today: Seek to encourage someone today and share the burden they are carrying.

When we were on a trip out west we saw a gorgeous home set up against the mountains. In front of it was an old weather beaten building that was about to fall down. I wondered why they didn't just demolish it as it blocked the view of the new house. Did this old building become an attachment for the owners of the new house? Were they unwilling to let go of it? It spoiled the beauty of their present house and limited their vision. Do we hang on to things in our own lives so that they become idols that we don't want to let go of? Is our vision of the Lord and His kingdom limited? How important it is to let go of anything that hinders us in relation to the Lord. When Paul was writing to the Thessalonians he commends them for their faith and turning from their idols to serve God. I Thess.1:8-9 (The Message) says "The news of your faith is out. We don't even have to say anything anymore—*You're* the message! People come up and tell us how you received us with open arms, how you deserted the dead idols of your old life so you could embrace and serve God, the true God." Let us let go of anything that hinders us from our relationship with Him. What we gain far exceeds hanging on to any idol.

Challenge for today: Ask the Lord to show you anything that stands in the way between you and Him and give it up

When we arrived at our son Kurt's home, one of the first things the grandchildren asked was to play a marble game with them. We all sat on the floor and used shooters to hit the marbles in a center square in order to claim them. We could also hit the marbles in front of others and keep them as well. Grant, being only 5, was so happy when he had a pile of marbles in front of him. But when they were taken away he was disappointed and his countenance fell. Quite different from when he hit several of grandpa's marbles and jumped up and down ecstatically. I thought of how maybe we are not so different from Grant in our spiritual lives. Isn't it great when everything is going super well and we have *piles of blessings* before us? But when they seem to disappear suddenly or when we see someone else gets showered with them, can we be happy for them?! We are told in Rom 12:15 (Amplified) "Rejoice with those who rejoice (sharing other's joy), and weep with those who weep (sharing other's grief)". Let us be happy in whatever state the Lord has us in at the time, and just like Paul, let us be content in plenty or want.

Challenge for today: Thank the Lord for how he is blessing someone you know.

We made a quick trip to the cities for the get–together of my childhood friends that were from my home church. We have done this periodically through the years and time keeps marching on. It doesn't seem that long ago that we were sitting on the floor playing jacks at a slumber party and telling our secrets to one another. We did not know then that one of us would lose a son in his youth; or that one would go through a divorce; or another would have stage-4 cancer; or that one would lose her spouse to brain cancer etc. We were so carefree! All of these childhood friends know the Lord and though we don't always understand His ways; we know we can turn to Him. When we go to my brother's home we sleep in the guest room that is on the upper floor with a balcony and sky lights. We can see the top of the trees, the birds flying about etc. and the view is quite different than from the first floor. In the same way, when we see things from only a limited perspective our situations may seem dark and hopeless ...that is until we look up to Him and see from an eternal perspective. Then the light breaks forth and we are able to walk through the most difficult times, holding tightly onto to Him. David said in Ps. 3:3-4a (Amplified) "But You, O Lord, are a shield for me, my glory and the lifter of my head. With my voice I cry to the Lord, and He hears and answers me out of His holy hill." May the Lord lift our eyes upward to Him for whatever comes our way.

Challenge for today: Ask the Lord to open your eyes to see more from His perspective.

There are times in our lives when we are to hang on in hope and other times when we are to let go. That calls for discernment and we need to hear what God is saying to us at the time. When I went to our Women's Bible Study this week more and more gals arrived and we tried to squeeze in a few more chairs around the tables. Lots of laughter and hugs and then we got to the lesson with sharing and prayers. Each of us goes home richer in our faith. I was told that some time ago there were only 2 or 3 that were coming and they could have made the decision to just disband. But they hung on in faith and watched as gradually the Lord added to the numbers again. I am so glad they didn't give up as I receive so much each week. But there may be other times when the Lord says it is the time to let go as He wants to do a new thing and bring us into a different season. Perhaps some organizations need to die as their mission has been fulfilled. Or maybe something has to be dropped from a full schedule so something new can be added. Each day we need to patiently wait to hear the Lord and discern His way for us. Then we may join David in Ps. 40:5 (NIV) when he says, "Many, O Lord my God, are the wonders you have done. The things you planned for us no one can recount to you; were I to speak and tell of them they would be too many to declare." Can we even imagine the wonderful plans He has for us?

Challenge for today: Ask for a discerning heart and thank Him for what He has planned for you.

Sometimes the Lord does things so completely beyond what we could ask or think that we know it could only be Him. One such instance was at our church in Des Moines when we had 3 big needs which included a jeep for our missionary in Bolivia and a roof for the church. A council member suggested we all pray as families for 2 months and then take up an offering. We were given cardboard cubes with scriptures to set on our kitchen tables and were to pray each day for what God would want us to give. I'm not sure how many of us really believed we would possibly meet the goal. The long awaited Sunday arrived when the offering was to be taken after our regular offering. Unbeknown to us at the time, there happened to be a fundraiser from the synod who was present in the pew. When the second offering was taken, men went out to count it and to bring back the results by the end of the service. We all waited in anticipation and then they came back with the announcement….the exact amount needed was taken in! Clapping and praising broke out as we were all giving thanks to the Lord for what seemed like a miracle. Ps. 115:1 (Amplified) expresses it as it says, "Not to us, O Lord, not to us but to Your name give glory, for Your mercy and loving kindness and for the sake of Your truth and faithfulness!" It was not us but the faithfulness of the Lord! That afternoon there was a synod gathering and this fund raiser that just happened to visit us that Sunday shared the unusual fund raising *method* used by our church!

Challenge for today: Give the Lord a particular need you have and pray and watch for how He answers.

Burr! The weather is colder now and the lake is frozen over. Change has come with lots of snow and no longer any open water on the lake. It makes me think of the condition of our hearts and how they can get cold and frozen just as the lake. We may get hurt from something said or done to us and our heart puts up walls of protection. Soon we are cold inside and may not even realize that hardening has taken place. When the winds of adversity blow upon us we may come to realize and acknowledge how really needy we are; in need of the Lord's warming love. Our heart starts to melt when we come into the presence of love and with it the courage and willingness is given to forgive others. It may take some time and is so gradual we may hardly know it is happening. But one day we notice our heart has thawed and softened and we begin to feel again. We are told in scripture that the Lord searches our hearts and we are warned not to harden them. Prov. 4:23 (Amplified) tells us, "Keep and guard your heart with all vigilance and above all that you guard, for out of it flow the springs of life." Let us be more alert that our hearts not turn cold and that the Lord can use us to share His warming love with others.

Challenge for today: Ask the Lord for a change of heart where it is needed.

When we were young we probably had a dream of what our life would look like. It may have been very idealistic and didn't turn out anything like we imagined. Our church in Remer had a senior group (The Hilltoppers) that were good sports and knew how to have fun. We invited them to Canaan's Rest for a dinner party and about 40 of them came dressed as *someone they wished they would have become.* We were not prepared for how they got *into it:* one came as a nun; another as a stewardess; two came as lumberjacks with beards and axes slung over their shoulders; one came as a homeless man (he was trying to sell his house); I came as a ballerina etc. The opera singer had it staged so that when she sang her highest note, she had a wardrobe malfunction. Lots of laughter and fun! Many had dreams that were never fulfilled but was it their dream or God's? The Lord has a picture and plan for each of us and there is great joy when we come into that place. The Lord says in Jer. 29:11(NIV) "'For I know the plans I have for you,' declares, the Lord, 'plans to prosper you and not to harm you, plans to give you hope and a future.'" God's plan for our life is perfect for the gifts and desires He has placed within us. Each one of us need to discover what that plan is for the day as well as, for our calling. Life is exciting and full of deep joy when we are in the center of His will and plan!

Challenge for today: Ask the Lord to show you any place where you are not in His plan and to help you make the necessary change.

I think we have all met people that we would consider a saint as they seem to radiate His presence and have a carefree way about them. A friend described a saint to be someone who can truly be themselves: that is being all who God made them to be and using the gifts He has given. That is my desire but I have a long ways to go. This friend asked if she could record a session in which she would give me spiritual direction as it was a requirement for a class she was taking. How blessed I was as she asked me questions of the Lord's work and leading in my life. She stopped midway through to ask us to be quiet for 5 minutes to hear the Lord and what He was about in my life. A picture came to me of a chick breaking out of the shell and the feathers were all moist and matted down. The sun suddenly came in the window of the prayer porch where we were quietly sitting and just warmed me inside. I felt the rays and it was like my feathers were getting fluffy and I was coming forth. When I described it to her she just gasped in surprise for she had the picture of me as a hen and giving nurturance to others. How encouraging it was that this little chick would grow and become more of what the Lord has planned and nurture others. Let us become our true selves, in Him, and know that freedom of being real. Paul says in Eph. 3:20 (The Message) "God can do anything, you know—far more that you could ever imagine or guess or request in your wildest dreams! He does it not by pushing us around but by working within us; His spirit deeply and gentle within us."

Challenge for today: Ask the Lord to help you be real and become your true self in Him.

This week our son is coming up to the cabin with two friends for their bi-annual guy's time. For a few days they forget their work and relax, enjoying time by the camp fire, cooking up some gourmet dishes etc. Last year when Bo drove his minivan down the steep hill to the cabin to unload everything, Al warned him that he needed to watch the weather as he did not have 4 wheel drive to make it back up. There was more snow and since he delayed he made 4 or 5 attempts and each time had to back down to try again. Finally, he took a fast drive up with 2 of them pushing before he got to the top. Had he waited any longer, he may not have made it. Timing is important in our lives. God has a time table and we need to be in sync with it. Otherwise we may be spinning our wheels and not getting anywhere or even backsliding. Sometimes God gives us warnings, like the warning Al gave the guys, and we need to pay attention. It may be easier to stay put than to move out like Abraham when he was asked to leave his country; not knowing where God would lead him. It takes faith and obedience but the safest and best place to be is in His will and on His time table. Jesus was a wonderful example for He paid close attention to His Father's timing. One thing we know for certain as it says in Hosea 10:12b (NIV) "... it is time to seek the Lord, until He comes and showers righteousness on you."

Challenge for today: Seek to know His timing and follow with obedience.

What does it mean to leave everything to follow the Lord? I was reading today from Matt. 4 of Jesus walking along the beach when he came upon Peter and Andrew throwing their nets into the sea. He extended the invitation to follow Him and He would make them into a new kind of fishermen that would catch men. What was their response? It says in verse 20 (NIV) "*At once* they left their nets and followed Him." When the Lord gives a directive to us, do we say "but Lord" and question Him? Or are we like Mary that said in Luke 1:38b (NIV) "May it be to me as you have said."? The disciples responded to Jesus' invitation and left everything and their lives were forever changed. I imagine the transformation of their character as rough fisherman to followers of the Lamb of God did not take place overnight! It reminds me of the process of our moving from one parsonage to another. What a mess with stacks of packing boxes everywhere. Some things simply didn't fit into our new life and had to be discarded or left behind. Change happened! At first it seemed insurmountable; but each day progress was made and the house gradually was transformed. Isn't it amazing how the Lord can change selfish beings such as us to become more like Him? Along the way He reveals behavior, habits, and attitudes that need changing. But as we spend time with Him, and follow His example, He changes us to become more like Him. Perhaps that is one of His greatest miracles of all!

Challenge for today: Ask the Lord to reveal anything in your life that is hindering you from following Him whole heartedly.

God is a loving Father full of surprises and we may miss them if we are not paying attention. Sometimes we wake up to the moonbeams streaming in the window and He may be saying, "Just enjoy the display of My creative handiwork this morning!" Or maybe He prompts someone to send us an e-mail telling us how loved we are. Could He may be saying, "I love you so much, far more than your friend, and more than you can comprehend!" Or He may send a gift in the mail that was so totally unexpected as if to say, "I have untold riches to give you and this is just a taste!" This morning at breakfast we had an unexpected surprise when Al readjusted his placemat. I was getting the coffee and He exclaimed, "Hon, there is money underneath my placemat!" From underneath he pulled out a $20 bill and then he told me there was more; and another $20 bill; and one more after that. Well, you can imagine how excited we were and we thanked the Lord for his good gift. We soon realized that dear friends who came to Canaan's Rest must have hidden it there, and probably knew we would not want to accept it. But the Lord's way, as it says in Ps. 84:11b (Amplified) "No good thing will He withhold from those who walk uprightly." Let us humbly thank Him for His surprises and give Him praise.

Challenge for today: Ask the Lord to make you more aware of his good gifts and surprises.

God has created us to be dependent on Him and desires that we be deeply rooted in His love. Last time when we drove through the thick forests of the Blue Ridge Mountains, we saw trees on high ridges that almost seemed to be growing out of the solid rock! We wondered how they could grow in places that seemingly had so little soil. They must have a deep root system as they were growing so tall and straight. A townsperson told us that their secret is that they grow very slowly and push their roots down into the crevices between the rocks. They look for any little space they can find and have been known to even split rocks apart. It's so important that we sink our roots deep down into the Lord. When we do this the power of the Holy Spirit within us will cause us to stand against the devil's schemes and to break through difficult circumstances. We are told in Eph. 3:17 & 6:13 (Amplified) "May Christ through your faith (actually) dwell (settle down, abide, make his permanent home) in your hearts! May you be rooted deep in love and founded securely on love"... "Therefore put on God's complete armor, that you may be able to resist and stand your ground on the evil day (of danger), and, having done all (the crisis demands), to stand (firmly in your place)." Let us grow deeper into Him and stand firm in His power.

Challenge for today: Spend some time reading the word and asking the Lord to expand your heart to be more deeply rooted in His love.

Isn't it amazing how God chooses what is weak and insignificant in the world's eyes to shame the wise and give glory to Him? I remember when I was asked to have 2 workshops at an international conference, my *flesh* said no a hundred times. But my heart said yes in obedience to the Lord and I prepared weeks in advance and went over my talk many times. When the day of the conference finally came I had a headache and lots of feelings of inadequacy. The room they gave me seated about 200 and prior to my talk prayer warriors came in the room to pray for me. I could hardly believe it as one of them was a guy from my home church that I had known since childhood. He knew me well and my hesitancy to speak and prayed the words from I Cor. 1:27-29 (NIV) "But God chose, the foolish things of the world to shame the wise; God chose the weak things of the world to shame the strong. He chose the lowly things of this world and the despised things-and the things that are not-to nullify the things that are, so that no one may boast before Him." It is now years later and I remember it as if it was yesterday for those were the words I needed to hear. I felt weak and insignificant and yet God strengthened me and chose me that day to give His message. When we got back to the hotel a stranger in the elevator told me he liked my talk. Since I thought only women were present, I believed he was kidding. But he was a professor and sitting in the back of the room. How glad I was that I didn't know it at the time! Yes, God can use imperfect and weak people that all may know the glory goes to Him.

Challenge for today: Recall a time when the Lord brought you through a difficult time and give Him wholehearted praise!

Have you noticed how God prepares us for all that He calls us to do even when we are not aware at the time? When I was only 10 or 11 years old my mom's sister asked me to be her helper as she had a big house and 2 little girls at the time. It ended up to be years of working for their family after school, and during the summers, until I graduated from high school. It seemed like a new baby arrived nearly each year until there were 8, so help was always needed! My aunt was very kind and encouraging and we enjoyed working together. My uncle who was a doctor would often call at the last minute to say he was bringing home company and we would scurry around getting everything ready. We learned to work very fast and be creative. When they had parties I would help waitress and also plan a game as an ice breaker. Now I didn't realize at the time how all of this was preparing me for being a mother and a pastor's wife until I was actually in those roles. So often unexpected company showed up at the parsonage; or there were parties to plan for the youth; or the need to improvise at the last minute. Yes, God used those childhood years, preparing me for what He had planned all along. Maybe we don't see the purpose of the Lord's ways at the time, but He is getting us ready for what is ahead. Prov. 16:9 (Amplified) says, "A man's mind plans his way; but the Lord directs his steps and makes them sure."

Challenge for today: Thank the Lord how He has prepared you for the serving He has called you to do.

It's hard to believe that a small item like a computer can be a treasure one minute and a frustration beyond words the next. One sad day the unthinkable happened and my computer crashed. It could not be *resurrected* so a new one was needed. Our son Mark ordered one on line that he thought would be the right one for me. Unfortunately, they were out of stock and I ended up waiting over a month. Finally on the day the Fed-Ex delivery man came to our door I was not home and a note was left that he would be back the next day. You can imagine, I was nowhere but home when his truck finally came down our road! So often we miss out on what the Lord is saying to us when we are *not home* in the sense of listening to Him and may be pre-occupied with other things. It could be that we are sick or depressed or over-whelmed by pressures; but we must not let it keep us from being alert to His voice. It is good to pray daily to be attentive to the sound of His voice in our ordinary day. Find time to be alone with Him to reflect and listen to Him. He said in Rev. 3:20 (Phillips) "See, I stand knocking at the door. If anyone listens to my voice and opens the door, I will go into his house and dine with him and he with me." It is one thing to welcome the Fed-Ex delivery man, but quite another to *be home* and welcome the King of Kings who waits at our hearts door. Let us not leave Him standing there but open wide and let Him in.

Challenge for today: Begin to plan into your schedule a time alone with Him.

We are told in scripture that no one does good and we are all sinful and in need of a Savior. It says in Rom. 3: 22b-23 (Phillips) "For there is no distinction to be made anywhere: everyone has sinned, everyone falls short of the beauty of His plan." One weekend in the fall season our son came to Canaan's Rest with his friends. He had been on the lake only a short time before he stopped by the house to tell us he dropped his I-Phone in the water. He was quick to put it in rice in an attempt to save it but it wasn't until later that he told us the whole story. He had been standing on the side platform of the boat and all of a sudden he lurched and went overboard backwards. He threshed around in the water as his clothes and shoes weighed him down and then tried to rescue his phone. How much are we like that as we don't admit the whole story? We may feel we aren't as bad as someone else who has committed murder or rape. But the truth of it is, we are all lost and drowning without the Lord. Our righteous acts will not save us and we can thresh around and do all kinds of good things, but we need a Savior. Our part is to admit our guilt and ask Him for forgiveness. When we only admit we aren't as bad as someone else, we aren't admitting the whole story...we are drowning! Our righteousness is no more than filthy rags. Let us admit our sin and ask for His forgiveness and restoration.

Challenge for today: Before you go to sleep, acknowledge your sin and ask the Lord for forgiveness.

Winter time at Canaan's Rest is beautiful and quieter than the other seasons. It's wonderful to see nature at its best and there is so much activity going on that we can't see. When I go for my prayer walks I always see tracks in the snow of many kinds of animals. Today it looked like a family of deer had a party in my cousin's driveway by all the many prints left behind. I also saw 2 eagles on the ice eating fish left behind by the fishermen. Often in our spiritual lives we *know* the Lord is in something but is rather hidden. We see His print, like the deer tracks, but it is not obvious and we must trust our discernment. Sometimes we have more obvious signs of God at work and just know it is the Lord. Such as a specific word that is just what we needed to hear or the warm heat of His healing touch. But what about the times we can't *feel* His presence or see His answer to our prayers. If we look closely, often we can see His *tracks* and know He has been there before us. But even when we can't seem to, we have His promise that He is with us and answers our *every* prayer. Yes, it is nice when it is visible but He wants us to trust even when we can't see. We have the promise in Deut. 31:6 (The Message) "Be strong. Take courage. Don't be intimidated. Don't give them a second thought because God, your God is striding ahead of you. He's right there with you. He won't let you down; He won't leave you."

Challenge for today: Look for evidences of the Lord's hand in your daily life.

Sometimes less is more! Sometimes simple is better! Outside on our back porch Al has hung a single lighted angel that he bought to replace last year's ornament that had *expired*. It stands out in the night for only the outline of the angel is all lighted up. Now if we had lots of lights on our porch or on the whole house I doubt you would even notice the angel. But since it is the only decoration, it stands out. Why do we *need* so much when a little may be more? Years ago at Christmas children received only one main gift and that gift was cherished. Now they receive so much and still want more to satisfy their wants, not appreciating any one thing in particular. Before our present church had a building, we met in a house that had been converted into the office for the Christmas Eve service. Only 50 or so attended and the service was very simple and meaningful. There were lots of children and they helped pass out the candles, bulletins etc. Pastor had a ceramic figure of baby Jesus in a wooden box and before he unveiled it, he talked about the preciousness of the gift. We will all remember the sermon as it was simple and yet profound. Let us not miss the significance of something simple when we think we *need* more. Let us be all about the main thing which is Jesus. It says in Matt. 6:33 (Amplified) "But seek (aim at and strive after) first of all His Kingdom and His righteousness (His way of doing and being right), and then all these things taken together will be given you besides."

Challenge for today: Put the Lord first in your life and let Him be the main thing!

Not everything is as it seems on the outside and one must ask for a discerning heart. We have a cabin that our children and grandchildren have named *The Silver Chateau*. It has two bedrooms, a main room with a kitchen and a storage area. Now you might think it sounds like a beautiful structure and want to book it but take a second close look. It is very old and made of wood that is covered with aluminum, including the roof. The only heat is an old wood stove and you may even see a mouse or two! The guys like it as their *man cave* but their wives are NOT likely to stay there. I thought of how we may have titles of being a CEO, a doctor, a politician etc. but that is not indicative of what is on the inside. Even though we may have an impressive title or name (as *the Silver Chateau*), the important thing is the real person. Are we persons of integrity, persons that reflect the character of Jesus or are we just full of *hot air*? I think we have all be shocked as things come out about the hidden lives of entertainers, politicians, and even spiritual leaders. Does what others see of us outwardly match what is on the inside? Do we have hearts that are divided or ones that are devoted to Him? It says in Ps. 86:11 (The Message) "Train me, God, to walk straight; then I'll follow your true path. Put me together, one heart and mind; then, undivided, I'll worship in joyful fear."

Challenge for today: Ask the Lord to continue His work in you so that what people see outwardly is a true reflection of Jesus in your inward person.

A couple weeks before Christmas we went to the children's Christmas program and what a delight. There were readings of scripture as each of the characters in the Christmas story slowly came down the aisle. When they had all made their entrance and were in their places they were quite angelic at first. But before long; one of the angel's halos began to tilt and soon the little girl was making faces and picking through the hay in the manger etc. Then two of the Wiseman began playfully punching each other and others became restless. I wonder how we are like those children as we try so hard to be good, especially when others are watching. But, so often our *flesh nature* acts up and we call attention to ourselves instead of pointing them to the Lord; or we give someone a punch by our insensitive words. Even when we act up and blow it, He offers us His love and forgiveness. How wonderful that He continues to delight in us; just as we do toward those precious children when they act up. Isn't His grace amazing?! Eph. 2:8-9 (Phillips) says it well, "For it is by grace that you are saved, through faith. This does not depend on anything you have achieved, it is the free gift of God; and because it is not earned no man can boast about it."

Challenge for today: Next time you *blow it* thank the Lord for His grace to you!

Throughout the seasons we often see the doors of many homes decorated beautifully for a particular holiday. Our door is presently decorated for Christmas with a pine bough wreath tied with a decorative ribbon. Open doors are invitations to enter and like a passageway to where we are going. The opening of our heart's door is also important and will help us to see more of the treasure of who He has made us to be and His presence within us. How do we prepare our hearts so that they are open and are inviting to Him and others to enter? We need to spend time quietly before Him and ask the Holy Spirit to reveal blockages and barriers to His love and healing. When we go to worship it is good preparation to pray beforehand that our heart would be softened to receive what the Lord has for us. We can ask the Holy Spirit to search our hearts to reveal the things that need forgiveness and surrender them to Him. Maybe when we are with others instead of insisting on our own way, we put ourselves in neutral and ask what the Holy Spirit desires. I am preparing for retreatants coming tomorrow for a few days. If I waited until they were at the door before I prepared for them, think of how much I would miss! I want to be ready so I can graciously welcome them whole-heartedly and spend time together. Above all, let us also welcome the Holy Spirit to open wide the door of our hearts to receive Jesus. In Matt. 7:8 (NIV) He says, "For everyone who asks receives; he who seeks finds; and to him who knocks, the door will be opened."

Challenge for today: Take time for soul care and don't rush through your day without letting the Lord prepare your heart.

God's love is so amazing and knows no barriers of age, color, sex, or culture. In 1981 Al and I were honored to be included in the 28 people from the USA to be invited to the Renewal Conference in Finland. Eighteen nations, which included representatives from each of the continents, were there! We learned much from one another. It was amazing how we so quickly felt *one in the spirit* as we worshipped and fellowshipped together. Jesus was in our midst and joined our hearts and hands in unity. The talks given expressed a sense of urgency that the church needed to prepare for the coming days but also the promise that God would shine through His church. Even though we didn't understand each other's language we still seemed to communicate through our hearts. One memory that is still vivid is the day a bus took the women downtown to shop and I was with a mother from Africa looking for t-shirts for her many children. I didn't understand her words and yet we communicated and the job got done. So much love flowed amongst the many varied people and we felt renewed. We came home so full of love and grateful to those that made it possible for us to go. Paul tells us in Rom. 13:8 (NIV) "Let no debt remain outstanding, except the continuing debt to love one another, for he who loves his fellowman has fulfilled the law."

Challenge for today: Seek to get to know and share Christ with someone who is not like you.

The Body of Christ seems fragmented and we need to come together and quit splitting off. When we traveled south it seemed like there was a small church around each bend in the road with such names as: Original Church of God, Second Baptist Church, Half Way Church, Primitive Baptist church, The Salvage Yard, Divine Church, Awaken Church, Faith, Freedom, and Deliverance Church etc. There are many churches and expressions of our Christian faith and we should come together with our gifts and personalities. He wants us to get to know and recognize what He is doing in and through and among us. We have so much to learn and give to one another. When we are open to each other's expression we will be mutually encouraged and impart gifts to one another. Our part is to come together as living stones for it says in I Peter 2:5 (NIV) "You also, like living stones, are being built into a spiritual house to be a holy priesthood, offering spiritual sacrifices acceptable to God through Jesus Christ." Let us focus more on what unites rather than what divides us.

Challenge for today: Show interest and ask questions of someone who has a different expression of faith.

Often we glean profitable lessons from hard circumstances in our lives as we trust God in all things. At the time it may not seem pleasant but when we look back we may find we have grown and learned much. A practical lesson happened over Christmas as we got an e-mail from the hotel the day before we were to check in saying we would have no water in our rooms from 7 a.m. to 5 p.m. on Dec 26th. Of course we realized that would mean no showers, no flushing etc. and wondered how they could do that as we had about 10 rooms reserved for the relatives. But at check-in time they offered us a free buffet breakfast at the hotel café and a free night in the future because of our inconvenience. Well, it turned out on Dec. 26th we all went to Mall of America to shop and eat and go on the rides so we didn't get back to the hotel until afternoon. Shortly after that the water came on and we really hadn't suffered at all....plus we were left with the benefits promised. Some relatives stayed a third night with the free coupon so it all worked out well. We have a choice when unfavorable things happen to us: We can go around complaining and playing the martyr or give it to the Lord to work good out of it. Rom. 8:28b & 39b (Message) says, "That's why we can be so sure that every detail in our lives of love for God is worked into something good....... absolutely nothing can get between us and God's love because of the way that Jesus our Master has embraced us." Let us praise Him in all our circumstances.

Challenge for today: Whatever happens today, give Him praise.

Isn't it wonderful to be known in our hearts and fully understood? We get a taste of what that feels like when the Lord gives us special friends and confidants; those who look past the outward things and see what is going on inside. What a gift that is! When I use to go to see my blind friend, I didn't have to dress up before- hand or put on make-up. I could just go as I was since she couldn't see if I had a spill on my clothes or how my hair looked. She could *see* only what was on the inside and we had such pleasant talks. Friends have partial insight to know our hearts but the Lord sees it all and is a perfect *heart reader.* It says in I Kings 8:39 (Amplified) "Then hear in heaven, Your dwelling place, and forgive and give to every man according to his ways, whose heart You know, for You and You only know the hearts of all the children of men." Sometimes others assume they know what is in our hearts and get it all wrong. Even our explaining may not help. But God is the only one who truly knows us; inside out and loves us unconditionally. He wants to draw us closer to Him and have an intimate relationship with us. Too often we care more what others think more than the One who knows all our failures and shortcomings but sees the best in us. Let us seek Him who loves and knows us best!

Challenge for today: Be honest and open before the Lord and tell Him all the concerns of your heart.

Our relationship with God is the most important thing in life and He wants to walk with us, talk with us and have deep communion within us. We can do all kinds of things *for* Him but He wants us to live our lives *with* Him and *in* Him. When the gals in our women's Bible study took turns leading it, often they would have an object lesson to emphasize their points. One gal brought her bike to class and put it upside down in the middle of the group. She proceeded to manually push the pedals around and said one of them was grace and the other works. You need both pedals to make the wheels go around. So often we get caught up in works and get overly busy *doing* things for the Lord. Our schedules get so full that we have no time to just *be* with the Lord. But when we are bathed in His grace we know how good it is to spend time in solitude, silence and listening to Him. We come to appreciate the gift of grace and know it is nothing we do but all Him. We must know first and foremost that we are His beloved child and then the works He has planned will flow out from that. Eph. 2:8-9a (Amplified) says, "For it is by free grace (God's unmerited favor) that you are saved (delivered from judgment and made partakers of Christ's salvation) through (your) faith. And this (salvation) is not of yourselves (of your own doing. It came not through your own striving), but it is the gift of God; not because of works." Let us put first things first!

Challenge for today: Commune with the Lord as your eternal best friend as you go about your day.

Today I read the words from Mark 6:50b (NIV) "Immediately He spoke to them and said, 'Take courage! It is I. Don't be afraid.'" The disciples were on the sea in a terrible wind storm somewhere between 3 and 6 in the morning. They must have been frightfully scared and then Jesus showed up and climbed into the boat with them. I thought of all the times I have been fearful and wondered what was going to happen. Even as a child, I remember being afraid of storms and my stomach would just turn when the sky got dark and eerie. But one day His words got through to me and I was no longer afraid of storms. It was like a miracle. I felt peaceful and had the assurance that He was with me and it was alright. I wish I could say that all my fears flew away at once but I know now where to go with *frightful* things. We can have peace in Him in the midst of the storms of life, *knowing* that He will get in the boat with us and calm the winds. Even though the economy may go down-hill, or we get old and feeble, or we miss out on a job opportunity we can be at rest. David was in a tough situation when he said in Ps. 56:3 (Amplified) "What time I am afraid, I will have confidence in *and* put my trust *and* reliance in You."

Challenge for today: Give every concern to the Lord that comes your way and rest in His peace.

The Lord awaits us! Each day He has our day planned and ready for us to step in and walk it out. When we visit our daughter's family in Texas I rise and shine a little before 5 a.m. Our son-in-law does something I appreciate so much; He grinds the coffee the night before and sets the timer so it is all done brewing when I get up. What a wonderful aroma to greet me when I come down the stairs and the coffee just hits the spot. It is a reminder that the Lord is always there waiting for us each day and desires to satisfy our soul's thirst. Jesus says in Matt. 5:6 (NIV) "Blessed are those who hunger and thirst for righteousness, for they will be filled." I love having my devotional time in the quiet morning hour as it is just what my soul is hungering for. It is like a jump start for the day! Later when everyone gets up we have devotions together as there is also a need to gather with others in the Body of Christ. When scriptures are read, more viewpoints are given and we may find new ways of seeing things. We don't need to get stressed for what the day holds as we are not on our own. We have so many promises of the Lord's constant care over us. Let us greet the Lord as we start our day and step into His plan.

Challenge for today: Enjoy a few minutes of just sitting and soaking in His presence.

When we enter each new day or the New Year, it is good to ask ourselves the question, "What am I after?" Is it money? Is it power? Is it prestige? The apostle Paul was after spreading the gospel so the fact that he was in prison only gave him more opportunities to spread the news. Every 2 hours they changed guards, so he had a new one chained to him with whom he could share the gospel. His joy was full because of what he was after. If he was after comfort and ease, he would not have had joy. When we go after pleasure and riches and that is not happening, we may fall into depression. If we find ourselves missing out on joy maybe we are going after the wrong things. When our desire is to draw closer to Him and to share Him with others, then we can rejoice even in our trials for it is accomplishing that. In Hab. 3:18-19 (NIV) the prophet said that even though his crops and herds fail, "Yet I will rejoice in the Lord, I will be joyful in God my Savior. The Sovereign Lord is my strength; He makes my feet like the feet of a deer, He enables me to go on the heights." I have an idea that his joy was not found in material things! Let us go after that which will last for all eternity.

Challenge for today: Rejoice in the Lord today, no matter what happens.

The Lord comes to us in so many varied ways and wants to draw us close to Him. He is always speaking to us and the sound of His voice should make our hearts leap with joy. We had two young people in our former congregation that each had a lamb. They named them and when they would come home from school, they would call to their lamb. Each lamb knew the voice of their master and would come bounding over to them when they heard their name called. I was amazed as I stood by the fence and saw how they instantly discerned the voice calling to them. I wonder about us? Do we recognize when the Lord is calling out to us. He may do it through a dream; through a word of scripture; through an impression or picture; through a sermon; through another person speaking something that you have asked of God etc. How often do we miss His voice when we are not alert and may be too busy or preoccupied? Jesus said in John 10:14 & 27 (Amplified) "I am the Good Shepherd; and I know and recognize My own, and My own know and recognize me—The sheep that are My own hear and are listening to My voice; and I know them, and they follow me." May we be intently listening for the voice of our Good Shepherd in whatever way He desires to communicate with us. His voice of Love can reach us no matter where we are at.

Challenge for today: Humbly tell the Lord you want to discern His voice and listen intently.

Al and Judy

Hendrickson family

Our grandchildren

Lake view of Canaan's Rest

Road view of Canaan's Rest

Great Room

Sauna

The Wildmen

The Silver Chateau

Contemplative site

Relative gathering at the Point

Family Fun

Family times by the Lake

Quiet waters

Recreational time

Winter at Canaan

Women's retreat

Cabin at the Point

Contemplative time at the Point

Sunset over Man Lake

CPSIA information can be obtained at www.ICGtesting.com
Printed in the USA
LVOW12s1810121214

418588LV00001B/1/P